TOUGH LOVE

The Amazing True Story of a Boxing
World Champion Turned Lawyer

Lovemore Ndou

First published in 2020 by New Holland Publishers
This edition published in 2021 by New Holland Publishers
Sydney • Auckland

Level 1, 178 Fox Valley Road, Wahroonga, NSW 2076, Australia
5/39 Woodside Ave, Northcote, Auckland 0627, New Zealand

newhollandpublishers.com

A record of this book is available from the National Library of Australia.

ISBN 9781760792848

Group Managing Director: Fiona Schultz
Publisher: Fiona Schultz
Project Editor: Liz Hardy
Designer: Yolanda La Gorcé
Production Director: Arlene Gippert

10 9 8 7 6 5 4 3 2

Keep up with New Holland Publishers:
 NewHollandPublishers
 @newhollandpublishers

TOUGH LOVE

The Amazing True Story of a Boxing World Champion Turned Lawyer

Lovemore Ndou

Foreword by
Linda Burney MP

NEW
HOLLAND

FOREWORD

Ability may get you to the top but it takes character to keep you there.

Lovemore Ndou's life story is so inspiring that it may well play a significant role in helping young people all over the globe reach that little bit higher and find true meaning in their lives. At a time when Black Lives Matter has become a rallying call for indigenous people around the world, Lovemore's story is graphic evidence of why we need to be successful in bringing about change.

Here was a young black boy who faced the hourly life-and-death reality of growing up in a humble town on the South Africa–Zimbabwe border, with the edifice of apartheid beginning to crumble in South Africa and civil war raging in Zimbabwe. He only ever started fighting to protect himself, his parents and his siblings. But he became so good at boxing, he became a triple world champion!

Lovemore did not get the opportunity to go to school until he was nine years of age, yet he was committed to educating himself and making the most of his life and epitomised the value of education. Today, he is a successful lawyer with a thriving legal business in Sydney, and with no fewer than six university degrees to his name.

Like he did as a boy trying to protect his family, Lovemore is today committed to helping as many people as he can.

A question we have heard a lot in recent times is, 'Why do black lives matter when all lives matter?' No-one is arguing against the idea that all lives matter but at this time in history, with the recent deaths in the US highlighting yet again the injustices toward black people that happen on a daily basis, people from all indigenous cultures and ethnic backgrounds are feeling the pain of the victims' families and the global ache of yet more racism.

Now in his late 40s, Lovemore – a proud Australian – one day hopes to join me in the political realm … in his case eventually returning to his roots to play his part in shaping the political landscape of a land of countless contrasts and contradictions wrought by ongoing upheaval and inequality in the post-Nelson Mandela era. I wish him well in his endeavours.

Eloquently told here in the book *Tough Love*, his life tale is as evocative and harrowing as it is ultimately inspiring.

I hope you enjoy Lovemore's story.

Linda Burney, MP

CONTENTS

CHAPTER 1

THE ELEPHANTS GO TO WAR

'It always seems impossible until it's done.'

– Nelson Mandela, former South African president and 1993 Nobel Peace Prize winner

Thoughts of my childhood consumed me as our hire car cut through a landscape of shrubs and baobab trees, illuminated by bursts of crimson from giant impala lilies, and shades of tangerine and scarlet from a setting African sun.

It had been seven years since I'd last seen my hometown and my mind whirred during the meandering five-hour journey north as we left the media scrum that greeted my arrival at Johannesburg airport far behind us.

Nearing my birthplace of Musina, formerly known as Messina, 15 kilometres from the Zimbabwe border in the arid lands of South Africa's far north-east, I remembered the boy I was back then: growing up in a deprived and dangerous place where the life path for an angry youth like me was either jail or ending up dead in a street fight, or maybe both.

Travelling with me were my two younger brothers; the thoughtful and analytical boxer-turned-pastor Ruddock, and my self-appointed 'bodyguard' Moffat, a hot-tempered but lovable rogue more conversant with pistols than punching. They were pontificating and prognosticating over what lay ahead for me on this crusade back to my roots. Their chatter was all about the real reason I was back in South Africa.

But my mind was elsewhere and their words wafted away on the sultry breeze as we passed the countless plywood and corrugated-metal shantytowns, which ignited vivid recollections of where it all began for me.

Finally, we were there, pulling up at the rusting cast-iron gates of our destination – Musina Cemetery. The headstones were prosaic; no polished marble or quartz in this final destination for the departed, just masonry and simple inscriptions of lives lived and lost. Lying side-by-side in adjoining plots in the sun-scorched scrub were my parents; mother Emma-Mina and father Freddy-Jachacha Ndou, unified in death as they were in life.

I was jet-lagged, stubble-chinned and hollow-eyed after the fifteen-hour flight from Sydney and the dusty trek north to my ancestry. It's a tradition of the Venda tribe I was born into to pay respects in this way, without any form of delay.

My parents both died young: Mum was only forty-one and Dad fifty-seven. In South Africa, where the average life expectancy is just fifty-six, their deaths were no statistical anomalies, more the stark reality for our country's impoverished underclass. My mother died of a heart attack and my father of kidney and liver failure, though for him it came as a form of salvation because he'd lost the will to carry on after her passing.

As I knelt at their graves, I recalled the child I was back in the 1970s in this small outpost of roughly 20,000 people, where the population sometimes swelled to twice that figure as an endless flow of humanity passed through each year on the busiest road in Africa, following the compass south as far away from the Zimbabwe border as they could get.

To me, this was always the middle of nowhere. I was just a boy with a combustible temper in a town of drudgery, desperation and dreamers. Many of the town folk were escaping the vicious civil war that raged on the other side of the border as Robert Mugabe's ZANU–PF resistance movement and other factions wrestled to overthrow the colonial white rule in what was still Rhodesia. Like some of those fleeing I too carried the dream gene, imagining a life beyond the confines of my birth.

Rising to my feet, the reels of my mind fast-forwarded. It was thirteen days and counting. The clock was ticking on my boxing future, and whether I even still had one. I needed to draw strength from the spirits of my parents as I prepared to face my own destiny in the ring.

My opponent for the vacant IBO world welterweight title at Johannesburg's Emperor's Palace Casino on 11 July 2009, had not only invaded my core, he was seeping out of every pore.

All I could hear were his taunts: 'You're too old Lovemore. I am going to retire you. Your time has passed Lovemore. I am the *Thohoyandou* now,' (a word which to us of the Venda tribe means 'head of the elephant' or, 'head of the state').

His verbal jabs gnawed like an open sore.

Anger was molten in my mind and an eruption was close. The fact we were of the same people somehow made it all the worse. My nemesis bore the same 'Ndou' surname as me. It translates from Venda to English as 'elephant' and is as common with my people as Smith is to Australians.

He shared the same roots and the same birthplace in the northern province of Limpopo. At the age of thirty, Phillip Ndou was seven years my junior and thought I was more suited to a rocking chair and a porch than the ring.

It wasn't always so. Back in the amateurs, he was a callow and respectful teenager who looked up to me and sought my counsel during my time as the captain of our regional boxing team. Now, thirteen years on, as the undisputed pound-for-pound champion of South Africa and a fighter of the year on numerous occasions, he was intent on taking me down and applying the last rites to my sixteen-year professional career. In his eyes, I was going to be his patsy, his plaything.

I'd been earmarked as his thirty-first knockout victim in thirty-four professional fights. He was tall and languid yet could hit harder than your worst hangover and claimed I was an imposter who had forsaken South Africa to live a life of comfort and privilege in Australia among the 'whites'.

In the media frenzy which had engulfed the build-up to 'Ndou versus Ndou' I'd make the point that while I no longer resided in South Africa, I'd helped put the country on the boxing map, not least by winning the IBF world light welterweight title two years earlier. According to Phillip, though, I no longer belonged among Nelson Mandela's people. A wise man once said you must know your limits – but Phillip didn't know his.

Boxing's like a hall of mirrors where the line between reality and fantasy is blurred and the only things that ultimately count are ticket sales, pay-per-views and titles. Phillip's heckling and hyperbole had guaranteed a full house for our intra-tribal war. He'd done his bit to promote the battle, but he'd also lit a fire within me.

Beyond his baiting, there was something else just as primal fuelling my determination not to be humiliated in my homeland. Years of legal fights with my ex-wife Florence over the custody of our three kids – Maxine, Marion and Lovemore junior – had left me just about flat broke after shelling out several hundred thousand dollars in lawyer's fees. I needed the winner's purse as much as I needed to put my gloating tormentor in his place.

Controversial losses in my preceding two fights had plenty of people buying what Philip was selling. The first was a split decision in my rematch against New Yorker Paul Malignaggi in Manchester in 2008, where only a knockout would have been good enough for me on a Ricky Hatton promotion. Malignaggi had already signed to take on the former champion and there was no way I was going to be allowed to win by any other means than a fight-ending shot. The acrid whiff of judges being bought and sold singed my nostrils.

Five months later I'd lost on points to Puerto Rican wrestler-turned-boxer Kermit 'The Frog' Cintron in an IBF world welterweight title eliminator in Nashville, Tennessee. I had little to croon about in the home of country music that night. It was a step up in weight for me and I also had the weight of the world on my shoulders over the ongoing fight about access to my kids. It was a battle I thought I could lose. I feared back then I might not see them again after my ex-partner had made unsubstantiated allegations of assault against me. Mentally, I was in another place far away from the ring that night. And not a good one.

Phillip thought he was on a banker. He believed the 'Black Panther' – my nom de plume between the ropes – was about as threatening as the Pink Panther. While I still had my supporters and believers, I knew that my record had been tarnished by those losses.

To be given the chance by South African promoter Rodney Berman to fight for a world title again was a cherished prize. Berman had a reputation for giving older fighters a shot at redemption. Maybe, in my case, he just had a soft spot for an ageing 'elephant'.

I was on a tight schedule. Court orders back in Australia meant I could only leave the country for a maximum of two weeks, or risk losing my hard-won temporary custody of the kids. Since it takes at least twenty-one days to adjust to the 1700-metre altitude of Johannesburg, it was just another stumbling block. Luckily for me, I found a gym with a hypobaric chamber where I could accelerate the acclimatisation process, do some pad work and work out how I was going to suffocate the menace of my opponent.

For me, it was the opportunity to become a two-time world champion in separate weight divisions; for Phillip it was all about being served up an opponent who looked to have Father Time, not so much tapping him on the shoulder, as gripping him in a choke hold. He'd only lost three fights and one of those was against Floyd Mayweather Jr – pound-for-pound the best fighter in the world.

I didn't care about all that. It was my first big fight on home soil. After all the years based in Australia and taking title bouts across the world, I just wanted to win it and dedicate the victory to my lifetime hero, Nelson Mandela.

———

Five days and counting … judgment night was beckoning and there I was at two in the morning, pounding the streets of Johannesburg trying to reset my body clock to the nine-hour time difference between South Africa and Sydney.

In a city where muggings and an off-the-scale murder rate are the narrative of everyday life a car cruised alongside me, keeping pace with my strides as its two shadowy occupants eyed me off. A raised voice from the passenger seat barked out from the gloom: 'Come on man, what you think you are doing? How do you think you can get away from armed muggers running so slowly? You're easy prey!'

The attempt at humour from my brother Moffat, who knew something of being on the wrong side of the law after doing jail time for shooting at the police, brought a brief smile to my lips as I ploughed on into the night; my watchdogs along for the ride – Ruddock behind the wheel and Moffat making the wisecracks.

Four days and counting … 'Lovemore, you haven't come here for a holiday show me something,' chided Harold Volbrecht, the grizzled, moustachioed trainer who I had first hooked up with as a raw twenty-one year old. He was back in my corner again as I traded blows with one of my sparring partners at a secluded gym in Boksburg that the media knew nothing about. An Afrikaner ex-welterweight champion with a sardonic sense of humour, Harold also had a track record of training champions.

'Show me you mean business, show me you want to be a champion again,' he goaded. 'Have you come here just to make the other Ndou famous? He's the baby elephant and you're the old bull. Don't let him replace you.'

In front of the media we trained across town at Harold's Hammer Gym where I deliberately took it easy in front of the reporters and TV crews, showboating and coasting to lull them into believing I would suffer plenty of collateral damage in my meeting with Phillip 'Time Bomb' Ndou.

There was another familiar face in my entourage – Divas Chirwa, the former security guard-cum-boxing trainer who had taken me aside as a troubled fourteen-year-old. I had never been near a boxing ring before but knew well how to get into a fight with little or no provocation.

He was an amateur heavyweight boxer in his own right who went by the nickname of 'Makhaza' (the cold one) thanks to his knack of leaving his opponents freeze dried on the canvas. He was the man who introduced me to a boxing gym for the first time and became a mentor and an older brother rolled into one. Having him around again meant a lot to me.

It's fight night … I was losing track of time. I knew the bell would sound soon and could hear the chants of the crowd from my dressing room, some singing my name, others bellowing Phillip's. Several coach loads of fans had journeyed from Musina to support me, including the mayor, who was once my schoolteacher. You couldn't miss them on the TV screen in their white Lonsdale T-shirts with my name emblazoned across their chests.

A who's who of South African celebrities were ringside – actors and singers there for the primeval spectacle. But I was reclining on a makeshift bed, sidetracked and removed from the theatrics unfolding around me, immersed in another world as I devoured the words of a favourite book *Gaspipe: Memories of a Mafia boss.* A true-life tale of New York mobster turned informer Anthony Casso, a man personally responsible for over fifty murders. It helped cast my feud with Phillip in a whole different light and soothed my mind.

My reverie was interrupted by the words, 'Wake up Lovemore – are you a librarian or a fighter?'

They came from the mouth of Harold, perplexed by my laidback preparation. His intervention jolted me, and I looked up at the photos of my kids placed on a table in front of me. They were the main reason I had continued to fight on into my thirties. It was all about them now and before every bout I tucked a picture of them into my socks and carried it with me into the ring like a lucky charm. I also had my girls' names inscribed on the front of my boxing trunks and my son's on the back.

Relaxation gave way to niggling anxiety. It was my sixty-first professional fight and I had been down this road many times. If there are no nerves then you're either on drugs or you're crazy. I swapped the book for some R & B CDs and I jived to the beat as my hands were taped. And then I was shadow-boxing – the face of Phillip Ndou a moving mirage weaving and ducking in front of me.

I turned to watch myself in the full-length mirrors; I was smeared in Vaseline, my torso ripped and cut. The face staring back at me had a dark malevolence. It was time to get busy.

'Remember, you're his captain, you'll always be his captain,' bantered my brother Ruddock.

He handed me a cell phone and my kids were on the other end. I knew they were watching on pay TV back in Sydney. They were excited and all speaking at once; I told them I loved them and I was doing it for them.

The crowd was singing the old Zulu mining anthem 'Shosholoza', which boxing followers had adopted as an anthem to hype up fighters – and when I saw a white man mouthing the words I realised how much society had changed since I'd been away.

THE ELEPHANTS GO TO WAR

Brandishing both flags, Australian and South African, I made the long walk to the ring with my theme tune, the Roy Jones Jr hit 'Can't Be Touched', thumping out from the sound system. That was just how I felt at that moment. Untouchable.

Phillip made his entry to a gospel song, which featured his voice crooning something about a comeback or a resurrection. Yes, I thought, but the resurrection will be mine.

When the national anthems came everybody's eyes were on me to see if I still remembered the words of the South African anthem. I was singing but Phillip just stared me down, his eyes boring into my soul, scanning for signs of apprehension or frailty. He had the majority of the crowd behind him but I had no qualms with that.

I did have qualms, though, with the referee Lulama Mtya. He was a one-time trainer/manager whom I had tangled with when I tackled one of his fighters, Mthobeli Mhlophe, for the South African title before relocating to Australia. Despite beating his man from pillar to post, I only got a draw. So I feared the worst.

'Stay on top of him, be first to the punch, get the action going … don't hold back,' Harold hectored as the bell rang.

Taking him at his word, I threw combinations to the body to slow Phillip down, but he fired back with his long-arm jabs. I stuck with the strategy for the opening rounds and was feeling light on my feet and throwing left hooks and looping right-hands that were catching him. Here I was, the outsider getting the crowd on my side against the local hero and that stung him almost as much as my body shots.

I could hear Ruddock yelling from my corner: 'Action and reaction Lovemore … action and reaction.'

For me, it was all about starting strong and finishing with a flourish – I knew well that's what judges remember most.

His breaths were getting deeper with each round as I tried to drag him into the sort of brawl that suited my style. I was all left hooks and right-hands and the crowd was at fever pitch. Despite the din around us I could pick up the TV commentators saying, 'Phillip's fighting the wrong fight … he has lost control.'

That gave me greater belief. The pundits were complimenting me, saying how my body shots were landing. He was fighting in spurts and by the seventh round I was fighting off the ropes, but Harold hated that, complaining, 'Stay away from the ropes. You are making him look good.'

I caught him with a left hook and right-hand in the eighth, which shook him, and I could see some of the life force drain from him as I followed up with a blur of combinations. He was just holding on and I thought maybe I could finish him then but I decided to be cautious. I knew he still possessed as-yet-untapped power to go with his pride and I had to be careful.

Here was a fighter used to quickfire finishes; going the distance was anathema to him and fatigue was at his door. I was talking to him … burrowing inside his head.

'Come here boy, I've got some candies for you. I am your master, you know I'm your master, you can't beat the master,' I taunted.

Provoked, he was hitting back with combinations. It was what I wanted. I needed him to punch himself out in the championship rounds.

'Come here, don't go away. Why are you running from an old man?'

He moved forward again but I caught him with jabs, saying, 'Go back, and take that with you. Come on now, I've got more for you.'

I'd learned something of the art of psychological warfare from my time as a sparring partner for the great Floyd Mayweather, and knew the knee jerk, instinctual reaction it could elicit.

Mayweather would tell me 'C'mon bitch, come and take this' during our time together at his Las Vegas gym.

I caught Phillip with a huge right at the end of the eleventh round and only the bell saved him as he staggered back to his corner. Another five or ten seconds and it would have been over.

In the twelfth round I suspected only a knockout would win him the fight, but I'd never been KO'ed in my career and it wasn't going to happen now. I grappled and wrestled while the crowd booed me and he searched for that big punch. But I didn't care … I'd given them eleven good rounds and I couldn't let myself get caught by a sucker punch.

When the final bell sounded, despite of the acrimony and the trash talk, we spontaneously hugged like brothers. The respect I'd seen from him all those years ago retuned.

'It's good to see you again,' he said, as if we'd just met like old friends on a street corner. 'Welcome back.'

The verdict was in and I'd won by unanimous decision. I told the crowd the win was for Nelson Mandela.

My brothers were hugging me, my trainer Harold and Divas slapping me on the back, and the noise was piercing. Yet I felt removed from the elation exploding around me, as if I was floating out of my body. Time stopped and a sense of emptiness overwhelmed me.

The people who should have been there to share the moment were absent. My children were back in Australia and my beloved mother, the woman who had sacrificed everything for her family, lay beneath the parched earth in her modest resting place at Musina Cemetery.

CHAPTER 2

SWIMMING WITH CROCODILES

'We were victims of elemental forces which wrought turmoil and turbulence across southern Africa.'

They say chance is everything in life. If that's true, then growing up in a perfect storm of civil war in Zimbabwe and the death throes of apartheid across the border in South Africa didn't bode well for the chances of me amounting to much. Toss in off-the-Richter-scale poverty and I was a poster boy for the underdog.

My odds were further diminished with the added risk of believing that a pure soul protected you from perils lurking in the crocodile-infested waters of the Limpopo River, near its source in the north-east of my homeland.

Growing up in a two-room corrugated-iron shack without running water, sanitation or electricity with my parents, four sisters and two brothers were the cards I was dealt when born in the shantytown of Nancefield, on the outskirts of Musina, on 16 August 1971, and named, with great creative licence by my mother, 'Lovemore'.

She enjoyed none of the comforts or protections of a hospital delivery, giving birth at home on a mat on a floor made of cow dung, with only my maternal grandmother by her side. In South Africa, black women are traditionally undervalued and that attitude was multiplied many times over by an apartheid regime which wouldn't have cared less had she given birth in the street and died in the process.

In those days, Lovemore was an unusual name, to say the least. But I never complained. To this day, I still don't know what my mum was thinking when she dreamed it up. If she were still alive, I'd ask her. In later life its novelty value stood me in good stead with the opposite sex … but those are stories for another time.

My father Freddy, who had a passion for Levi's jeans and motorbikes, grew up in the dusty Zimbabwean border town of Beitbridge. With a sculpted physique and an easy charm, he was a ladies' man by nature and a mechanic by trade, who portrayed himself as a sort of African version of 'The Fonz'.

My mother sold fruits, fish and vegetables on a market stall. They had eloped to Zimbabwe because her parents disapproved of dad's Lothario-like ways – plus the fact he had two children by a previous marriage. But they were more forgiving when the couple returned to South Africa with my mum pregnant with her first child, my sister Caroline, the first. (There are two Carolines in my family – my oldest sister and youngest sister are both named Caroline.)

I entered the world next as the firstborn boy of the family – a status that by tribal tradition bestowed upon me many responsibilities and expectations. Living up to these ideals was a burden I embraced as my siblings and I found ourselves unwitting extras in the bloody real-life drama of our people's fight for freedom from white oppression and the atrocities in neighbouring Zimbabwe, where we lived for three years.

We were victims of elemental forces that wrought turmoil and turbulence across southern Africa in the '70s and '80s. My subsequent life as a professional boxer was a theme-park ride into unending pleasure by comparison, even when I was getting smashed and bashed in the face by an opponent committed to knocking me senseless.

We lived in a shanty so perilous that if you strayed just a few streets away onto the turf of one of the many *tsotsis* (gangs) you risked being badly beaten and robbed.

The townships were awash with these thugs and people being relieved of their meagre monthly salaries were common. If they fought back, they sometimes paid with their lives.

Despite this ever-present threat, we kids found satisfaction in the simplest of things, like the little toys we moulded from clay, the cars we made from shaping strands of wire mesh, or kicking around the makeshift footballs we constructed by stuffing plastic bags full of paper and then tying them up.

Singing tribal songs, jumping rope – which proved handy in the boxing career to come – were also popular pastimes, along with hide and seek. The folk tales of our elders were also important in passing down the Venda tribal teachings to our generation, and we would sit rapt for hours at night listening to tales from our grandparents of what seemed to us a mystical and mythical time. It kept us in touch with our own history because what we learned at school under the apartheid regime's hated Bantu education system was all about white European history – I knew a lot about the Dutch settler Jan van Riebeek, Adolf Hitler, Christopher Columbus and Captain Cook; but little about my own people.

I took wry amusement from my own research, which revealed to me how the people of Africa were meant to have originated in the far north of the continent but had migrated east, west and south due to tribal wars. My people headed south, which to my logic, made me think we must have been the weakest tribe; one that never stopped running.

As children, we shared everything in keeping with the Venda motto of *vhana vha muthu vha nwatelana thoho ya ndziye,* translated in English it means, 'siblings share the head of a locust'. But what that really means is that siblings share the last bit of food during a famine.

To supplement the family's meagre income, I took my life in my hands by setting and emptying nets in the river, where crocodiles lurked in shallows and the shadows, without ever worrying whether or not I would make it out in one piece. The Venda people believed that if you were without sin the water gods would protect you. If you were unfortunate enough to be left crippled or maimed, or even lose your life to the crocodile's jaws, then in our culture it was seen as punishment for your misdemeanours in this, or another life, and the fates were teaching you a lesson.

When others were attacked, people would nod sagely and say in hushed tones: 'They have reaped what they have sowed. Now is the chance for them to turn their lives around.' When I look back on it now,

I realise it was all gibberish and I was blessed not to have become an entree at a crocodile's banquet.

We also used to poach from white-owned farms, setting wire traps for impalas and kudus, which we would cut up and take back to eat or sell. Sometimes the police would see us but turn a blind eye because they knew it was a way of surviving. The Venda people worship the spirits of their ancestors, rather than gods, and we always believed they would protect us.

There were other rituals we practised which, according to tradition, can never be discussed with Westerners – even now. Circumcision was mandatory at a young age and occasionally boys died from the infections that sometimes resulted. Death was a constant companion, not least in the shebeens – elicit bars where unlicensed booze was sold. Stabbings were commonplace among those who had imbibed too much and became embroiled in brawls.

The whites lived in smart houses with lush lawns in the centre of town while we blacks were ostracised to the outskirts, right under the toxic clouds that spilled out from the nearby copper mines. People often perished from mysterious lung illnesses and tuberculosis was rife.

When I was eight years old, my parents decided to take us across the border to Beitbridge in Zimbabwe, which was still then Rhodesia, where they thought we could get an education rather than the indoctrination on offer through the Bantu education system in South Africa, which was seen by black people as just another insidious tool of apartheid. It was a decision that almost cost my father his life – and changed mine forever.

The year was 1979 and the country was in a state of upheaval. There was insurrection everywhere and murderous rampages were common. Abel Muzorewa's United African National Council (UANC) had taken charge after the fall of Ian Smith's whites only government but a power struggle was still continuing, with black-controlled parties such as Robert Mugabe's ZANU–PF and Joshua Nkomo's Zimbabwe African People's Union (ZAPU) at each other's throats.

We had relocated to a village 20 kilometres from Beitbridge to stay with my uncle, and the memories of our time there still give me nightmares. There were seven of us – my siblings and two cousins – huddled together in my uncle's hut one night when my mother and aunt burst in and told all but me and a male cousin to enter a secret tunnel, the entrance of which, to our amazement, lay beneath a wooden crockery cabinet. Crawling on your belly for 15 metres, it led to a small door camouflaged with bushes. Above was a track that offered an escape route to a hiding place in the mountains. It had been dug out for emergencies, just like these.

'What's happening, why are they leaving like this?' I yelled at my mother in a state of blind panic.

My sister Caroline, the first, also started asking questions and she was told to shut up and do as she was told if she wanted to make it out alive. We were ordered never to mention this to anybody and I was told to go back to bed and pretend to be sleeping. The next thing my mother and aunt had disappeared.

Moments later I heard noises and footsteps outside. I got up and peeped through a little hole on the door of the hut. I couldn't believe what I saw. A large fire was burning under a huge tree barely 10 metres away. People were seated around the fire and some were naked. There was a group of men standing above them dressed in civilian clothes but wielding machine guns, and they were kicking and lashing out at some of those at the fireside.

'What's happening?' I asked my cousin, but he said not to talk and to go back to sleep.

I couldn't avert my eyes; though I wish I had. I saw my father in a group of men sitting on one side. He was in his underwear and shirtless, just like the other men. The women were also grouped together.

What I saw next has haunted me since. People were getting beaten with sticks, wires and gun barrels. Then a tall man who I knew was the village chief was ordered to lie on the ground next to the fire. He was naked and I had heard the men with guns accusing him of being a traitor. Some of the guerrillas were taking burning wood and placing it on his body. He was crying and begging for his life and imploring the villagers to confirm that he was a loyal follower of the ZANU–PF leader Robert Mugabe. But nobody spoke up on his behalf.

Then the guerrillas did the unthinkable. They took a sharp stick and shoved it up inside his rectum. They laughed, ate and drank while he writhed in pain.

A ringleader warned the others, 'This is what happens if you don't vote for ZANU–PF. This is what happens when you become a traitor.'

The bloodlust didn't end there. They then grabbed the chief's wife. The ringleader pulled out a large knife while two of his henchmen pinned her arms back, rendering her defenceless. The psychopath-in-chief ordered her to open her mouth. He reached between her lips and yanked out her tongue, and with a quick swipe he cut off a slice of it and threw it on the ground.

He then grabbed her upper lip, seared off a chunk of flesh as nonchalantly as a chef trimming fat from a steak and tossed it next to her piece of tongue, as she recoiled shrieking in agony. But he wasn't done yet; tugging at her lower lip and repeating the same ghastly act.

Tears welled in my eyes but I dared not make any noise in my hiding place only metres away. My horror intensified when I saw them take turns to rape teenage girls and the younger women.

I feared the worst: what were these monsters going to do to my parents? I knew where my dad kept his rifle and contemplated going to find it. Suddenly my aunt came towards the hut. She had been ordered to bring more food and alcohol. The moment she entered she told us to run for our lives.

'Don't look back and don't come back until tomorrow,' she said as she pushed the wooden cabinet aside. 'Hurry now and move.'

In the morning, after spending the night in the mountains to a haunting chorus of hyenas and wild boars, we managed to find the other kids before returning to the village, if, indeed, there was a village left to return to.

In our haste to be reunited with our parents, we had ignored the loud cries of my mother and aunt to come in via the side of the mud house, rather than passing the big tree in the front yard under which the atrocities of the previous night had taken place.

The guerrillas were gone but for the first time I saw a dead body – the charred, naked corpse of the chief, his head grotesquely swollen and the stick still wedged obscenely inside his rear end. The hideous spectre of his lifeless corpse gives me nightmares to this day, usually sparked by any reports I see of civil wars erupting across Africa.

The sickly-sweet stench of seared flesh wafted from his upturned and contorted carcass, and while I took in the gruesome scene in silence, some of my sisters screamed and wailed at venality of it all.

Being exposed to such horrors as an eight-year-old never leaves you, yet back then our elders were often already desensitised to the barbarism people inflicted on each other.

Drenching bursts of rain tumbled from the skies as if god was trying to cleanse the carnage. Thunder, too, and lightning struck the tree. A branch fell near the chief's body. It was smoky and smouldering.

I learned that my father had been attacked with an axe, a savage blow to his back just missing his spinal column. He was in a state of toxic shock and was pronounced dead on arrival at hospital, his eyes swollen shut and his head swollen like a pumpkin. Two hours after being placed in the morgue, two petrified nurses were seen running from the scene screaming and gesturing.

My father had arisen from the dead, perhaps resuscitated by benevolent ancestral spirits, demanding they give him some blankets to fend off the cold as they unloaded another corpse. He was transferred to another hospital the next day and it was three months before any of us saw him again.

My uncle Mathandaza believed in polygamy and had two wives at the time. But that didn't stop him forcing himself on my mother while my dad was recuperating. One morning we all left for the river to do some washing and fetch water while my mother remained behind to cook. My uncle stayed back too – and it bothered me.

I turned back and as I approached the mud house I could hear my mother screaming, 'Get off me.'

My dad had taught me as the first son it was my job to protect my family, and knowing where he kept his rifle, I fetched it. When I walked in my mother was fully clothed and fighting him off. His pants were by his knees. 'Get off my mother before I shoot you,' I shouted.

'Get outside before I smack the shit out of you,' he retorted.

I had seen him beat his children before and pledged to shoot him before I allowed that to happen to me, my mother or any of my siblings. That's when my eight-year-old finger pulled the trigger.

I wanted to shoot him in the chest but the bullet only grazed him on his bicep. He got up and ran from the hut, pulling his pants up along the way. I followed him outside and fired again, this time in the air.

My uncle was a changed man after that and began to treat my family with respect. But that didn't stop my father, on his release from hospital, going after him with a gun cocked before my mother intervened to defuse the potentially deadly situation.

Soon afterwards we all moved to Beitbridge where we began school, while my dad, shunning traditional medication, plied himself instead with alcohol to dull the physical and mental pain of his near-death experience.

I recall on the few occasions that my dad would visit the local hospital for medical check-ups on his back I would accompany him. On one of these occasions we ran into the chief's widow who was also there for a check-up. She looked frail. Her mouth was covered with a black cloth wrapped around her head like a hijab. She removed the piece of cloth to show my father her permanently damaged and disfigured face. It was not a pleasant sight. Her teeth were left permanently exposed. She had lost the ability to speak. I wish I had never witnessed this because to this day I have never been able to shake off the sight of that woman. As a child I would sometimes wake up screaming in the middle of the night from nightmares. The mental suffering is there for life. Even now, I sometimes wake up kicking and moaning, the mental picture of her mutilated face staring at me. I guess I'm also scarred for life.

———————

My father's drinking was getting worse and my mother, tired of his shifting moods and the endless rows over his alcohol abuse, finally whisked us all off back to South Africa before they reconciled and jointly swore never to leave their homeland again.

But the situation in South Africa wasn't much better. Apartheid's foundations were under siege from the civil insurrection orchestrated by the ANC (African National Congress), and mob justice was rife. The state was arresting, torturing and making blacks simply disappear in record numbers as the white government looked in horror at what had taken place in Zimbabwe with the end of Ian Smith's rule, vowing not to let the same happen to them.

In addition to the institutionalised violence all around us, blacks were also torturing other blacks they believed to be collaborators. Vengeance came in the form of the 'Necklace' – a tyre doused with petrol and strung around a victim's neck and set alight in the most brutal expression of township justice.

By the age of fourteen I had seen so many of these killings I had almost become desensitised to the butchery. The value systems instilled in me by my parents were warped beyond recognition. I saw how expendable life was and what had once been sacrosanct was cheapened and tarnished. I barely even valued my own existence anymore.

CHAPTER 3

DARK TIDINGS FROM THE SKIES

'I held him hard and told him to hang on – but he never even heard me.'

Resentment fermented and festered inside me during my teenage years as the fight to rid ourselves of the poison of apartheid gathered momentum. I took to the streets, along with other disaffected teenagers, to protest against the government filling our schools with white teachers, while not giving black teachers the same right to teach in white schools. That wasn't so surprising since we weren't allowed to eat in the same restaurants as them, use the same public toilets, ride the same buses or live in the same neighbourhoods – not that many of us could afford it anyway.

The demonstrations were a regular occurrence and the response from the authorities was to send in armoured police trucks, sometimes with army units along for the ride, just to add another layer of intimidation. They would normally fire off canisters of tears gas or shoot pellets at us but sometimes they used live ammunition with a clear intent to maim or kill.

Both my parents were members of the ANC, and I shared their hunger to rid ourselves of our Afrikaner rulers. Taking to the streets was a natural expression of that. But there was something different about one particular Thursday afternoon back in the summer of 1984; something that troubled me above and beyond the normal anxieties that gripped anybody who dared to challenge the government through open dissent.

My twelve-year-old best friend Phathu (which was short for Phathutshedzo, translated in English it meant Blessing), whom I had known since early childhood, was trudging through the streets of our township alongside me as we headed towards town to join a crowd of hundreds protesting the takeover of our schools. The piercing sunlight of yet another hot and dusty day suddenly gave way to an eerie half-light as dark, foreboding black clouds bubbled up from the north. Seemingly summoned by some hidden demonic force. Then, from the sudden darkness, a deluge poured down from the skies, leaving us running for cover to escape raindrops that within minutes had turned the streets into streams.

It was over almost as quickly as it had begun, but the intensity of the downpour made me uneasy, giving rise to a sense of dread over what ill fortune might greet us if we joined the angry throng. An inner voice urged me to turn back.

'I don't think it's a good idea to go on, let's go home,' I urged Phathu, who was as wringing wet as I was.

'No, what are you talking about?' he replied. 'What's wrong, are you scared?'

But it wasn't fear that was stalking me, more a conviction that something very bad was about to happen.

An hour later, in the midst of the chaos of the protest, as we sung our protest songs in the streets, shots rang out from the police rifles trained on a couple hundred teenagers from an armoured police truck barrelling towards us. Amidst the pandemonium, as people ran for cover and others hurled themselves to the dirt to try and avoid the bullets, I felt the weight of a body fall against me.

Phathu was slumped like a rag doll, his eyes rolling back in their sockets and arterial blood pumping from his neck with each beat of his heart as we both landed on the ground together. A bullet had passed through his neck and out the back of his skull and he was in my arms, the life pouring out of him. I held him hard and told him to hang on, but he never even heard me.

His face was expressionless. He was gone. At the age of only twelve all that potential, all those hopes blasted away by a single bullet.

He was not the first or last black soul, young or old, to fall victim to the apartheid regime – many others came before and followed later. But the deaths were never recorded, as if those who perished had never existed. Just another worthless Kaffir erased.

The police convoy disappeared out of sight as I sat there cradling him, tears lubricating the grief and anger overwhelming me.

His death reinforced my own fatalism, fuelling the conviction that the currency of my own life had been devalued. It was the inevitable consequence of a state that treated us worse than domestic pets and made us feel unwelcome in our own land. It was not uncommon to see a white man driving in his ute with his dog perched next to him in the passenger seat while in the back, exposed to the elements, was a black man, sometimes soaked to the skin if the rains were falling.

We were taught that being born black was akin to a curse and that white people should be worshipped. We had to refer to every white man as 'Baas' (boss) or 'Miesies' (madam) and their sons as 'little boss' and daughters as 'little madam'.

I could never comply, the words sticking in my throat and almost choking me with contempt for those who categorised us as a kind of subspecies, suited only to performing menial tasks. Put there to do their bidding, enrich them with our toil and make their lives more comfortable, while ours were deemed expendable and worth only pennies. My refusal to comply got me into trouble and cost me several domestic jobs, gardening for instance, which I needed to help the family make ends meet.

As I entered my fourteenth year all I could see ahead was struggle and conflict; there was no tangible or discernible sign of the career path that would soon unfurl for me.

I never visualised myself as a prize fighter although, ironically, fighting was part of everyday life in the townships. I had to fight to be accepted as an equal in the country of my birth, and I had to fight for the basic necessities like food and to gain the respect of the ubiquitous thugs who preyed on anybody who showed any inkling of vulnerability. As the eldest son, I felt it was my duty to protect the family – any way I could.

The no-holds-barred fights erupting around us were not governed by niceties such as the Queensberry rules. It was anything goes, with the use of knives, rocks, sticks and sometimes even guns.

Kids used to stab each other on a daily basis and sometimes the altercations had fatal consequences. There were even knife champions, who wore their titles like badges of honour. They didn't always kill their victims but would inflict so much damage that their targets would often be left scarred for life.

The weapon of choice was the *kappa* folding knife, which youngsters took pride in owning, polishing and sharpening as if they were treasured heirlooms. I wasn't allowed to carry a knife – at least that's what my parents were led to believe. The reality was I had very little choice.

In later years, it was guns that became prevalent. It always baffled me how, amid so much deprivation, these expensive tools of destruction were so readily obtainable. I even theorised that perhaps our apartheid rulers surreptitiously drip-fed them into our hands, in the expectation that black people would turn them on each other to cull our own population and save them the trouble of doing it themselves. This was the genesis of a gun culture, which now, in modern day South Africa, is a malaise that stalks all communities – both black and white.

I was not immune to temptation and also at various times owned these agents of death. But I am eternally grateful I was never tempted to use them, which considering my volcanic temperament at the time, was something of a miracle. Guns, like the drugs, were an elixir to those that carried them, generating a giddy feeling of omnipotence.

My own personal panacea was playing soccer, the sport of the people. It was a pathway out of poverty, much like marathon running and also boxing. Rugby, tennis, cricket, golf and swimming were seen as pursuits of the whites. Rugby, in particular, was heavily associated with apartheid. Soccer players were respected in the community; they were the rock stars of the townships, and always ended up with the most beautiful girls. Boxers, on the other hand, were respected and also feared.

Street soccer was a way of life and you joined a team closest to where you lived. Bets were often placed on results in these games between near neighbours and fistfights would often erupt, during or after games, as emotions spilled over.

In a sign of things to come, I was the king of these fights. I had a chip on my shoulder the size of Mount Kilimanjaro and it took next to nothing for me to ignite and begin lashing out at anybody I felt had wronged me. Whether it was a shove, a kick, a push or a late tackle, it was guaranteed I was going to retaliate – with my feet or fists. It was common for me to chase another player, rather than the ball, so I could kick or punch him. It was all about getting even with anybody who hurt me.

I got red-carded on a regular basis. It got so bad that people used to place bets to see how long I would last before getting sent off. It didn't take long before I had earned the nickname 'Mr Red' – whether I was playing for Makushu Primary School, or Musina High School, or my neighbourhood – and it was richly deserved.

Some kids were so fearful of me they would start apologising *before* games had even kicked off, in the hope of pacifying me. I was not the most skilful player but, because of my fitness, I could last longer than anybody else. And every time I got suspended the call would always go out to get me back in the team again in my role as an attacking midfielder. And so the cycle continued.

By this stage, I had decided that I wanted to be *somebody*, and sport was going to be the vehicle to achieve that. It was a ticket to being viewed as an equal in the racist regime of South Africa. But soccer wasn't going to punch that ticket for me. The course of my life was changed one day when, true to form, I became involved in yet another on-field incident in a school game against a team from nearby Thohoyandou. I ended up knocking a kid out cold as retribution for some minor infraction on his part. He had to be carried off and I was sent off and ordered to go home.

The incident was looked upon so dimly that the referee called a security guy to escort me from the premises. Instead of berating me the guard, a towering, thickset figure, looked solemnly down at me and said, 'What's up with you kid? Every time I see you play you get in trouble. I have seen you many times – and it always ends up the same. Why don't you try boxing? It might be better for you. I don't think you have much of a future in football. You're never on the field long enough.'

I told him I'd give it a go, and I accepted his invitation to come and train at a boxing gym owned by the local copper mine the next day.

The big brawny man was there again to greet me and introduced himself as Divas 'Makhaza' Chirwa. It turned out he was a fully-fledged boxing trainer and fighter in his own right and he had a quiet charisma about him, which made you want to listen to what he had to say.

There were other kids there too, a scruffy rabble who, like me, had been dragged off the streets — or soccer fields in my case — and urged to take another path by Divas. We all thought we'd come to lace on gloves and fight, but there was none of that. The first day in the gym was all-out fitness training: pull-ups, skipping rope, press-ups, jumping jacks, and within ten minutes half of the fourteen or fifteen boys there had already walked out. By the end of the session, there were only two of us left.

The next day, I was the only one who returned for more punishment. Why, I am still not sure, but my curiosity had been piqued.

Divas was surprised to see me, saying, 'Oh kid, you're back. Now I am going to teach you how to really fight. But, the first thing we need to work on is your anger. Temper doesn't work in boxing, it works against you. When you're angry, you don't think straight, you're rash and make mistakes. When you're relaxed your mind is clear and your body responds.'

I ignored his advice in my early days of sparring and allowed my inner rage to bubble to the surface all too often. But I soon realised that I was getting hit and hurt, and it wasn't what I had in mind. When I calmed my mind and my moods, I began to find I wasn't getting hit as much and I could counterpunch with force and effectiveness … the pieces of the jigsaw began to fall into place. My inner axis tilted and my anger inside and outside the ring subsided. It's what saved me from a destructive cycle which, I firmly believe, would have probably left me dead before the age of twenty, just like so many others around me, either claimed by gunfire or the blade of a knife.

I was no miner but that didn't stop Divas embracing me as part of his team, and I soon learned that many boxing champions had begun their careers this way. It was a path I chose to follow too.

Divas called it 'training' but stepping between the ropes down at his gym was more like entering a warzone — minus the bullets and guns. Each sparring session was an exercise in self-preservation. Even as a novice they put you up against seasoned fighters, boys older than me and some who had already made names for themselves in boxing and were seen as champions in the making.

I was a featherweight back then but that didn't stop them putting me in against welterweights and even heavyweights – there was no differentiation of the weight classes. And nobody was holding back: a lot of damage was done and some of these fighters became punch drunk – their brain functions scrambled and speech slurred – from the incessant punishment being meted out. Some were washed up before they had so much as stepped in the ring in a single professional fight.

Divas wasn't the only one at the gym intent on giving township kids an opportunity to channel their rampant aggression; a police detective we knew as Sergeant Peter Sinthumule was another. He believed in boxing's redemptive powers and its ability to instil discipline in wayward youths. They were the do-good double act, and they helped illuminate an alternative life path for us.

When I told my parents of my newfound passion, my father was fairly ambivalent, but my mother was worried. She agreed to support me, while at the same time vowing never to watch any of my fights. It was a decision she never once wavered from.

Blacks and whites fought in parallel universes, and for every division there was a black champion and a white champion, before finally a unifying body was formed so there could be one champion, irrespective of colour. The only problem was that black fighters could never win on points – they had to knock a white opponent out to win. Why? Because all the ringside officials were white. Knocking a white rival down numerous times often wasn't enough, with officials finding any excuse to disqualify black fighters if they thought they were on top.

I had a different sort of problem facing me in my first ever amateur fight, against a guy we knew only as 'Robert'. At the age of twenty-four to my fourteen, he was a miner built like the Incredible Hulk, whose mere presence in a room cast a shadow of intimidation. It was an intra-club bout, with the winner to be selected to represent the copper mine team against the local army team. But I wasn't cowed by him; my perspective on fear had shifted to the point where it was an irreverence. My disregard for my own wellbeing had reached a heightened level.

The death of my friend Phathu was fresh in my mind and my own mortality seemed of little consequence to me. I didn't care if I got hurt, didn't care if I died.

It was an obvious mismatch, and everybody in town was saying, 'Lovemore is going to get killed.' People were genuinely scared for me – a teenage and novice featherweight up against a seasoned welterweight. One uncle, who had tenuous claims to a fighting past as a boxer and a wrestler, even told me to cancel the bout. Some of my schoolteachers were also concerned, telling me to focus on my studies and forget about fighting.

But I spotted a flaw in this Godzilla who everybody thought was going to tear me apart. I had seen him train and had done my research. I knew he was a heavy drinker and a womaniser who wasn't taking me seriously.

The fight was, ironically, staged on the same soccer field that I had been escorted from in disgrace three months earlier. The field was packed with a crowd expecting to see me served up and dismembered like some sort of sacrificial offering. I was nervous but unafraid and that didn't change, even as we stepped into the ring and he trained a manic gaze on me that carried the implicit threat of systemic annihilation.

'Lovemore control your temper, stay composed,' Divas told me. 'Do that and you can win this fight.'

I could hear people in the crowd shouting 'You're dead meat Lovemore, dead meat.'

The bell sounds – and he's coming at me like a rhino with a grudge, so confident in his supremacy he has let his guard down. He's throwing some big punches but I'm evading them, moving out of range. I close my eyes, for some peculiar reason, crouch, and roll and snap back with a left hook which hits him flush on the jaw – and he's going down within the first minute. His huge bulk collapsing to the canvas as if all the air has been sucked out of him. He's out cold.

It was a lucky shot and it came from instinct and a bit of tactical tuition from Divas. He lay there for maybe ten minutes as his seconds (cornermen) moved in to revive him. There was a stunned hush in the crowd. Lovemore – the boxer – had been born.

Instantly, in the eyes of the township, I was a world champion in waiting. The next day at school the principal announced my feats at assembly, and everybody applauded.

I was happy to accept the accolades, but I knew it was a fortuitous hit. At the same time, it instilled in me a belief that I could achieve something and be somebody.

CHAPTER 4

UNJUSTIFIED INCARCERATION

'Injustice anywhere is a threat to justice everywhere.'

– Martin Luther King Jr

Word of my emerging prowess began to spread fast and it wasn't long before a commandant from the local army (the South African Defence Force), where my dad worked as a mechanic, had recruited me to fight for them, which I agreed to do so long as I didn't have to give up boxing for the copper mine team.

The commandant was an unusual man, in that he treated everybody the same, irrespective of whether they were black or white. It was incongruous with the prevailing wisdom of the white community and his open-mindedness set him apart. His broad face wrinkled with delight, and his eyes lit up like lanterns when his mind turned to boxing. In sport, and in life, he was not blinded by colour. He was captivated by the chemistry of the sweet science and never let anything or anybody blur his appreciation of ring craftsmanship. He opened my eyes to the wider world, and the possibilities of how far boxing might take me.

'Look Lovemore,' he would say. 'You have the potential and the hunger to succeed. I can see you travelling far and wide to fight, to other towns, and maybe even to cities like Pretoria, Johannesburg and Cape Town. Perhaps one day you can even box in other countries. There's no limit if you believe in yourself and maintain your dedication.'

For me, these were prescient words which further stoked my own smouldering ambitions.

Fighting for the army had its benefits: they provided us with the latest boxing boots and gear, and combining that with my bouts for the mines, my amateur career was humming along at a frenetic pace. I was riding a wave which ultimately saw me become a provincial champion and then a four-time national champion before, in the years that followed, I crossed the Rubicon and turned professional. Sometimes I would fight three times a day: in the morning, afternoon and evening. It was all consuming, but I had found my metier and even that brutal schedule didn't fatigue me.

Boxing was bringing me into the orbit of people whose wisdom and farsightedness I fed off voraciously. Another figure of enduring influence was a Venda tribal elder, who had watched many of my fledgling fights before introducing himself to me after a sparring session one afternoon.

Wilbert Madzivhandila was a man of substance and standing and I was flattered he had noticed me. When he told me I could become a totem for our people inside the ring, and an inspiration to youngsters in need of a positive direction, I found myself mesmerised. Wiry and fit, he may have been into his sixties, but he still moved with stealth and his love of boxing, and the toil it takes to master its myriad skills, was infectious.

He ran his own stable of fighters and was on a mission to put the Venda tribe on the boxing map. Back then we didn't so much play second fiddle to the Zulus, Xhosas or Tswanas; we weren't even in the same band. He saw that as a stain on our tribal stature and wanted to see honour restored. He owned several businesses and he adopted me as a de facto son, paying for taxis to ferry me from my home in Musina to his residence 134 kilometres away, where I would stay the weekend with his family and train in his gym with fellow Venda boxers.

It was all about preparing for bouts with the neighbouring Tsonga-tribe fighters such as Cassius Baloyi, who went on to become a household name as a professional. Wilbert schooled me on the realities of what the future might hold if I continued to follow the path of discipline and desire. He would drive me to Johannesburg to watch professional fights. Sometimes world titles were on the line, and I saw at first hand the ferocity and tenacity needed to excel at a level I could only aspire to.

He introduced me to the great Dingaan Thobela, the 'Rose of Soweto', who went on to become one of the icons of South African boxing. This was in 1991 when Thobela successfully defended his WBO world lightweight title against Antonio Rivera at the Standard Bank Arena. For me, as a twenty-year-old and already contemplating turning professional, to meet him, shake hands and mutter a few muffled words of admiration was further affirmation that I was on the right road. I saw the reception he got from the crowds, the awe he provoked, and I dreamed of being in his shoes, bathing in his aura, and feeling the adulation.

My province had never produced a fighter of any note, let alone a world champion, and I wanted to be the first. I used to tell anybody who would listen that one day they would be sitting at home watching me on TV fighting in Las Vegas or New York. They used to laugh. They thought I was crazy but I knew I could make it happen. I also knew that I was on the ground floor on an elevator of great expectation. That elevator lurched back to the basement level when I suffered my first loss, in my seventeenth amateur fight, at the age of fifteen.

I had made the 194-kilometre journey to the neighbouring Giyani, which is a Tsonga territory, to fight a kid called 'Paulos', one of their best up-and-comers in the featherweight class. I knocked him down three times and after three rounds of domination I instinctively raised my arms in a victory salute in anticipation of another win. I was stunned and shattered when the judges awarded a points decision against me. I was so mad, I even contemplated walking away from the sport.

I felt fleeced and wondered whether it was worth continuing when I was at the whims of such farcical verdicts. I would have expected an unjust decision had I been fighting a white boxer back then, but I never dreamed it could happen so blatantly against a fellow black teenager.

As my sense of grievance and indignation abated, I began to view the loss as simply one of those incomprehensible decisions that boxing throws the way of any fighter. It taught me that sometimes, no matter what, victory will be snatched away from you for reasons beyond your understanding. It showed me that you can't win every fight but that shouldn't stand in the way of chasing your dream.

The fight had been broadcast live on Radio Thohoyandou and the commentators were saying I had been robbed. It was a similar refrain on the streets when I returned to Musina. Plans were quickly made for a rematch. It was being billed on radio as a grudge battle and three months later the opportunity to turn the tables arrived.

I was so wound up that I wanted to hunt him down and annihilate him. The smell of vengeance in the air was so pungent that I frightened even myself with emotions I was feeling.

My fists exemplified the extent of my intent and before the end of the first round I hit him so hard he suffered a ruptured eardrum and it was all over. I heard later that he never fought again and was left with enduring problems affecting his balance and his hearing. His equilibrium was so badly comprised by that one blow that no matter how many times he tried, the authorities wouldn't let him back in a ring, fearing he would suffer even greater damage.

A sense of remorse nagged at me at his plight, and the episode was just another reminder, as if one were needed, of the precarious nature of the journey I had undertaken; and how it could all end in an instant.

As my fistic feats continued unabated, it wasn't just the black community that noticed me, some whites had too. A combination of incessant training and my father's alpha-male genes had turned me into the personification of fitness and youthful vigour. Hints of swagger, and even a touch of arrogance, were also emerging characteristics as my testosterone levels went through the roof. I was not averse to the attention, and plenty of it came my way at one particular location: the local supermarket.

Under apartheid rule, the perils outside the ring were an ever-present part of life – even when delivered in the most alluring of packages. I used to go there to buy goods and groceries for my parents. It was owned by a white man, whose teenage daughter used to sometimes do stints at the checkouts. It wasn't long before, on my visits there, she would tell the black employees to send me over to pay at her register. While we couldn't go into white areas and open shops, they had colonised ours with businesses of all descriptions, and this was one of them.

Some days she wouldn't even take my money, and would just give me the groceries for free, smile beguilingly, and I would be on my way. In my teenage naivety, I wondered what the hell was going on. But it wasn't too long before some of the black staff started whispering to me, 'That girl likes you. She's always talking about you.'

I had suspected it, but such was the taboo of black–white interaction of any kind, other than the master and servant relationship, I hadn't given it any thought. She was undeniably attractive, probably the same age as me, with long dark hair, violet-blue eyes and a figure fast turning from puberty to womanhood.

I knew by reputation that her father, even by South African standards, was an avowed white supremacist. He had a Greek heritage but had been brought up in my province, which was a bastion of hardline Afrikaners, and he had adopted their mantras with the greatest of relish. His wife was also Afrikaner. I knew that if he got even the merest inkling of any connection at all between us he would want to make me suffer the consequences. The prospect spooked me and I stopped shopping at his store, thinking little more of it until, out of the blue one day, a car pulled up outside our family home.

Peeking out of our living room window, I could see the driver was a black lady, and sitting in the back was the 'Greek-Afrikaner goddess'. A beautiful white face in a black neighbourhood, she and the gleaming red-coloured BMW E30 M3, attracted instant attention.

The driver stepped out and walked to our door. I answered and she informed me Sunette was in the car and wanted to speak with me. Seeing a white girl and a BMW car in our neighbourhood was rarer than a sighting of Halley's comet, and it wasn't long before a small crowd had gathered.

'What's going on Lovemore?' said my incredulous mother. 'Have you done something wrong?'

I reluctantly went out to the car, and Sunette said through the rolled down window, 'Step in Lovemore, we need to talk.'

I did as I was asked and when the door had closed behind me, she said, 'You know I like you. I haven't seen you at the shop for so long. Why is that? What's going on?'

I looked her in the eye, replying, 'What are you doing here? Are you trying to get me and my family killed? Because that's what will happen if your dad finds out you've been here.'

'Nobody has to know,' she countered.

But I interjected, 'If he finds out I'm dead meat and so is my family.'

In an effort to hasten her departure, I reassured her I would come by the shop and visit her from time to time, joking that I was in need of some more 'free' groceries anyway.

True to my words, I did begin going back to her father's supermarket. But it quickly got to the point that every time I stepped through the door, the staff would start staring and winking at each other.

Eventually, my worst fears were realised and I was told by one of the African check-out girls that Sunette's father suspected there was something going on between us. I vowed never to go back, but the genie was out of the bottle.

Several weeks later our family home received some unwelcome and unannounced visitors late one night, with six white and two black cops. Kicking down the door and bursting in, demanding I give myself up and come with them. They gave no explanation over why I was wanted, and with my horrified parents and siblings watching on, I was dragged away and hustled into the back of a police van and taken to the police station.

Once there, I was marched into a tiny holding cell where three of the six white cops that had burst into our home began to threaten me, a pastime which came naturally to them when presented with just another 'worthless' black.

'Who do you think you are Kaffir?' they railed at me. 'You don't mess around with white girls and get away with it.'

The bigger and burlier of the three slapped me a few times to try and soften me up while his partner, his pockmarked face barely centimetres from mine, accused me of getting 'sexual' with Sunette.

'This is crazy,' I said. 'Nothing ever happened. What am I doing here?'

The burly one snapped back, 'Shut up Kaffir. Jy is dood [You're dead in Afrikaans]. You won't ever be going back to your people in that cesspit where you live.'

Back then, the police could keep political activists locked up for ninety days without charge while they interrogated them or, in many cases, murdered them. The law had been abused to the point where anybody that the police or government took a dislike to was liable to be swept off the streets and then left to rot. Or worse.

My parents were told that I had sexually assaulted a white girl, even though word had filtered back to me that she had stated that nothing ever happened, which it hadn't, and would testify to the fact if charges were ever laid. But that didn't stop them caging me and then transferring me from Musina to the notorious Louis Trichardt prison.

The day of my transfer my mother was outside the jail with a loaf of bread and a carton of milk for me. Sergeant Peter, my mentor from the boxing gym, was also there. He had become a guardian angel for me while I was held captive, lobbying on my behalf and doing his utmost to get me released. He told his white superiors I was a good boy, a promising boxer and a juvenile of good character. But his entreaties fell on deaf ears. I had made a powerful enemy, who was rich, powerful and influential, and he wanted me punished, no matter what.

My mother handed the bread and milk to him and they were passed onto me. I was perplexed by her insistence that I drink the milk since I was lactose intolerant and it didn't agree with me. It turned out my mother had sought the counsel of a prophet to find a spiritual solution to my problem and had been advised that by drinking the milk I would be protected, wherever I went.

Guzzling down the milk was the same to me as ingesting a fast-acting laxative, which meant that an hour trip to Louis Trichardt wasn't the most comfortable for me, or my captors, with the police van having to pull over more than once while I relieved myself in nearby bushes.

I thought my destination would be the prison's juvenile section, but I was promptly thrown into a holding cell full of adults, some hardened criminals and some on trumped up charges, just like me. The expectation of the cops was that I would get beaten up, or perhaps better still, raped by the motley assortment of inmates, some of whom had been arrested for crossing the border into South Africa illegally from Zimbabwe, Malawi, Botswana, Zambia or the Congo.

There were over 100 men crammed into an airless and windowless pen where every inch of space was at a premium. Prisoners slept wherever they could and scuffles erupted like little brushfires over even the tiniest incursion into somebody else's space.

My entry awakened intense interest, not least because I was carrying a loaf of fresh bread, which in this hellhole had the allure of filet mignon. There were no pleasantries, or polite introductions: I was shoved across the threshold and the cell door slammed shut behind me as men from all directions zeroed in on me with outstretched arms and mean-looking stares; all looking to be the first to relieve me of my booty.

The biggest, baddest and loudest of them shoved the others aside and grabbed the loaf from my hands. He swallowed it almost whole, and I feared I might be next on the menu. But, instead of taking a pot shot at me, he placed a protective arm around me and led me away from the others.

'Kid, what are you doing here? This is no place for you,' he ventured.

We got to talking about sports, most particularly boxing, and I told him all about Divas Chirwa, the trainer-cum-fighter who had introduced me to my new passion. He recognised his surname as common moniker in Malawi, his home country. And from that moment on I became an instant blood brother to this George Foreman-lookalike with a cue-ball head, paws big enough to choke a zebra and skin so dark it looked like he'd been dipped in a vat of tar.

Now and again the guards came to check on me, no doubt hoping I had suffered some form of physical abuse at the hands of one of the more unsavoury characters in my midst. They looked crestfallen to see me sitting alongside this amiable giant, laughing and joking while he threw mock punches at me as I ducked and weaved.

When I told him I'd been hauled in over an allegation of sexually assaulting a white girl, rather than repelling my fellow captives it seemed to impress them and there were wry smiles all around. My alleged transgression was viewed by them as a kind of badge of honour.

The plan for me to suffer a beating, or worse, at the hands of these men had backfired badly from the perspective of my jailers, and it didn't take long for them to transfer me to the juvenile section, where I chanced upon some boys from my home town who were doing their time there.

There were still no charges forthcoming and the clock was ticking. My jailers kept telling me I was going to go to court soon, but nothing was happening. I didn't know much about the law, or much less my rights, but I did know they had to charge me with something. The older prisoners kept asking me if there had been any paperwork or official charge sheets, and there were none.

The days were drifting by and weeks were turning into months. My mum used to visit me every second week and she had no idea what was happening either. She had been talking to Sergeant Peter about my case, and he too was none the wiser. There were rumours back in Musina that I had been killed. Eventually, I was transferred back there and was told before being bundled into a police van that I would be charged the next day. With what, I had no idea.

When I finally made it into the dock just before 5 pm, the prosecutor stated that I had been charged with theft. Apparently, I stole something from the supermarket. I protested my innocence but the Afrikaner judge was having none of it and I was sentenced to 'six cuts', which was a common punishment for a minor infraction and meant I would be lashed with a bamboo stick until it drew blood.

I was hustled out of the courtroom and taken down to the cells below by four white cops, who were clearly looking forward to meting out the orders of the court. They were joking among themselves and one warned the other two, 'Boys, we need to be careful with this Kaffir, apparently he can fight. We're going to need to make sure he doesn't play up.'

I was stripped of my shirt and pants, handcuffed and held down by three while the fourth one took great relish in swishing the cane through the air for maximum velocity before sending it cracking down onto my bare buttocks.

They were hollering all the way, saying, 'How does it feel Kaffir. Are you going to mess around with white girls again?'

In an explosion of anger, I reared up at one of my tormenters and spat at him, telling him to go and fuck himself. It was not a wise move. Wiping away the sputum from his cheek, the leader of the police pack, a hefty, bearded figure who had been doing the whipping, fixed his gaze on me and calmly said, 'You're a dead Kaffir.'

He then kicked me in the face and every other part of my body with full force. With the kick to the face I felt his freshly polished boot crack on my lips and nose. Blood started flowing from my broken nose and busted lips. As I spat blood from my mouth I realised my front tooth had been chipped.

'Ek gaan hierdie kaffirtie dood maak. Bring my een van die honde,' he said (I'm going to kill this little Kaffir. Bring me one of the dogs, in Afrikaans).

One of them disappeared and within a few seconds he was back with a German shepherd on a leash. The dog was already growling and straining to get at me. It was hardly surprising, as all police dogs then were trained to attack and kill black people on sight.

The hefty, bearded leader of the police pack released the leash and set the mutt on me. I felt its sharp incisors graze the skin below my right eye, searing open the flesh, and just missing the socket by a few centimetres.

I couldn't do much to fend off the malevolent canine as I was handcuffed. All I could do was turn my body to the left side, and I felt the dog's teeth puncturing holes in my right arm. Within a few seconds the blood was gushing. I knew then what was going to happen.

Abruptly, the police then left with the dog in tow. I could hear them laughing uproariously as they went, while I curled my bleeding naked body on the floor.

I knew then what was going to happen. It was commonplace for prisoners to be placed in a cell alone and then mysteriously be found hanged hours later, with suicide recorded unquestioningly as the verdict. As a matter of fact, years later in 2006, human bones were found buried in the same police station. Construction workers who were refurbishing the dilapidated building stumbled across the remains while digging a ditch for water pipes behind the holding cells.

I can't say the news came as a shock to me, or anybody else with even the vaguest knowledge of how the police force, with a macabre glee, enforced their sub judicial role as the administrators of death to perceived enemies of the state. Sometimes supposed felons – usually political prisoners – were taken for a drive and when they purportedly attempted to run away were simply shot. The other method of choice to do away with blacks who presented a problem to the authorities was to take them to a high building where they would be tossed off, with police records reading that they 'threw' themselves to their deaths.

As I crouched in the cell, the grill opened and I could see the outline of a black face peering through. The keys jangled and the door creaked wide open. Standing there, with the weight of the world seemingly bearing down on him, was Sergeant Peter.

Before he had even entered, he said softly, in a tone of exasperation bordering on desperation, 'Lovemore, what have you done? You should have kept your mouth shut and taken the punishment. Do you know what they are going to do now? Do you understand? They are going to kill you. You're going to disappear just like everybody else.'

My cavalier approach to the concept of life and death predicaments had brought me to this point, and still his words didn't resonate. I was the victim of a mindset with scant regard for the sanctity of life. Even my own.

After staring long and hard into my eyes, before I finally bowed my head, he turned away and left the cell without saying another word.

Ten minutes later, the silence was broken by voices in the corridor outside. The loudest of them belonged to Sergeant Peter.

'Please don't do this, he's a nice kid. He's just angry. He doesn't understand what he's doing. He deserves another chance,' I heard him plead to an unseen white cop.

There was a lull, and then a harsh-toned voice barked back, 'Get off your knees and stop begging. You're losing all your dignity. Leave this to us.'

Then the footsteps were gone. An hour later, the cell door swung open and two white policemen sneered at me, 'Get up and get out Kaffir. If we ever see you again you're dead.' They took the handcuffs off me.

With the pain from the welts in my buttocks, the kicks to my head and body, the dog bites to my face and body throbbing, and the lifelong scars forming, I said nothing and followed their instructions. I was free again. But there was no sense of joy or deliverance. I just felt numb inside.

I dragged myself out of that cell. I was weak. I had lost too much blood. I started walking towards the hospital. I knew I needed medical attention right away or I would risk bleeding to death. The 'blacks only' hospital was about 3 kilometres away and the further I walked the weaker and more drowsy I felt. Although I had no watch on me, I figured it would have been after 7 pm as the sun was slowly setting.

There were hardly any blacks roaming in town around that time, as was the law then. The curfew laws meant that by 7 pm most blacks had already hurried back to the townships to avoid being victims of targeted police brutality. Urban areas were forbidden territory at night for blacks. As I was walking, I heard the sound of a motor vehicle approaching. I turned around to look and I noticed it was a police van approaching.

The first thing I thought when I saw the police van was that they were coming to finish up what they had started. It didn't bother me or faze me at all at that time. I was ready to be taken out of my misery and didn't care anymore for life. The police van pulled next to me. It was Sergeant Peter. I could see tears in his eyes as he opened the passenger door and helped me into the van. He kept telling me 'It's gonna be alright son,' as he drove towards the hospital.

By the time we arrived at the hospital I was almost unconscious. I woke up the next morning with a drip connected to my right arm, a cast on my left arm and stitches on my right cheek just below my eye. My mother was sitting next to me with a Bible in her hand. She was not rigorously religious and to see her with the Good Book in her hand made me realise that my death might not be far off. Her first words were, 'I love you son. God is great.'

When I lay in that hospital bed a lot of things crossed my mind. I thought of hunting down those police officers and petrol bombing their homes. I thought of petrol bombing the courthouse and the police station. But the more I mused the more I felt I had a purpose to serve in this world and I should not throw it all away.

That's when I made a decision, right there in that hospital bed, that I was someday going to become a lawyer and a politician. I was going to use my law degree to help others fight the injustices of the world. I have been asked many times why I decided to become a lawyer, but never before have I told anyone else apart from my children that this was one of the reasons I decided to study law.

I have also been regularly quizzed about the scar on my right cheek but never before have I told anyone the truth about it. People often assume it's a badge of honour from years of boxing and I just go along with it. Sometimes I tell people it was from a car accident when I was young. I have studiously avoided talking about it to avoid triggering traumatic memories. Even up to this day I do not like to talk about it as the thought of what I was exposed to stirs so much anger inside me. I have been able to mend my chipped tooth with beautiful veneers but the scars on my face and buttocks are a constant reminder of my teenage life in a country that was once torn apart by racial discrimination and injustice.

The draconian punishment dished out to me hardly fitted the crime, even if one had actually been perpetrated. Six lashes and incarceration for ninety days alongside hardened felons – as well as a smattering of fellow sufferers of rough justice – for supposedly stealing 50 cents worth of lollies was the personification of overkill. In any civilised nation, as a sixteen-year-old juvenile with no prior criminal history, I'd have walked away with a warning or fine, even if I had been guilty of the trifling misdemeanour. But to be banged up in remand, not even knowing what I'd been charged with, was par for the course in what passed for justice in apartheid South Africa.

The whipping was all about revenge for the crime of consorting, however tenuously, with a white girl. It was the mission of the prosecutor and a complicit judge to make sure I suffered lifelong consequences for breaching those boundaries erected by our white rulers.

They knew exactly what they were doing and it had nothing to do with the alleged theft of confectionery.

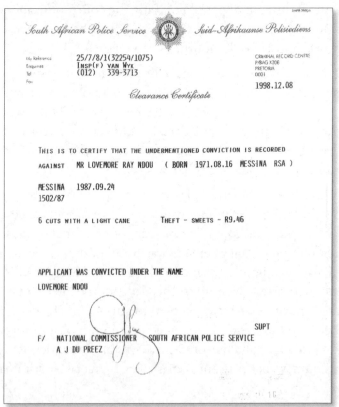

A copy of Lovemore's conviction record as a result of trumped up charges in South Africa at the age of 16. Lovemore was sentenced to six cuts with a cane.

CHAPTER 5

THE SCHOOL OF HARD KNOCKS

*'Instinct and a streetwise intuition, both inside and outside the
ring, were my closest allies.'*

The notion of freedom was a subjective term in apartheid South
Africa. What passed for liberty could be snatched away from you
at any moment, as I had discovered. I had no inclination to renew
acquaintances with the agents of law enforcement, or what masqueraded
as the justice system, any time soon, as I licked my wounds and sought
to regain my equilibrium following my brush with the authorities.

The angry, raised welts on my back and buttocks were a painful enough
reminder of my incarceration and the lashing and beating I'd received.
The lacerations on my face from the razor-like teeth of the hound from
hell unleashed on me by the cops, were another unsightly consequence.
But what worried me most was the broken left arm bequeathed me by
my tormentors.

I was in a cast for several weeks and in my darkest days a gnawing
depression descended on me as the fear of never being able to box
again took on its own reality. It was a reality I wanted no part of, and as
the weeks ticked by I resolved to fight back. When the cast was finally
removed my arm was withered and, even worse, it was at a slight angle.

My mum was worried and after consulting with my dad, money was
found to pay for a medical consultation. The news wasn't good, with
the doctor decreeing that without surgery I'd never have full range
of motion again in my damaged and painfully swollen left elbow. I

was diagnosed with elbow bursitis, commonly known as Popeye elbow. Surgery was scheduled at a nearby clinic, and a full anaesthetic was administered while the surgeon went about his work.

Things didn't go according to plan, and my boxing future seemed the least of all concerns after I failed to awaken from the anaesthesia in the prescribed time. Not only that but my body – so I was later told by the medicos – suffered a series of epileptic seizures while I was supposedly recovering in the post-op area. The convulsions jerked my frame so violently that I was thrown off the hospital bed in a semiconscious state, crashing face down onto the tiled floor. Oddly, the impact shook me out of my dreamlike trance and into full consciousness, much to the relief of the doctors and my distraught mother.

She joked later that the fall was actually a preordained act of God, designed to activate my previously dormant cerebral cortex. Her reasoning was that I excelled at my studies in the months after the incident, much to the delight of my tutors.

I wasn't buying her half-baked theories and attempts at humour but was just relieved no further damage had been inflicted, other than a smorgasbord of bruises and a top lip so swollen it looked like I'd just gone the distance with an opponent who had used my unprotected face for target practice.

Despite the operation, my arm continued to be at a slight angle. I became my own physiotherapist, collecting bricks and using them to do arm curls to try and strengthen and straighten the arm. It got to a point where I'd have a brick at my bedside at night, and if I awoke in the wee small hours I'd do several sets of curls before dozing off again.

My brick obsession proved a blessing one night as the family slept, crammed side-by-side in my parents' two-room shack. There had been a rapist stalking the area, as if we didn't have enough troubles already, and he decided to pay the Ndou household an unsolicited visit.

I was awoken by a shadowy figure moving deftly from one sleeping sibling to another, doubtless looking for a female victim. When it was my turn, I reared up and caught him flush on the jaw with a punch. He recoiled, turned and leapt through the same open window he'd emerged from. Screaming at him, I jumped up and followed him through the same window, my trusty brick in my right hand.

He was still within range, and my aim was true: the brick, carrying all my wrath with it, catching him on the back of the head and bringing him to earth in the half-light. He was left semiconscious and though unknown to us at the time, he turned out to be instantly recognisable to police, who were soon on their way, as a wanted serial molester and rapist.

My spirits were lifted, but the aftermath of my healed fracture at the elbow was still an issue and continued to be throughout my career.

For a while I went through a period of depression. I was angry with the world and also fearful that I might never step into the ring ever again. Egged on by my uncles, I began to experiment with alcohol, the poison of the townships. And much to my mother's disapproval, I started hanging around with some sinister characters at the shebeens (the illicit bars where alcoholic beverages were sold without a licence).

Shebeens came with all the shenanigans one can think of. Sex for the exchange of alcohol was at the top of the list. That also meant a spread of sexually transmitted diseases including HIV/AIDS. Fights flared like brush fires, and they were often over women.

A friend paid with his life in one such incident, in a stark warning to me that I needed to get out of these dens, for good. He confronted a local hooligan who had slapped his girlfriend on her buttocks and before we knew it, it had escalated into a deadly fight. It was typical of the casual disregard men back then had for women. I am not sure if it is still the case today. In a country like Australia such behaviour amounts to a case of indecent assault and carries a jail term but in South Africa back then it was all part of the daily fabric of life. My friend was stabbed in the neck and bled to death before he'd even made it to the hospital.

A few days prior to this incident the perpetrator had tried to pick a fight with me. He had called me a *mpintshi,* which was a street vernacular for 'moron', to the delight of his buddies and female companions. I had seen the big dagger tucked in his pants and protruding through his shirt so instead I bit my tongue, although I knew I could have easily knocked him out cold in a fair street fight. He was notorious in the neighbourhood, with a string of previous stabbings – some of which led to fatalities – part of his portfolio of sins.

The episode showed me that I was in grave danger of morphing into my father by resorting to alcohol to deal with my inner demons.

I finally felt strong enough to return to training, albeit in an unorthodox fashion. To rebuild my left arm, my trainer Divas would tie my right hand behind my back, forcing me to use the suspect limb. I would spend hours jabbing, throwing left hooks and body rips. It was relentless. As my career unfolded, those torturous sessions paid dividends, with the most damaging weapon in my arsenal strangely enough my left jab. At times, it's unerring penetration and power could literally win me fights on its own.

The preceding seven months of inactivity had left me unable to perform any manual odd jobs to earn the money I needed to supplement my school fees. I needed to find a way to pay because it was beyond the means of my parents, with so many other siblings to also consider, and living perilously close to the breadline as we were. So I decided to devote myself to scholarly pursuits and I began hiring out my services to do other kids' homework. It proved a lucrative pursuit, and I would collect a small fee or maybe they'd give me their lunch box. It also made me a better student and an ever-willing receptacle for knowledge.

Back then electricity was a luxury far beyond us, and our street, and those throughout the neighbourhood, were plunged into darkness each night. We relied on candles and paraffin lamps for illumination. When streetlights were finally installed one day, it felt like we'd moved into the space age. From then on, I could be found outside at night under a lamp, pouring through my books, while my contemporaries played games around me.

With my boxing hopes on hold, I'd had an epiphany and now viewed education as another possible avenue of escape from the remorseless poverty which seeped into every recess of existence in Musina. Visions of a utopia far away were a constant show reel in my unconscious and conscious minds.

Those daydreams were fuelled by the infamous 'bucket system', which was as good as sanitation got back then in dealing with human waste in our neighbourhood. I used to dread Tuesdays, the day the truck that picked up all the faeces-filled buckets would come by. The whole street reeked for hours of excrement, an invisible, eye-watering cloud of pong invading every nook and cranny of your senses.

It was the only day I couldn't bring myself to sit outside and study. The foul odour was filtered by closed doors and windows but still detectable. Escaping that stench was another powerful tool of motivation, as if one were needed, to get as far away from Musina as I possibly could.

I knew the Bantu education system imposed on us by our white rulers was designed to fail black people, but it was all we had. I'd go to libraries and devoured books about Martin Luther King Jr. I dissected Karl Marx and Friedrich Engels's *The Communist Manifesto*, Aristotle's *Politics*, and *The Social Contract* by Jean-Jacques Rousseau. I read books on Hitler, Winston Churchill and African heroes such as King Shaka, King Mzilikazi, King Lobengula, Emperor Haile Selassie, and the Mansa of Mali, Musa Keita. I read anything I could lay my hands on.

My parents encouraged me in my pursuits. My mother had limited education but could at least read and write in Venda, whereas my father Freddy had to teach himself to write his own name, and often struggled with that. He confused his b's with his d's, thus landing him the family nickname of 'Frebby', though none of us dared utter the pseudonym within earshot of him.

There was even an incident where he had to go to hospital and signed the paperwork incorrectly. When the white doctor came out asking for a 'Frebby' it didn't go down well with him, and he barked in exasperation at the perplexed medico, 'What's wrong with you? First you come and take our country, now you want to change our names!'

———

It was nine months from my beating to my first fight back with the team from the local copper mine. I won it but I was rusty and bereft of confidence. It took several more bouts fighting for the local copper mine's team, and also the local army team, for my belief and swagger to resurface, as my amateur career began to gather some lost momentum.

For some reason, the mine workers, the ones with me in the boxing team, saw me as some sort of conduit between them and management. I made presentations to the head of sports at the mine, a man named Njozela, pleading for better equipment like new punching bags and gloves. He was from Nelson Mandela's Xhosa tribe, and highly educated. He seemed somehow out of place in such an environment. He asked me to put it in writing, probably thinking he'd seen the last of me.

When I returned with a list of requests articulated in a letter, he perused it and said sagely, 'Kid, did somebody write this for you?'

He was shocked and told me I could end up being more than just a boxer, and to keep up with my education.

A meeting was arranged with the mine's white managers, to which I was invited, to press the cause further. As a final request, I implored them to stop forcing their black fighters to ride in the back of trucks on dirt roads for sometimes up to 200 kilometres to get to fights, while the white boxers were ferried about in cars and buses. Sometimes you got to a bout and were exhausted before even lacing your gloves on.

A week later, a new ring and equipment arrived and suddenly I was seen by my fellow fighters as a master negotiator and the natural mouthpiece to articulate their desires. The prevailing wisdom, much to my astonishment was, 'If you need something done, you need to go and speak to Lovemore'.

I did the same with the army, where my father was a mechanic/labourer, requesting through the commandant that they let us eat the same diet as the white fighters, rather than just scraps and leftovers. Suddenly, we were allowed to all travel on the same bus and even stay in the same accommodation, which was unheard of in those days.

My amateur bouts were coming thick and fast and by the time I was done and ready to turn professional I was a four-time national champion, with a record of sixty-six wins and only two losses.

Instinct and a streetwise intuition, both inside and outside the ring, were my closest allies. Which brings me to my chance meeting with Malawi-born fighter Mtendere Makalamba, who had fought the legendary American middleweight Roy Jones Jr at the Seoul Olympic Games in 1988, finishing outside the medals but distinguishing himself nonetheless. He was an amiable scrapper with a gold front tooth and the ability to deliver a vicious upper cut when the mood took him, which was often.

He wanted a pipeline to some reputable boxing promoters in South Africa to further his aspirations of transitioning into the professional arena. We became friendly and I put him in touch with a number of them. One of them, Thinus Strydom, was interested and signed him up.

He made a storming start to his pro career, knocking out his opponent in his first fight while I watched on TV. Afterwards, he publicly thanked me through the press for helping him on his new path. I was touched and I went to Johannesburg for his third bout. Again, it was a short-lived affair, with his opponent knocked out cold in the early rounds.

My companion, Mr Wilbert Madzivhandila, planned to make the drive back to Musina that night. But Makalamba was anxious for me to stay back for a few days to hang out with him, promising to drop me off at Musina, en route to Malawi in his spanking new car. Normally I'd have accepted such an invitation, and part of me wanted to, but another part told me not to. I'm not sure what it was but a small, but insistent voice, urged me not to go with him.

I made my excuses, saying I had a lot on my plate and needed to rush back. But really, there was nothing pressing. A few days later, news filtered through to Musina of a flipped and burned out car by the side of the road 10 kilometres out of town. The driver was scorched beyond recognition by the flames ignited from an exploding gas tank.

The car was traced to him and I was asked to go to the mortuary to identify the body. Before instinctively recoiling and averting my gaze from the charred remains, I was able to see the one trademark feature which had survived the inferno. That unmistakable gold tooth.

CHAPTER 6

TEARS IN THE DUST

'Her wearied face creased into a smile, as if to reassure me that everything was going to be okay, but I think we both knew, in that moment, we would soon be parted.'

The one constant in my life in those days of endless uncertainty was my mother. She was my closest confidant and supporter, although she could never bring herself to attend any of my fights, for fear of seeing me badly beaten, or worse.

She would wake me up at 5 am each morning for my morning run. When I returned, she had prepared warm water for me to bathe in before I went to school. We had no electricity, so it meant she had to make a wood fire and boil water for me while I was out jogging. She never wavered from the routine, even as the heart condition she'd been diagnosed with three years earlier began to slowly suffocate her life force. She'd just turned forty, and yet her symptoms worsened a little with each passing month.

She would make me porridge and a cup of tea before school and, cobbling together the little money she made from selling fruits and fish at the markets, she made sure I had proper boxing boots, trunks, mouthguard and shorts. She also ensured I had enough money to travel anywhere around South Africa to compete as an amateur.

I could scarcely bear to acknowledge it, but this totem of love and stability in my life was close to falling. Festering fears over her failing health cast a shroud over me, affected my studies, and when she began to spend several days in hospital at a time, before eventually returning home, I began to understand that the most important person on earth to me might soon be lost forever. We couldn't afford the medications she badly needed, and it tore at our souls to visit her propped up in bed amongst the desperation and drudgery of the public hospital.

The day she passed away – 24 November 1992 – was the worst of my life. How can you ever truly prepare for the day when your mother, the very essence of your own existence, is taken from you. She was the foundation of my life, my inspiration and motivation. The day she died was probably the last time in my life I've ever cried.

I can still feel the gut-wrenching despair of her passing as if it were yesterday. I had just finished writing my Year 12 exams (called Matric in South Africa). My brother Ruddock and I went to visit her in hospital in the morning. She wasn't herself but put on a brave face. She pulled me close, looked me in the eyes, and said, 'Never forget to chase your dreams. You will make me proud.'

Her wearied face creased into a smile, as if to reassure me that everything was going to be okay, but I think we both knew, in that moment, we would soon be parted.

Ruddock and I went to the gym to spar, neither of us saying much, both consumed by a sense of impending doom. The welling grief in us morphed into anger inside the ring. Tears welled in both our eyes as we went at each other with a ferocity which had never before surfaced. Ruddock, who went on to have seven professional fights, was a mean puncher and we were doing our damnedest to knock each other out. Other fighters in the gym stopped what they were doing to witness the surreal scene of two brothers going to war, tears streaming down our cheeks.

The spell was abruptly broken by the entry into the gym of my father, for the first time ever. It portended news we didn't want to hear, my dad declaring solemnly, 'Boys, you need to stop now. I have something important to tell you.'

He didn't need to say anything else. We both knew only too well why he'd come, and all three of us just melted into each other's arms, sobbing and embracing. No more words were needed, or uttered.

I carry my mother's memory with me everywhere: her gentle determination is a guiding beacon and the hearty laugh she uttered in moments of levity echoes still in my mind.

While we mourned her loss in our own ways, my father was the most profoundly damaged by her passing, turning with a grim gusto to the crutch of alcohol to numb his grief. When Mum was there, she tempered his leanings towards cheap, illicitly brewed booze, but without her the boundaries were torn down. He borrowed money to buy *mukumbi* (marula beer), *chibuku*, or the deadly *tototo*, a noxious concoction made by fermentation and distillation from grains like millet, maize and sorghum. The drink is sometimes adulterated by adding substances like battery acid to give it more 'kick'. He was guzzling it like there was no tomorrow and had creditors knocking down the door after spending beyond his means each month to buy the stuff on credit. I had to threaten exposing them to the authorities to ward them off.

For all my father's faults, there was still a deep love there between us and he always taught me to stand up for myself and speak my mind. He also taught me that sometimes what it takes to get respect from people is to get even with them. You might say being vengeful or vindictive. I used to quote him biblical text, declaring grandly, 'If one strikes thee on thy right cheek, turn to him also the other.'

His response was always a terse and unforgiving, 'Only if you are a fool like Jesus would you do that and end up hanging on the cross like him.'

He would then tell me that at least Jesus was imbued with the gift of rising from the dead, adding pointedly, 'But if you die your ass is never coming back. You will just end up buried next to the other fools who also turned their other cheeks.'

He was an eye for an eye, tooth for a tooth type of guy. Case in point was an incident where he fell foul of a hardline Afrikaner boss who had ordered all his black employees to refer to his five-year-old son as 'klein baas' (little boss) instead of referring to him by his first name. This was very common in South Africa back then.

My dad, the would-be Fonz with easy charisma and burning sense of injustice, wasn't having any of that and suggested to his boss he should 'go and fuck himself'.

Needless to say, the invitation went down about as well as an arsenic capsule and the infuriated employer stormed off to get his gun, so he could teach the insolent, uppity Kaffir a lesson in front of his fellow workers.

On his return he found my father waiting for him with his own loaded old rusty rifle, cocked and ready to fire. The shocked boss wasn't willing to pull the trigger in fear of his own life. And the stand-off ended with him sacking my dad, who left with a box full of spanners as a parting gift.

Canny and cunning, he taught me to be a hustler – but in a good way. It was by using his street smarts that he always found ways to feed his family even when times were hard.

The deep wound of my mother's death had barely even begun to scab over before more bad tidings rolled in to Musina. With my father in a self-destructive free-fall, I felt an even heavier burden upon me, as the oldest child, to step up and fill the void left by my mother. But, as ever, the pathway was more like an obstacle course. The local copper mine began laying workers off as talk of an impending closure gained currency and my trusty trainer, Divas, was one of those tapped on the shoulder. He left for Johannesburg to find work, and I was deprived of another hugely positive influence on my life.

CHAPTER 7

DIRTY TRICKS AND GREAT ESCAPES

'In the 1980s and 1990s amateur boxing rings were largely monochromatic. Forget weight divisions, the biggest division was along racial lines: there was one for blacks, one for whites and one for coloureds (mixed races).'

'Wake up Lovemore, it's time for your run – there'll be breakfast and a hot tub waiting when you get back …'

I awakened with a jolt expecting to see my mother's familiar, soothing face staring down at me. But reality kicked in as I gazed out from under the sheets. There was nobody crouched over me and the only sounds were the rhythmic inhalations and exhalations of my still sleeping siblings, and the muffled crowing of a cockerel somewhere a street or two away. A familiar paralysing pang of longing and sense of loss enveloped me, before finally subsiding into an echo of emptiness.

That same dream of her at my bedside to awaken me had become a recurring theme since her death. It was as if the umbilical cord that tied us from before birth could be stretched but not irrevocably severed. It was her presence, in spirit if not human form, that was driving me. And the message was simple: don't lose sight of your goals.

It was then that I made the unbending decision that I was going to turn professional, no matter what it took. I knew I had the talent to become a champion, if only I was given the opportunity. But the words 'opportunity' and 'black' were rarely mentioned in the same sentence back then. I'd witnessed too many talented black boxers fall into apartheid's vortex and end up on the scrap heap before coming close to fulfilling their potential. There were others who became world champions only to be mercilessly ripped off and bled dry by unscrupulous promoters. If they were 'lucky' enough to get the chance to fight overseas, the promoter would more often than not end up siphoning off the lion's share of the purse.

Promising white fighters, on the other hand, were spoon fed sponsorships and had promoters fawning over them in another example of the sport's lack of equality. I knew all too well as an amateur that being black, in the eyes of referees and judges, was a cue to skewed results and perverted natural justice.

I needed to find a promoter who was essentially colour blind, and the name of legendary former South African World Heavyweight Boxing Champion, Gerrie Coetzee, kept jumping into my mind. Although I got responses from other promoters, it was Coetzee who I set my heart on. I respected the way he'd conducted himself during his boxing career. He was polite and gentle outside the ring, at odds with the beast-like presence the pasty-faced, moustachioed mauler exhibited inside the ropes. Most tellingly, he had publicly denounced racism to win the affection of many among our nation's black majority.

In the 1980s and 1990s amateur boxing rings were largely monochromatic. Forget weight divisions, the biggest division was along racial lines: there was one for blacks, one for whites and one for coloureds (mixed races). This was despite South Africa lifting the ban on interracial fights in 1973, and legalising 'mixed bouts' in 1977, along with discarding the system of 'white' and 'supreme' titles.

The truth was that deep-seated beliefs and prejudices perpetuated boxing's colour bar. Boxing clubs remained segregated and multiracial fights were studiously avoided. When they did occur a light shone brightly on apartheid's absurdities and inequalities. I was, of course, not immune to this and had to play with the cards in front of me.

I foresaw turning professional as a pathway to a future in which South Africa, and its rotten system, would be left far behind in my rear-view mirror. It had nothing to do with despising my homeland but a lot to do with being treated as just another servile member of the great underclass in the land of my birth. Sport was a further reflection of that.

I had to learn to fight dirty as an amateur, as beating a white opponent on points was virtually unheard of. The officials who ruled on 'mixed bouts' were white and racist to the core, especially in my home region of Northern Transvaal. There, the hue of prejudice was blindingly vivid. The hardline white supremacist political party Afrikaner Weerstandsbeweging (AWB) was headquartered there, as was its arch-bigot grand wizard Eugène Terre'Blanche. The group operated as a self-governing, self-styled vigilante force, equipped with an army-like arsenal of weapons, and they exacted summary justice, very often fatal, on 'unruly' blacks or anyone who espoused pro-democracy views.

Each time I boxed against a white fighter in Northern Transvaal the odds were he either came from a family that was associated with the AWB or his trainers were members of the AWB. Or one of the officials was associated with the AWB. It was common to hear baying white crowds hollering and screaming, 'Donder die Kaffir' (Hit the Kaffir, in Afrikaans).

It was also commonplace to see a white fighter wearing 8-oz gloves and a black fighter wearing 12-oz gloves while officials turned a blind eye to the obvious advantage afforded to the former.

Luckily, I had a trainer in Divas, prior to his untimely departure to Johannesburg, who was an expert in the art of dirty tricks. He taught me so many underhand ploys and shady tactics that by the end of it I felt like I'd graduated with first class honours from the Harvard school of chicanery and subterfuge.

One of the low-down acts I mastered was how to break noses using the elbow. This was the best way to cement a knockout and be guaranteed a win. Then there was standing on my opponent's foot to stop them from moving around the ring and then unleashing heavy blows to their body. Otherwise, if you allowed them to dance around the ring they would win the fight without landing a single punch. Without a clear-cut knockout, victory was impossible against a white opponent. You could outfox, outbox and pretty much beat your man to a pulp in every round, or knock him down ten times, but as long as he made it to the end still standing he had won.

Another ruse employed by racist referees was to simply disqualify a black fighter for a mystery infraction, if he felt that he was on top and a knockout was imminent. Then there was the old slow-motion mandatory count routine, where referees would hesitate over every number they enunciated in the count to ten, in the hope the dazed white fighter would regain his sensibilities and stagger back to his feet. If that looked like it might fail, the official might halt the count and march over to the black fighter's corner and issue a theatrically stern warning over some imaginary misdemeanour to try and buy even more time. But we learned to fight fire with fire, hence Divas's dossier of dirty tricks.

It was not unusual to hear a black trainer screeching to his fighter 'Phuli impumulo' (break his nose in Zulu). This wasn't easy to do considering fighters sometimes used to wear headguards in the amateurs. What didn't assist white fighters though was their often long and pointy noses which invariably protruded through their headguards. All you had to do was make sure the referee was out of view and throw a hook that missed the nose, or just grazed it, but your elbow hit the target. You had to do it fast though, otherwise you risked getting disqualified or banned for years, if not life. Fortunately for me they didn't have banks of TV cameras back then covering every angle of the ring, as is the case today.

Do I regret resorting to deeds that were more Marquis de Sade then Marquesse of Queensbury? No, because boxing is a fight. It's not like soccer or tennis where you play ball. You do not play boxing. You go to war. Your opponent is trying to render you unconscious. He is unleashing blows which can potentially kill you. So you make sure you do it to him before he does it to you. And you make use of anything, and everything, you can to achieve your objective.

While well versed in the intricacies of the unorthodox and the outlawed, I outdid myself on one memorable occasion in which I was fortunate to escape with my life. I was participating in the provincial championships in a town formerly known as Pietersburg. Today it's called Polokwane. It was a staunchly pro-white stronghold whose ruling inhabitants tended to treat their dogs better than they would the local black populace. At such events you would sometimes fight up to three times a day, eliminating each other until the last two fighters in the division battled it out for the championship.

I had blazed my way to the final with a chain of knockouts and found myself matched against a tall, lanky white fighter in the decider. My sharp-featured and sharp-tongued opponent kept referring to me as a 'Kaffir'. The referee could hear but did nothing about it, telling me to 'shut up and fight', or he would disqualify me, when I complained.

For the first time in a very long time I resorted to what had got me into boxing in the first place. Unrestrained anger. I lost my marbles. I hated being called a 'Kaffir' and, in the heat of that moment, I wanted to kill this sneering, condescending kid, whose noxious bile exemplified everything I wanted to see end in my homeland.

I knocked him down more than eight times in the first two rounds, yet they were all ruled slips. The trash-talking beanpole then resorted to dirty fighting. He would step on my feet, push me, intentionally head-butt me and elbow me. Unsurprisingly, the referee saw nothing untoward and made no interventions.

My brother Ruddock, who had taken over as my trainer when Divas left town, could see the tempest brewing inside me was about to erupt. He yelled at me repeatedly, 'Stay calm Moore.'

I returned to my corner at the end of the second round, and he said matter-of-factly, 'Moore, they're going to take this fight away from you. They are either going to disqualify you or give it to him on points.'

My response was instant and unabashed: 'If that white boy fights dirty again I'm gonna give him a present for life. Be prepared to run for it.'

Though he knew my temperament all too well, Ruddock thought on this occasion, and in this hostile jurisdiction, I must surely be jesting. But I was deadly serious, and the instant the white kid came firing with his dirty tricks again, I took the most drastic action of my boxing career. He missed me with his elbow. I took a step backwards, as if I was going to take a penalty shoot and, martial arts style, kicked the kid in the nuts as hard as I possibly could. Not daring to wait for a reaction, I vaulted out of the ring, a shocked Ruddock right behind me, leaving the kid doubled-up in pain on the canvas clutching his groin.

The ripple effect throughout the auditorium was instantaneous, with every black fighter and spectator that was in the hall sprinting for the doorway. We all knew hell was about to break loose, in the form of white retribution. The racist locals were capable of shooting anyone and anything black. Within ninety seconds we were tearing down the street away from the scene of the crime, our bus driver screeching to a halt in the middle of the road allowing us to jump aboard. Moments later we heard gun shots, as a furious mob of pursuing whites fired volleys of bullets into the air to see us on our way.

The disqualification was my second loss and was the last time I ever fought in Pietersburg.

It was Johannesburg, the city known as Egoli (the City of Gold), that held a magnetic attraction for me as my plans for national and international recognition germinated into a fully-fledged obsession.

CHAPTER 8

WELCOME TO THE CITY OF GOLD

'Everything is good is nice. You come baas Gerrie's Gym and we get the fights, don't worry.'

The pay phone swallowed the coins and, after a short delay, the line rang three times before a gruff voice answered with a curt, *'Yebo'* (hello in Zulu).

The sharp manner was instantly replaced by a warm, syrupy tone when I introduced myself as, 'Lovemore, the boxer from Musina …'

I didn't get another word in before Jonas, Gerrie Coetzee's right-hand man and owner of the disembodied voice at the end of the line, interjected, 'Yes, Lovemore, greetings, baas Gerrie [boss Gerrie, in Afrikaans] has tell me all about you … you go be famous my boy.'

There it was, his sales pitch, delivered in broken English.

'Everything is good is nice. You come baas Gerrie's Gym and we get the fights, don't worry.'

I tried to switch to the alternate tongues of Zulu, Xhosa, Tswana and even Afrikaans, but Jonas was having none of it, ploughing on in his splintered abomination of the Queen's English. His lack of English language skills was matched by an obvious and glaring absence of boxing know-how, as he rambled on about his work with Gerrie's stable of fighters, and how he'd take me to the Promised Land and make me a household name. He explained, in his fractured lexicon, how he was a foreman in a trucking company owned by Coetzee but would be acting as my manager while Gerrie would be my promoter. None of what he said resonated, at least not in a good way.

But, at the age of twenty-two, the dice was cast, the seat on the sixteen-seat minibus to Johannesburg was booked, and there was just enough money in my pocket to pay for another phone call on my arrival. Not that I needed to call anybody, with Jonas promising to pick me up and whisk me away to my new lodgings. There was no turning back; the compass pointed south, and my future lay in the same direction.

My brother Ruddock, who had become my de facto trainer, fitness coach and sparring partner, was there to see me off on the five-hour haul down the N1 highway to Johannesburg. His normally unflappable demeanour cracked, just a little, as we hugged and promised to stay in touch, his eyes moistening and his head bowed as we stood there in the dust at the Musina bus and taxi rank, a chaotic cacophony of travellers and traders, people clambering into buses and mini-vans bound for destinations near and far.

As I stepped aboard the minibus I turned and told Ruddock, 'Don't worry, once I'm settled in the City of Gold and you have completed your Matric I will make sure you come join me and turn pro too.'

I barely even glanced back other than to notice Ruddock standing stone-still with his gaze fixed on the minibus. My eyes were diverted to Musina's featureless single-storey concrete blocks and tin shacks sprouting from the orange dust, as the driver negotiated his way through the throngs of vendors, hawkers and traffic before picking up speed to leave the town of my birth far behind. There were no pangs of sentiment or nostalgia, just a feeling of expectation of what possibilities lay on the road ahead.

As we drove past Louis Trichardt, the first major city, about 90 kilometres from Musina, I flashed back to the ninety days I'd spent incarcerated at its corrective centre when I was just sixteen years of age for a crime I never committed.

Another 110 kilometres down the N1 and we were in Pietersburg (now called Polokwane). We stopped at a petrol station to refill and stretch our legs. I reminisced, with a wide smile crinkling my face, about the time I kicked an opponent in the testicles during the provincial championships before hightailing it out of town.

'What are you smiling about, young man? We are not there yet. This is Pietersburg. We are only halfway to Johannesburg.'

It was an elderly lady, journeying south to visit her son, whom I had spoken with earlier. I didn't reveal to her the source of my mirth but continued to reminisce fondly of my past encounter with the racist whites in this city.

Nearly three hours later we had reached Pretoria, around sixty minutes from our final destination. The chatter in the minibus became a soothing balm for my senses and I nodded off.

'Excuse me young man, we're here, it's time to get off,' said a voice in my ear, interrupting my reverie. It was the same elderly lady, journeying to visit her son.

It was almost 8 pm, and the crowds at the Joubert Park taxi rank near Noord Street were dispersing and scurrying in myriad directions. Clutching my small weather-beaten holdall, I wandered around the taxi rank looking for Jonas, who was supposed to meet me. But there was no sign of him, and no way of contacting him because I only had his work number.

The light had already faded. It was dark and I was at a loss of where to go, or what to do. Eventually, in a state of some dismay, I headed for the nearby Joubert Park, a Johannesburg landmark, which was within a couple of minutes' walk of the taxi rank. I didn't even have enough money for food. But I had my bag, which contained my boxing gloves and tracksuit and some other scrunched up items of clothing.

The frigid mid-autumn air forced me to rug up as best I could, and I curled up on a bench, strategically placed near the toilets. I'd slept out in the savannah surrounding Musina with my brothers on occasion during our teenage years to a chorus of hyena cackles and jackal barks, and the threat of becoming a late-night snack for a lion or a leopard.

But being out alone at night in a city teaming with *tsotsis* (gangsters) was probably an even more foolhardy venture. People had returned to Musina in coffins after falling foul of Jo'burg's criminal classes.

Another concern was the volatile political landscape. The recent release of Nelson Mandela had precipitated violent and bloody black-on-black clashes between supporters of the ANC and the Buthelezi-led

Inkatha Freedom Party, known as the IFP. The latter represented the interests of the Zulus and their quest for self-rule. It took me back to the turbulence and carnage I'd witnessed in Zimbabwe after the fall of Ian Smith's whites-only government.

Taxi ranks and hostels were often venues for outbreaks of violence between ANC and IFP activists, which was a reason I had declined an offer from a concerned driver to sleep in his minivan on that first night. I thought taking my chances in the park was the lesser of two evils.

The IFP had decided to boycott the looming free and fair elections of 1994, the poll which marked the historic end of white rule. People were dying in large numbers, left on the streets suffering fatal wounds from attacks by perpetrators carrying clubs, sticks, iron bars and *pangas*, the machete-like trademark weapon of the Zulus. Semiautomatics were also used in some assassinations.

The rumour was that Zulu leader Mangosuthu Buthelezi had been granted illicit funding and weapons by the ruling National Party, led by President FW de Klerk, to instigate the attacks. In return, so it was claimed back then, the Zulus had been promised an autonomous homeland in KwaZulu-Natal, their ancestral stronghold. It was viewed as the last desperate, treacherous act of a party facing the prospect of political oblivion, as the tide of reform following Mandela's release after twenty-seven years of incarceration on Robben Island engulfed everything in its path.

Fortunately for me, the night passed uneventfully, other than being accosted by a couple of hobos who looked even more bedraggled than me. They left me alone after assessing I had no form of sustenance or succour to offer them.

The next morning, I dusted myself off and called Jonas. It turned out he'd been there the night before but had left before I arrived. Stepping out of his dented and dirty car, I was greeted by an unshaven bear of a man, his corpulent belly poking out from under his T-shirt, his eyes frog-like and his broken English in full flow. He was dressed in a stained white T-shirt, tracksuit bottoms and sandals, and explained the next stop would be Gerrie's Gym in Witfield, which, much to my surprise, turned out to be my less than salubrious new home, about 30 kilometres from the City of Gold. There, in this run-down suburb, situated in the equally nondescript satellite town of Boksburg, lay Gerrie's Gym.

Once inside its sweat-soaked confines, Jonas introduced me to Jansie Coetzee, Gerrie's brother and my new trainer, telling him he was going to turn me into a 'Venda warrior'. There were a smattering of small dingy rooms around the back of the gym in a separate concrete block where some of the blacks that worked with Jonas in Gerrie's trucking business resided. Jonas, too, was headquartered there in a cramped box room that reeked of stale cigarettes and dirty laundry. He offered to share his accommodation with me but it was so unkempt I opted instead to sleep in the gym. It became my hotel.

After training each night I'd open the windows to let the acrid stench of blood and sweat escape, set up my mattress and go to sleep. Keeping the gym clean became my part-time job. But no matter how hard I tried, the all-encompassing odour never fully dissipated.

Two years earlier I'd spent a month in Jo'burg in very different circumstances. I'd travelled by bus to the iconic Rotunda terminal where a trainer named Solly Selebi was proposing to help turn me pro. There was no slumming it in the park. No hardships, just a glimpse of a better life. Solly, his wife and baby boy lived in a voluminous apartment in what passed for an upscale neighbourhood in Johannesburg back then. His main claim to 'fame' was attacking the national boxing authorities during the years of apartheid. He was seen as the only black licensee who did not fear the then iron-fisted national executive director, Stan Christodoulou. Years later his 'fame' was further cemented by being appointed a board member of BSA (Boxing South Africa), the current national boxing authority. He is also known for being the brother of the disgraced former National Commissioner of Police and Interpol chief, Jackie Selebi, who was sentenced to fifteen years in jail for corruption.

Solly was a former fighter turned trainer, and a formidable and charismatic presence. He and his wife joined me for my 5 am morning jogs. Their home was situated in Berea, which is near Hillbrow, the Kings Cross of Jo'burg, a haven for drug dealers and prostitutes. Every time I ventured out for a run, or a stroll, I was accosted by beautiful women, a sight rarely, if ever, seen in Musina. Their lascivious language and brazen approaches were music to the ears and eyes of a testosterone-propelled twenty-year-old. Even though I knew that a price tag was attached, I felt flattered by the attention as I passed on by.

After a month in what was to me a rough approximation of heaven, the desire to complete my Year 12 studies overcame the desire to turn pro there and then, and I headed back home.

Memories of those days of comforts and female advances filtered through my mind as I inhaled the fetid air at Gerrie's Gym and swallowed down yet another plate of 'pap', a bland and less than nutritious porridge made from maize. It was hardly the diet of champions but was all Jonas had to offer his 'Venda Warrior'. Even in the toughest of times in Musina we'd occasionally have vegetables, meat and fish to tickle our palates and nourish our bodies.

Eventually I got to meet Gerrie Coetzee, but he was largely preoccupied overseeing the careers of his nephew and another promising Zulu fighter, Johnson Tshuma. My presence seemed to barely register with him initially. But, as time wore on, I began to accompany Johnson, my new housemate at the gym, to Gerrie's home for weights training.

Gerrie was softy-spoken and bashful. If you quizzed him enough he'd tell you about how he became a world champion and he'd speak of his relationship with God. But he was happiest talking about his fighters, and their futures.

The fine-tuning on my transition to pro fighter was nigh, but first I had to progress through some trials, involving sparring, shadow-boxing, skipping rope and other tests, to prove I was worthy under the regulations of the day.

My trainer Jansie took me to Nasrec, where the South African Boxing Board of Control was located at the time, for the trials. I was put in the ring with a series of partners, and after I'd knocked the third one out Jansie hollered at me in exasperation, 'Lovemore, if you keep this up you'll be sparring all day because the adjudicators aren't bothered about your power. They want to see your boxing skills. They need to see your footwork and defensive ability.'

I was granted my licence, and my moment of truth arrived several weeks later on the undercard of a bout between the then South African middleweight champion, Johnson Tshuma, who was promoted by Gerrie, and Gerhard Botes, a tough, white boxer who had an aggressive style and always pushed forward, fast and strong. I trained like a demon for what I saw as a coming of age, a springboard to untold riches and the ability to share the fruits of my success with my family.

My preparations were interrupted and besmirched though by news on the eve of the fight of the assassination of one of my long-time heroes, Chris Hani, a freedom fighter whose idealism and realism had won my admiration. He was a leader of South Africa's communist party and chief of staff of uMkhonto we Sizwe, the armed wing of the ANC. It was on 10 April 1993, and his life was ended, aged fifty, at the end of a gun wielded by a far-right extremist from Poland, Janusz Waluś, outside his home in Boksburg. His death cast a pall over my debut against a tall, lean fellow novice called Enoch Khuzwayo. Distracted and demoralised, I won the bout on points, with little fanfare and minimal celebration.

My downcast demeanour wasn't helped any by the prize money, or lack thereof. The blood, sweat, toil and sacrifice of eight years in the underworld of the amateurs was distilled into a winner's purse of ZAR250 which is the equivalent of A$25. Even that miserly sum dropped to A$21 after I'd paid Jonas his 15 per cent manager's fee.

As I stepped from the ring, I ruminated over my choices. Just months earlier I'd been offered a scholarship by Venetia diamond mine, located 80 kilometres from Musina, to study mining engineering. It had presented me a future of stability and the opportunity to further my learning. Had I forsaken higher education for this? A measly A$25. Was this going to be my future? A two-bit card-filler hurting another human being for peanuts. Where was the majesty and dignity in that?

Jonas put his beefy arms around me and assured me this was just my first fight, and that the only way was up. As I counted my meagre winnings, I wasn't convinced.

CHAPTER 9

FROM RAGS TO GLITCHES

*'This was my first exposure to the flagrant lies, deceit
and deception woven into the fabric of professional boxing.
It wouldn't be my last.'*

The weeks came and went after my underwhelming professional debut, and there was no sign of a follow-up fight in sight. I had virtually no money and relied on the pap dished up by Jonas at the gym to keep the hunger pangs at bay. A creeping sense of foreboding was festering inside me, along with a sense of guilt at not being able to send funds back to my siblings. They'd huddled around a TV in Musina to watch my pro debut and like all Africans, once they'd seen me up in lights fighting in front of the cameras, they'd assumed I'd become an instant celebrity, with untold riches to match. Nothing could have been further from the truth, as I buckled and tottered under the weight of my own embarrassment at being too impoverished to help them.

Before leaving Musina I'd bragged about my impending role as a family benefactor, and I wasn't even close to delivering on the pledge. I didn't know how to tell them I'd received so little from my pugilistic pursuits that I'd probably have been better off remaining in Musina tending white people's gardens or washing their cars.

I'd taken to referring to Jonas as 'the Englishman', in a sardonic reference to his stubborn insistence on mangling the mother tongue of the missionaries who had colonised our country before the Dutch. Having a command of English was viewed as a status symbol and something to be flaunted in a somewhat bizarre tribute to our early oppressors.

The image of the dapper English gentleman carried great currency and cachet and spouting the lingo was a mark of a certain refinement, and proof positive of a higher level of education. Not that Jonas, whose linguistic liberties were of egregious proportions, was fooling anybody. The pseudonym stuck, with the other boxers and the resident workers housed at the rear of Gerrie's Gym adopting the moniker.

While mocking Jonas provided some light relief, it wasn't getting me any fights, much less desperately needed sponsorship. Being born with the wrong skin colour in South Africa had many pitfalls, and even world-ranked black fighters found attracting sponsors a painstaking and often fruitless pursuit. There were companies like the telecommunications giant Nashua, and foodstuffs producer King Korn who did scatter a few morsels the way of indigenous boxers. Others were Crossbow Cider, which produced apple cider drinks, and Black Like Me, purveyors of hair care and grooming products.

While some of those firms provided small cash donations, King Korn didn't and only offered fighters batches of yeast to make beer and maize meal in bulk dumped in their dressing rooms, along with one-size-fits-all boxing shorts and gowns. It was slim pickings and frustration had become my constant companion.

Bottling it up any longer became impossible, so I confronted the Englishman over my future. Just so there were no misunderstandings, I purposely phrased my enquiry to him in broken English.

'Englishman, when is me fight again?' I queried one afternoon, making no attempt to hide the disdain in my voice. 'Two months I no fight now, you promise make me Venda warrior. No fight, me go other manager.'

His response was immediate and categorical. 'Don't worry my boy, you fight June 26. I work hard every day to find right opponent for you.'

That was the date of the WBA world lightweight title rematch between hometown hero Dingaan 'The Rose of Soweto' Thobela and American Tony 'The Tiger' Lopez, and Jonas assured me I would feature on the undercard of the show which was being promoted by Gerrie Coetzee.

For all his bravado and bluster, I had my doubts over the veracity of his claims, especially since the main event was only two weeks away and there was no sign of a contract. My cynicism was further stoked by the fact that no opponent had been mentioned for me on a card dubbed 'The Day of Judgement'. However, in my desperation, I wanted to believe the Englishman was telling me the truth.

He was tied up running errands for the Lopez team as their designated driver and general dogsbody. Our paths hardly crossed but when they did, a big toothy smile would spread across his pockmarked face, and he'd crouch into a playful shadow-boxing stance, before intoning knowingly, 'Venda Warrior, make sure you ready for the big show. You going to be big news.'

But there was still no opponent on the horizon and my trainer Jansie, his face peering down at me from atop his wiry 6-foot-5-inch frame, said with sincerity, 'Lovemore, I wish I could tell you what's happening but I don't have a clue. Just keep training hard.'

With the fight just six days away, the Englishman was nowhere to be seen. It turned out he'd moved into a hotel adjoining the Lopez camp's headquarters, so as to be at their beck and call day and night. My worst fears were realised a day later after Jansie quizzed Gerrie on where I would feature on the undercard, only to be told I had never even been considered in the first place.

This was my first exposure to the flagrant lies, deceit and deception woven into the fabric of professional boxing. It wouldn't be my last. When I finally caught sight of the Englishman again on the eve of the show, and asked for an explanation, he said, with all the plausibility he could muster, 'Of course, you have opponent but he chicken out when he learn he fighting great Venda warrior. He too afraid to step in ring with you.'

Thobela beat Lopez on points winning the WBA lightweight world title but no defence was scheduled for at least six months on Gerrie's next promotion. That was far too long, and I knew I had to make a move, or my fledgling career would have been over before it had even got going.

Money was so scarce that I started looking for odd jobs to earn a few rand. I'd queue up with other unemployed hopefuls on Main Street in

Witfield, at a spot where whites looking for cheap day labour would cruise by in their vans and pick-ups and pluck a lucky few for a few hours of manual work in a factory or a building site. I had little choice but to offer my services for next to nothing.

My relationship with the Englishman wasn't getting any better either, and it was about to get a whole lot worse. Unbeknown to me, he had developed a crush on one of two maids who worked at Gerrie's house, where I would go and push weights in his home gym from time to time. The prettier of the two, Sonia, who was young enough to be the Englishman's daughter, was of mixed race, with delicate features and a demeanour which seemed to light up whenever she saw me. She would quiz me on my career and playfully flirt with me. I thought nothing of it, especially seeing her and her fellow domestic smoking, and even drinking on the job. For me that was the opposite of an aphrodisiac. One morning in the gym, the Englishman, his face taking on a beetroot hue and his eyes locking on me with a stony stare, marched my way with malice in every step.

'Me feed you, you sleep with my girl,' he barked belligerently.

For some peculiar reason, the Englishman had got it in his head that I was attempting to snatch away the woman he believed he had claims on. At first, I thought he was joking, but the way he was invading my space and glowering at me told a different story. Had he not been all too aware of the malevolence which resided in my fists, I have no doubt he would have tried to throw some punches of his own my way.

I eventually took the heat out of the situation by calmly insisting that there was nothing clandestine going on between myself and Sonia, and that he'd come to a wrong and hasty conclusion. But it was the final death knell in my failing and fractured relationship with the Englishman, and we barely spoke again after he turned tail and sullenly ambled out of the gym, shaking his head, and no doubt cursing me under his breath.

I continued to go through the motions of training and sparring but became increasingly distracted. One evening, amid the hubbub of grunting and hollering in the gym, I was approached by one of the guys I'd sparred with several weeks earlier. He wasn't much of a boxer and stood out more as a dapper dresser who arrived at Gerrie's in a gleaming car, with shiny shoes to match, sharp dress shirts and the latest in designer pants. With the aromatic scent of aftershave oozing from every pore, and a cocksure confidence in every move and gesture, he portrayed himself as a fighting Don Juan, although I imagined he scored more points outside the ring than in. He reintroduced himself as Tshehla but said everybody referred to him as simply 'T'.

When he found out I was living at the gym and struggling to make ends meet, he said he was a member of the South African police force and was connected with a Serbian businessman called Vlado, who dabbled in boxing and sponsored several fighters. He said he might be able to arrange an introduction for me with this great boxing advocate and would-be backer. He suggested we rendezvous the next day, after which he'd drive me to meet Vlado, who in my imagination immediately took on a saintly presence; a dream maker perhaps sent by the Venda spirits in my hour of need.

True to his word, 'T' cruised by the gym and picked me up for a meeting I hoped might be a circuit breaker, even a life changer. Forty-five minutes later we pulled up outside a smart-looking cafe in Pretoria, Vlado, my benefactor-in-waiting, stood out from the crowd. But not in the way I'd envisioned.

Puffing on French cigarettes and sitting in a cloud of vapour, sandwiched between two glamorous looking blondes, he was a study in middle-aged excess. Round of face, and rotund of waist, his cheeks were ruddy and what was left of his wispy, matted brown hair was landscaped across his scalp to try and camouflage a balding pate. He wore what he later bragged was an Italian suit, his well-padded stomach asking almost impossible questions of the buttons done up at his midriff.

When 'T' introduced me as Lovemore, Vlado, much to his own amusement, and that of his giggling female companions, turned it into 'Loverboy'. He made no mention of sponsorship, but spoke in grandiose tones of how he could make me a lot of money.

After several minutes, he rose up off his haunches and motioned for 'T' to step outside with him, leaving me at the table with the two women, whose glassy-eyed stares made me increasingly uncomfortable.

A black man sitting with two white women was a sight rarely seen back then, and after my ill-fated experience with the shopkeeper's daughter in Musina, I was all too aware how this might be perceived. To make matters worse, both of them seemed out of it somehow, maybe high on some drug or other.

To my relief, Vlado returned and before resuming his seat, he dug into his pocket and pulled out a roll of notes, handing me 500 rand with a curt nod. It was twice the amount I'd made from my debut fight. He said it was the first payment and that there'd be more where that came from, explaining that the next day 'T' would take me to nearby Rustenburg, and he would meet us there.

And with that, he waved his hand dismissively and decreed, 'Okay Loverboy, *hamba hamba* [which is Zulu for go].'

The women giggled inanely again, and I was on my way in a state of confusion over what had just transpired.

I asked 'T' why we were going to Rustenburg, translated as the City of Rest, an hour's drive from Pretoria at the foot of the Magaliesburg Mountains. He said we needed to help Vlado's boys 'offload some goods'. It wasn't the most forthcoming of answers but he kept me tethered to the hook by insisting that Vlado wanted to sponsor me and provide me with some of the accoutrements of boxing, like gloves, robes, shorts and boots. He even joked how Vlado wanted to change my ring name to Loverboy, saying he was flush with cash from his import/export business and was generous to a fault.

The Loverboy line didn't amuse me in the slightest but what concerned me more was the seeming implausibility of this entire scenario. Troubling too was 'T's mastery of the slang tongue of *tsotsitaal*, the language of the gangs. It's a mixture of English, Afrikaans, Zulu and some other African dialects and he spouted it with an effortless fluency. I wondered how, and why, a supposed cop would be so proficient in this patois. But, in my eagerness to explain it all away, I rationalised it as perhaps a lingo he had mastered when going undercover to infiltrate gangs.

On the way to Rustenburg the next day we stopped at the ramshackle township of Mamelodi, on the fringes of Pretoria, and to my surprise picked up two more guys, one who looked about sixteen and the other my age. 'T' said they were both boxers, though yet to turn professional, who would also be recipients of Vlado's largesse. As the car meandered along, we talked about women, boxing, and soccer. But each time Vlado was mentioned, 'T' would change the topic.

After decamping at our destination, a brand new four-bedroom house in a street lined with acacia trees on the outskirts of town, we trudged through a fully furnished lounge room to three adjoining rooms. They were stacked with packing boxes piled high, one on top of the other. We also noticed from a window a large shed in the backyard with enough locks and bolts to rival Fort Knox. My suspicions, which had been steadily fermenting, were hardly eased by this.

'T', meanwhile, had ripped open one box and was pulling out its contents: snazzy looking shirts and pants, similar to those he wore with such elan.

'Boys,' he said. 'Get changed, you need to look the part, you need to look good.'

This was enough for me to take 'T' aside, theatrically toss my bundle of designer threads to the floor and ask him pointedly, 'What the fricken hell is going on here? You need to be honest with me. We're in this house, there are boxes everywhere, a shed bolted up at the back, it looks like nobody lives here. What exactly are we doing here?'

It was then, in a moment of candour previously absent, 'T' laid it on the line for me. He explained brazenly that Vlado was in the drug trade, adding with a flourish that he also dabbled in stolen goods. Vlado was looking for mules, although 'T' spun it as 'pick-up and delivery personnel' to perpetuate his business model. That, of course, was where we came in.

Undeterred, 'T' continued, 'It's a chance for you to make some serious money, because you surely aren't making any from boxing. Give it some thought. You'll get to travel around the world, all expenses paid. I'm trying to help you here.'

Horrified by this proposal from a cop, if that's what he really was, I looked blankly back at 'T', realising that the police uniform in his car and the badge he'd shown me on the journey were all a charade.

This boxing hanger-on was a walking billboard for corruption. But I didn't want to inflame matters and create a cascade of retribution from Vlado's criminal network. So I chose my words carefully, appearing as grateful as possible in telling 'T', 'Look, thanks for looking out for me and trying to help me better myself. But, I have to be honest, this is not for me. I can't do it.'

Then, reaching into my pocket, I pressed the 500 rand Vlado had bestowed upon me into his hand. Without waiting for his reaction, I turned and made my way towards the front door. Not caring to look back, I headed out into the street, got directions from a local to the nearest taxi rank, and boarded a minibus back to Jo'burg.

I wondered whether 'T's charm offensive had seduced the other two guys. Was this his modus operandi all along? To float from one boxing gym to another recruiting hungry and desperate characters such as me for a 'better life'.

After my showdown with 'T', I decided to confront Jansie on my boxing trajectory, and why it was pointing down rather than up. With trademark frankness, he laid bare my situation like this: 'Lovemore, you have lots of talent, but you need to find a manager and promoter who can keep you active. You need to be able to build up your record. You won't make any money until you do that.'

He expanded on the theme, explaining that Gerrie was only concerned with promoting once in a while, and having the world champion Dingaan Thobela in his stable, all his energies were focused on him. He said I needed a manager like Harold Volbrecht, who was a professor of the sweet science, and a promoter like Rodney Berman, a prolific fight figure who staged shows almost every month. But to get to Berman, he explained, I would have to go through Harold, get down to his gym and make an impression.

All well and good, I thought. But I didn't even have the minibus fair to cover the 20-kilometre ride to Harold's Hammer Gym in Benoni.

But staying at Gerrie's Gym any longer wasn't an option. Not if I wanted to amount to anything more than just another broken soul in the City of Gold.

CHAPTER 10

WELCOME TO THE HAMMER GYM

'Look fellas, we've got Shaka Zulu in the house, Mandingo's in the house.'

A blast of frigid air greeted me as I stepped out of Gerrie's Gym in the half-light of a hazy winter's morning. In my hand was my gym bag and in my back pocket a crumpled piece of paper on which I'd scribbled a rough route to Harold's Hammer Gym, some 20 kilometres away in the featureless back blocks of New Modder, in the township of Benoni.

There was purpose in every stride as I braced myself against the icy wind which seemed to pierce deep into the marrow of my bones through the thin layers of my tracksuit top, T-shirt and vest. Asking people for further directions along the way, my mind turned to what might await me at my destination.

Harold's fame was long established. He was a former South African welterweight champion who had guaranteed his place in local boxing folklore by successfully defending his title a record nineteen times across fourteen dominant years. He had only fallen short on the biggest stage, losing two world title shots. The first was in 1980 for the WBA crown when he was stopped by Mexican Pipino Cuevas in the fifth round. He returned for a second tilt seven years later; this time he was stopped in the seventh round by American Mark Breland.

Short and nuggety, and with an expression of deep concentration seemingly forever etched across his broad face, his grace and balletic foot movement inside the ring belied his prize fighter-like appearance. He sported a neatly manicured moustache, the trademark alpha-male Afrikaner accessory of the day, but his voice, squeaky and small, was incongruous with his rugged and uncompromising persona.

His stable of fighters was a who's who of South Africa's most gifted prospects, and a continuous flow of aspiring champions beat a path to his door in the hope of being sprinkled with Harold's miracle dust. Corrie Sanders, who went on to knock out the great Ukrainian champion Wladimir Klitschko in two rounds for the IBF world heavyweight crown in 2003, was one of Harold's most luminous proteges. Sadly, at the age of forty-six, he was shot dead in 2012 during a botched armed robbery at a restaurant. Typical of his warrior spirit, he perished throwing his body in front of his daughter to protect her as bullets flew when his family gathering was gate-crashed by three bandits.

Harold also had another diamond in his cluster of gems, a lightweight named Philip Holiday, who went on to claim the IBF world title. I'd seen him dispatch a catalogue of opponents on TV and, in my musings, I viewed him as a potential adversary, as he fought in the same weight division. But the bout, which I saw myself winning, never made it beyond my imagination, and we ultimately went on to become great stablemates.

He was more feisty than flamboyant, and his attritional style wore away at the foundations of his opponents until the entire edifice crumbled. He was a human wrecking ball, who came at his prey from multiple angles, spraying body punches, hooks and an over-hand right which became his 'money punch'.

That was the landmark weapon which floored Australian Hall of Famer Jeff Fenech in the second round when they collided in Melbourne in 1996. Fenech, who had already won three world titles, was making a belated comeback, in the time-honoured boxing tradition of trying to revisit former glories.

It was begot by an addiction to the ring, which I well understood. It's a common delusion that shrouds boxers from their own mortality, even when that harsh reality is quite literally hitting you in the face. Fenech wasn't immune from the affliction. Nor were his corroded twitch fibres and reflexes. His career was effectively ended by Holiday's executioner-like demolition that night. Fenech at his peak might have penned a different story. But the parable of fighters overstaying their welcomes is a lesson rarely heeded.

Harold had yet another hot prospect in super lightweight Naas Scheepers, who was so tall and slim it looked like he was fighting on stilts, his southpaw stance and ability to weave away from incoming bombs making him an elusive quarry. The problem was that his default mode was to brawl first, box later and that left him open to canny counterpunchers.

All this accumulated wisdom was gleaned from my time in Harold's orbit, first as a satellite of little significance but before too long a budding supernova in my own right.

I thought I must have been given the wrong address when a New Modder local pointed me towards a sprawling, austere, red-brick federation-style building set back off the road and fringed by a verdant lawn and freshly painted white fence. Parked on the street out front was a gleaming convertible BMW, and next to it a white Volkswagen with the names of sponsors daubed over the bonnet, roof and doors, to go along with that of its owner, Philip Holiday. If this was the Hammer Gym, it was very different to any I'd ever encountered.

It turned out that Ron Howe Hall, as the inscription on the gate read, also served as a makeshift church on Sundays. But during the week it was Harold who was dishing out the sermons.

As I gingerly stepped through the door, I was shocked by the absence of the grit and grime I'd always associated with such places. It wasn't just 20 kilometres from Gerrie's Gym, it was light years away. The walls were festooned with glitzy posters, and framed pictures of fighters in action, and even the sweat somehow smelled less pungent. In my direct line of sight was Philip Holiday, the name of his sponsor, Lasch Services, a crane company, embroidered into his tracksuit. Also there going through a shadow-boxing routine was the lean and lanky Naas Scheepers.

From the corner of my eye I spied Harold, fiddling with some pads. I overheard him saying to one of the other fighters, 'I bet that lazy bum won't be here today. He's got so much talent. He can beat any heavyweight if he gets his shit together.'

I figured he was referring to Corrie Sanders, who at the time was the only heavyweight of note in South Africa and the reigning national champion.

My presence in the gym created barely a ripple, and if I had been noticed the assumption would have been I was just another wannabe fighter, or maybe a starstruck fan on a mission to collect autographs.

I hadn't come there to just gawk, and collecting my thoughts and my courage, I strode up to Harold, looking somehow smaller in the flesh than on TV fight nights, and said in a mixture of Afrikaans and English, 'Hallo, my naam is Lovemore, I would like to join your gym.'

His response was terse and to the point. Clearly ill inclined to waste time and energy on yet another aspiring fighter he knew nothing of, he replied in a mixture of English and Afrikaans, 'Have you actually had any fights? Is jy 'n professioneel?' (Are you a professional, in Afrikaans.)

I explained I'd had one pro fight which I'd won on points and sixty-eight amateur bouts for sixty-six wins. I added I was a four-time national amateur champion.

Furrowing his brow slightly, Harold paused before shooting back, 'So are you contracted to any promoter or manager?'

I told him I had neither but had turned pro on a Gerrie Coetzee promotion and that his younger brother Jansie had trained me for that fight. I added that it was Jansie who had recommended I come and talk to him.

Glancing at my battered old kit bag on the floor a few metres away, he asked, 'Do you have your training gear in that bag?'

I nodded in the affirmative, and he said, 'Okay, get changed and hit the punching bag for me.'

I was relieved that he hadn't asked me to get my sparring gear on because I was exhausted from my four-hour hike to reach his hallowed hall, and I hadn't eaten all day.

I returned from the changing room to be greeted by the sight of Philip Holiday going through a choreographed shadow-boxing routine in the ring. He was two weeks out from a fight against an international opponent and Harold's attention was focused on him, his deep set, owl-like eyes, monitoring his every move.

I pulled out my skipping rope and began a routine I had long since mastered with some alacrity. I wanted to use it to lasso attention my way because I knew I had to do everything to impress to have any hope of being invited into Harold's inner sanctum and become a part of his 'cult'. The word cult has its connotations. But that was how I characterised his stable of boxers, each under the spell of this magnetic man. I wanted to add my name to the list.

Sweat beaded on my brow as I completed fifteen minutes of skipping, a little cameo which had attracted some attention from some of the other fighters, most of whom were white, scattered around the gym.

I turned to shadow-boxing, knowing that Harold's gaze was upon me, weighing up whether I had the raw material that might be fashioned into a thing of boxing beauty. I started throwing some slick jabs, following up with straight hands, and left hooks. I pivoted on my heels after each combination, glaring and sneering at my imaginary opponent, telling him he couldn't lay a glove on me. I saw his punches coming, ducking and slipping out of range before counterpunching to catch him exposed, landing body shots that drained some of his spite and evaporated his venom. Now, I was on the offensive, telling my make-believe advisory to 'go back and take this with you', as I unloaded a flurry of punches.

'Come here boy, come and take some more of this candy,' I goaded, as I danced and blocked, bounced and fired off more shots.

If a psychiatrist had been in the house I'd probably have been advised strongly to seek an emergency appointment. But those in boxing's inner circle are familiar with such audible eccentricities.

I'd ape the Ali shuffle, and add, 'I'm too good boy … you can't even get close.'

My peripheral vision allowed me to glimpse Harold and his assistant trainer Eddie Sekwebo exchanging knowing glances and smiling at each other. They were enjoying my little show. And on cue, I overheard Harold saying to his sidekick in Afrikaans, 'Ek dink hierdie outjie kan boks,' (I think this little man can box).

At only 5 feet 7 inches I was short of stature but long on ambition, and proud of a physique which was cut and ripped, despite a subsistence diet of pap porridge, lacking almost all the essential minerals and vitamins. Not to mention any semblance of taste.

After three rounds I was pretty much spent but wasn't going to show them that. Next, I grabbed my gloves from my bag and Eddie was suddenly by my side lacing them up for me.

'Good boy, I like what I see. I like the jab. That's your money punch. Keep it going,' he said. 'The hand speed and footwork is there. Show us some more.'

Eddie was an imposing figure, with a slightly crooked, beak-like nose, and attentive, inquisitive eyes. His frame was pudgy, yet he seemed to glide effortlessly on his feet, as if defying the laws of gravity. I took his comments to heart and began pistol-whipping the punching bag as if I had a personal vendetta against it.

At the end of the round, Eddie was there at my side again, wiping sweat off me and giving me water. I produced more of the same for two more three-minute rounds. Mercifully, Harold called a halt before the mounting fatigue took hold, instructing me to do some ab work next. My shirt was soaked, so I pulled it off to replace it with a dry one from my bag.

When it came off, I heard audible whispering around the gym, and an amused Eddie, in reference to my chiselled abs and defined pectorals, bellowed loudly, 'Look fellas, we've got Shaka Zulu in the house, Mandingo is in the house.'

The place erupted into an infectious laughter, which I chuckled along with in mock embarrassment.

I finished off several sets of ab work, and once the commotion had died down, I sauntered off to the change room feeling pretty pleased with myself. After changing and packing up my gear, I re-entered the gym and formally introduced myself to a few of the fighters, including Philip Holiday.

He was on the floor doing his ab work, and his only reply to my introduction was a clipped and curt, 'Hi', and nothing else.

I didn't appreciate his rudeness, but then rationalised that maybe with a fight coming up he was thinking only of that, wanted no distractions, and was simply focused on the job ahead. I pondered that theory for a moment, but after some deliberation and deep reflection still concluded he was a fuckwit.

Harold pulled me aside and asked me if I had mouth and head guards, which I should bring with me the next day for sparring. I hesitated, happy to have been enlisted in the 'cult' but wondering how I'd get back the following day.

He told me he would try and have me included on the next Golden Gloves Promotions bill that was coming up in four weeks. He then asked me where I lived. When I told him I slept in Gerrie's Gym in Witfield, he wanted to know how I'd got to Benoni. I said I'd walked and was planning on walking back. That seemed to stop him in his tracks.

After a pause, he said, 'Why walk so far? Why not catch a taxi?'

'I couldn't afford it,' I admitted.

Shaking his head in disbelief, he replied, 'Okay, bring all your stuff tomorrow and I'll sort out something for you. I might have a room here for you.'

He turned to Eddie and told him to take me to the nearest cab rank, and he'd cover the fare from there. Eddie went one better, offering to ferry me all the way to Witfield, and promising to pick me up the next day with all my belongings. Not that I had much.

I was thankful that the gods had answered my prayers, even if there was something oddly eerie about my new home to be.

CHAPTER 11

STRIKING BLOWS FOR DEMOCRACY

'Reflecting on that initial loss, I had few regrets because it taught me that with defeat can come a humility and wisdom which prepares you for almost anything in a sport where controversy is a constant companion and you can be a loser, even though you know you have won.'

As promised Eddie was there early in the morning to pick me up, and I didn't linger as I left Gerrie's Gym for the last time. There was nobody there to send me on my way, and that was probably for the best because there was little inclination on my part for any fond, sepia-tinted farewells. Especially where the Englishman was concerned.

A room had been readied for my arrival at the rear of the Hammer Gym building, in a dimly lit alcove. It was basic and spartan with a single bed with blankets neatly folded on top. Down the adjoining hallway was a communal kitchen used by the black domestic workers, who served the live-in caretakers, an elderly white couple. The same facilities were used when the hall was hired out for weddings and birthday parties. There was a separate shower and toilet, and the ambience of my new lodgings exuded five-star luxury in comparison to my previous abode.

As an extra bonus, Harold's wife Christie, a sweet-natured and angelically alluring woman in her early forties, had him bring cooked meals to me during the first week of my stay, and thereafter provided me with pots, pans and cutlery to do my own cooking. Christie would come to the gym and make sure I was settling in okay, and as a young man not oblivious to the allure of the opposite sex she presented a figure of beauty: petite, with lustrous blondish light-brown hair and a smile that could appease the darkest of moods. While of course unattainable, she became like a second mother to me, as I responded to her nurturing instincts.

The building had an eerie quality to it. It was almost as if some kind of entity, be it benign or otherwise, was observing you. On my second night I awoke in a state of some alarm for no apparent reason, the hair on the back of my neck standing on end and a feeling of unease assailing me. I strained to discern any untoward noises. But all I heard was silence. And that was somehow even more unnerving. It was still winter, but the temperature in the room seemed even colder than it was outside, and I was shivering under my blankets. I asked the Venda spirits to protect me from whatever it was that was giving me goosebumps. Finally, reassured by my one-way conversation with my ancestral guides, I regained my equilibrium and slowly drifted off, back into a fitful sleep.

When I stirred in the morning, I chastised myself, saying, 'Come on Lovemore, toughen up, this is the Hammer Gym, not the Hammer House of Horror.' More than anything, I saw it as Harold's House of Hope.

Contravening the social norms of the day, Harold and Christie didn't treat blacks with the same casual disregard and disdain meted out by most of their brethren. And as time progressed I began to view the couple as a de facto or adopted family. I was shocked to even be invited to the wedding of their eldest daughter. Other than the hired help, black faces at white weddings were rarely, if ever, seen.

Christie would attend all my fights, and with the wisdom of her years, proffered sage mother-son type advice, urging me to be wary of ringside groupies, who'd latch on to up-and-coming fighters in pursuit of a cushy lifestyle and a blank cheque on legs, not that my meagre resources at that stage of my career made me much of a catch.

She cautioned that the life goal of these avaricious women was to bask in reflected fame. She warned, in her disarming and enchanting way, that predatory females presented a far greater threat to me than any opponent I'd ever be likely to face inside the ropes. I think she was oblivious all along to my infatuation with her, which in time morphed simply into unabashed admiration.

All of which made the news, some two years later, that Christie had inexplicably committed suicide almost impossible to fathom, let alone endure. I couldn't sleep for many nights afterwards, replaying our conversations and her kindness over and over in my mind. The numbness and desolation that swept over me the day Harold told me, as he sped to the gym to escape a media circus outside his home, was akin to the passing of my own beloved mother.

It was after meeting Christie for the first time during my first week at the Hammer Gym that Harold informed me I'd be sparring with his prize asset, Philip Holiday, to help him prepare for an international bout two weeks down the track. I was ordered to avoid throwing any damaging punches and simply concentrate on the quantity of blows and on speed work. Philip was tapering his training towards the big night, and it was all about maintaining his sharpness.

We sparred for six rounds – the first of over a thousand in which we were unleashed upon each other. We were perfect protagonists and after that first session the coldness and aloofness I'd encountered from him when we first met began to thaw. There was a budding mutual respect, which all warriors of the ring ultimately share as a common bond.

No matter what is said or done before battle, this unwritten code of honour abides when combat begins. That respect between us grew into friendship, though I always harboured the conviction that but for the entrenched mantras of apartheid within the boxing fraternity my career would quickly have surpassed his, rather than lagging in its wake.

There was no inkling of it then, but Philip and his beautiful family shared a similar trajectory to me by taking a path which also found its destination in Australia, where he resides in Queensland to this day.

True to his word, within a month of stepping into his gym, I was lacing up my gloves for my first fight under Harold's banner. It was nine days after my twenty-second birthday on 25 August 1993 at the Carousel Casino in Hammanskraal. I was scheduled to fight on what was known as a 'swing bout'. You had to be ready at a moment's notice to step in should, as was often the case, one of the advertised fights on the card finish ahead of the scheduled number of rounds, leaving a gap in the show that had to be filled.

On promotions featuring several heavyweight contests smart promoters always had swing bouts on standby to maintain the flow and keep the punters happy, in the knowledge that duels between the big boys of boxing were invariably decided by knockouts.

In my case, I stopped my opponent Joseph Sihlangu in the first round of a scheduled six with a flurry of upper cuts and body punches, and as a reward picked up the biggest purse of my short career, a princely 3500 rand (about A$350). On top of that came another 500 rand (A$55) from sponsors, a crane company called Lasch Services. For Lasch read cash, as I basked in the money glow. I paraded their logo on my shorts and in addition they provided me with a gown. Harold had also struck a side deal for them to pay me 500 rand per month as part of an ongoing sponsorship arrangement. At a time when a black family might have to survive on a subsistence sum of just $30 per month, it was not to be sniffed at. And for the first time since leaving home I was able to start sending funds back to my siblings. It wasn't going to change their lives, nor mine in any meteoric sense, but it was enough to help make ends meet.

If I thought it was to be the beginning of a plethora of bouts, I was mistaken. In fact, my next fight wasn't until fully six months later on 19 February 1994.

Though I was inactive, I at least had the sponsorship income trickling in each month. It wasn't, however, enough to dilute a growing sense of indignation, fed by the perception I was being sidelined, purely because the shade of my skin made me less marketable to a public spoon fed great white hopes rather than black wannabes.

This feeling of neglect was intensified by watching on as Philip's career moved in an upward arc, while I was cast in the role of perennial sparring partner. Seemingly forever in the shadows. In those intervening six months Philip had three more fights, against Mike Juarez at the Morula Sun Casino, Sugar Baby Rojas at the Carousel Casino and Jorge Palomares in Las Vegas. He was fighting almost every second month while I skulked and sulked in the background. It made little sense in my febrile mind. A novice, as I was at the time, should be busy building his career. This, after all, was why I'd come under the wing of the great Harold Volbrecht in the first place.

I was also being used as a sparring partner for Naas Scheepers to help him further his future with fights every second to third month. What these fighters were making from sponsorship alone was dwarfing my fight purses and I was beginning to become embittered. What made it worse was that I handled both Philip and Naas with an almost nonchalant ease in sparring, not that it seemed to earn me any kudos.

———————

While I toiled for recognition a far more seismic battle was brewing on the political front as the first elections in which blacks were allowed to vote were looming, and white fears of being disenfranchised by a newly liberated black majority were manifest. Those misgivings permeated every strata of society, and boxing was not exempt. The white far right were in contortions over the implications of what they saw as a genetically inferior subspecies of near Neanderthals being bestowed the levers of power.

The national boxing authority, a bastion of white dominance and influence, shared the disquiet at the prospect of the emergence of a potential CEO, high-powered promoter or, God forbid, chief of one of the TV sports networks with the wrong skin colour. Not to mention the possibility of a black being crowned the best pound-for-pound fighter in the nation.

Most whites feared that a South Africa ruled by blacks might lead to land reforms which would see farmers stripped of their ownership rights, as had been the case, to catastrophic effect, under Robert Mugabe's ZANU–PF in Zimbabwe. Their farms had been summarily seized by Mugabe's henchmen and placed in the hands of his cronies, with farmers fleeing for their lives. Or simply being shot. That feeling of fear among whites, whether in the cities or the veldt, was palpable, and many were stockpiling as much money as they could with the intention of seeking refuge abroad.

When the day came on 27 April 1994, euphoria engulfed the black community as the unthinkable happened and they were allowed to cast a vote. It was a Wednesday, and the day dawned with the news that a car bomb had gone off at Johannesburg's Jan Smuts airport, later renamed Oliver Tambo international airport. The story went that a young white extremist parked his car at the departure terminal then disappeared from sight before it exploded. Luckily nobody was killed. It was one more despicable act from the ultra-racists to derail the elections and invoke a climate of chaos. But it didn't stop me, or millions of others, who were prepared to die to cast their ballots. A similar explosion just days earlier claimed the lives of nine innocents outside the headquarters of the ANC in downtown Johannesburg.

The elections and resulting landslide for the ANC swept Nelson Mandela to power, while my sense of personal powerlessness became even more acute as my career ambled from one sparring session to the next.

With anger welling, I began to turn the normally strictly choreographed sessions into mini-wars in an attempt to prove a point and show I had more to offer. One day, things got particularly heated in a session attended by Philip's mother at a temporary ring set up in a car dealership in Benoni to promote one of Philip's upcoming fights. She was a member of the fringe blou rokke, or blue dress religious cult, also known as the Latter Rain Mission. It was a Christian offshoot which had found its genesis in South Africa in the 1920s. Its female followers eschewed make-up or jewellery, or anything ostentatious, and their garb was the ubiquitous long, dowdy blue dresses.

Also there that day was Peter Karam, a mean-looking monolith who had come on board as one of my sponsors through his steakhouse businesses. He looked like a latter-day Hulk Hogan but was in fact a genial and jovial giant, and one of the few whites I could call a friend back then. He was a boxing aficionado who would watch sessions whenever possible. Both were ringside as I stepped in to face Philip for the umpteenth time.

The spectacle had attracted a media throng, a gallery of sponsors and assorted fight fans. It was a showcase for me to unfurl the full monty of my boxing armoury. Convention be damned, I went out at full tilt and what was meant to be an exhibition of friendly fire degenerated into a brawl. I was dishing out left jabs, counter right upper cuts and left hooks, and goading Philip, telling him, 'You can't fight boy, eat these jabs. I'm better than you.' Philip wasn't bashful, fighting back with all the ferocity he could muster.

Harold wasn't happy with this turn of events and called an abrupt halt after three hellfire rounds, fixing me with an icy glare and shaking his head as I stepped from the ring.

Philip's mother was more vocal in her displeasure, striding up to me and screaming loud enough for the numerous onlookers to hear, 'Lovemore, what do you think you're doing? Are you trying to embarrass Philip in front of the media?' Her plump cheeks a vivid crimson, she stood toe-to-toe with me as if ready to continue where her son had left off.

Before I had a chance to say anything, Peter interjected. 'He's here to box, not to kiss and hug your son. Give him a break. It's not like he's getting paid for this,' he said.

The pair continued to exchange a visceral lingo not normally used in the realms of the Blue Dress brigade as I exited the scene.

I was accosted by a boxing reporter named Pete Moscardi on my way out. Smelling a story he wanted to elicit a few juicy quotes from me having heard Philip's mother's rant. I resisted the temptation to comment, but we later forged a friendship as my career unfolded.

Finally aware of my frustration, Harold stepped up his efforts to get me on Golden Gloves Promotion undercards and on 19 February 1994 I made my third professional appearance against Mlungisi Mlugwana in another swing bout, winning by KO in the first round. Just under two months later I fought again against a journeyman named Ben Mdinisi and won on points over four rounds.

In all the fights under Harold, I was provided with a blank agreement to sign, meaning I had no idea what my purse would be, or who my opponent would be. I found this odd but I was too young, naive and desperate for action to question any of it, and I would blithely sign the document.

I was on a mini-winning-streak until 19 July 1994 when I suffered a rude awakening with my first pro loss. I was scheduled to fight Jerry Malinga, a junior lightweight with a string bean frame, a long reach and a battle-hardened record. The bout agreement however made no mention of my purse.

Prior to this bout all my fights had been at lightweight, which has a weight limit of 61.23 kilograms. At junior lightweight it's 58.97 kilograms, a difference of 2.26 kilograms between the two weight classes. Harold felt with a stricter diet I could comfortably compete in this lower weight division and be a strong force in the class where the competition wasn't quite as fierce.

Malinga was a stablemate and main sparring partner of Dingaan Thobela and had already established himself as a national and international contender with a record of thirteen wins, one loss and one draw. On the face of it, facing such a well-seasoned opponent posed a serious risk to my unbeaten record over six fights, particularly as shedding those kilos was problematic. I had also never been beyond four rounds.

My situation wasn't improved by coming down with a heavy cold seven days out from the fight. I needed to keep my fluids up, leaving me still 5 kilograms over the weight limit with only three days left.

This created a crazy cascade of weight shedding. I was training three times a day and contorted my baby-oiled body into plastic stretch suits moulded from garbage bags to promote a sweat reaction. I'd wear a layer of clothes on top of all that and would eat only a single portion of baby food each day, washed down with a glass of water.

The night before the fight my body was cramping so badly due to the lack of electrolytes that I barely slept.

Back then the weigh-in was on the morning of the fight, unlike today where there's a twenty-four hour gap and you have time to rehydrate. They changed the system around the world after a string of ring fatalities. Needless to say, when I stepped onto the canvas I was as weak as a newborn antelope. I dominated the first two rounds of a bout scheduled for six. But from the third round on I was fighting purely in spirit, my physical reserves spent. My reactions and strength compromised, I was simply holding on and could offer no antidote to his constant pressing. I lost unanimously on points but my devastation was tempered by the knowledge that with my physical attributes undimmed he would not have been able to cope with me.

And so it proved four years later when I stopped him in the fourth round of a bout that was scheduled for ten. But after being poleaxed by a barrage of body blows, he was never going to make the distance.

Reflecting on that initial loss, I had few regrets because it taught me that with defeat can come a humility and wisdom which prepares you for almost anything in a sport where controversy is a constant companion and you can be a loser, even though you know you have won.

Sometimes fighters used to bathing in a balm of easy wins find they are ill equipped to deal with the adversity of defeat, and that chink in their armour can be career ending. I was never going to let that happen to me.

CHAPTER 12

AN AUDIENCE WITH THE
AFRICAN QUEEN

'Awusemhle. Uyinkwenkwezi ekhazimulayo. Yingakho namhlanje lusuku oluhle.' (You are so beautiful. You are a shining star. That's why today is such a beautiful day.)

The loss to Jerry Malinga didn't linger long in my mind, and two months later I was back in my preferred weight class and suitably buoyed by a fourth-round knockout victory over a canny but outclassed opponent called Hope Sole. The fight was scheduled for six rounds but was never going to go the distance.

It was an uplifting outcome but not half as uplifting as the arrival of my brother Ruddock, a more than proficient lightweight in his own right, journeying from Musina to join Harold's stable. He fought on the same card as me that night, overcoming his opponent on points, also over four rounds, in a case of sibling synchronicity. It was a long-awaited reunion and fulfilled the promise I'd made on leaving Musina to bring him to Johannesburg at the earliest feasible opportunity.

Ruddock set up home alongside me in my cramped little room, and our camaraderie and rivalry was as intense as ever as we quickly got back into the old routine. The ritualistic morning runs of our amateur days were revived, each driving the other's competitive juices.

For all his steadfast and reserved nature, Ruddock had a deep aversion to losing, no matter whether it was during a run or a sparring session. He would often lap me during our morning jogs, but I'd take a short cut back to the gym and, much to his disgust, would already be doing my sit-ups by the time he would bound through the door, breathless, drenched in sweat and cursing me for my deceptive tactics.

Ruddock stood just shy of six-feet tall and his rangy boxing style, and long reach, made him an awkward and often elegant opponent. That was all very well when he chose to box, rather than simply brawl. It was during these vignettes that he put his physical attributes to most effective use.

His right hand stung worse than a swarm of bees, and he once radically rearranged an opponent's nose with one particularly devastating right-hand. The resulting deformity made the unfortunate victim's beak look like a bulldozer had mistaken it for a parking bay.

His weakness, though, much like Naas Scheepers's, was his tendency to get sucked into a street fight, as opposed to a boxing contest, thereby sacrificing the advantages of height and reach. Harold would studiously avoid letting my brother and Naas spar together because he knew all too well it would degenerate into bar-room type free-for-all, with all boxing craft left outside the ropes.

The fates took another turn in my favour when no less than Brian Mitchell, arguably South Africa's best ever pound-for-pound fighter, joined Harold's inner sanctum. The former IBF and WBA junior lightweight world champion was on the comeback trail after a three-year sabbatical, and while his powers were dimming, he was still a luminous presence. He was known as the 'Road Warrior', in reference to winning most of his fights outside South Africa due to sanctions imposed by myriad other countries over the extremes of the racist apartheid regime. But he didn't let geographical impediments stand in his way, successfully defending his WBA title on twelve occasions in far-flung destinations before adding the IBF crown to his collection of bling.

With his rapier reflexes, slick looks and carefully groomed moustache, Mitchell, at 5 feet 6 inches, resembled more a pocket-sized buccaneer from the set of an action-adventure movie of swashbucklers and galleons, than he did a boxer. He was known for his all-action, aggressive style, throwing an array of punches which often left bewildered opponents in a defenceless daze. Affable and engaging outside the ring, he was demolition man when in fight mode, raining blows to the torso and the head that epitomised the old boxing adage of 'chop the body and the head will follow'.

He was a fat-free zone, as lean and lethal looking in his thirties as he was in his twenties, and his prowess was well recognised beyond the borders of South Africa with his induction into the international hall of fame. Mitchell was in his pomp at the same time that fellow junior lightweight Dingaan Thobela was on the rise. Even today, some twenty-five years on, debate rages over who would have won had they ever fought. I've always believed it would have been a beguiling spectacle: two boxers with equal measures of class and artistry, but Thobela wedded to by-the-book technique and Mitchell the quintessential brawler, with a touch of finesse tossed in.

Had they ever stepped into the ring together it would have had the ingredients of the all-time classic between Julio Chavez Sr and Meldrick Taylor, a war for the ages back in 1990, decided by one of boxing's most contentious ever refereeing decisions. Each was making the third defence of his respective belt – Mexico's Chavez the WBC and American Taylor the IBF. When Richard Steele theatrically waved his arms in front of Taylor's face with just two seconds remaining at the end of the twelfth and final round of a brutal battle, three lives were altered forever. Taylor, who was on course for a split-decision victory, was caught with a right flush to the face and sent spiralling to the canvas. Steele, who never lived down his decision to call a halt on humanitarian grounds, claimed Taylor was not responding to his questions as he got up at a count of five. It was his first defeat and one which lit the touch paper on a ruinous fall from grace. Conversely, Chavez escaped his first loss to take his record to 69–0.

Mitchell was the closest we had to a boxer of the stature of either Chavez or Taylor. His presence at the Hammer Gym created a new energy, such was the reverence his record commanded. Harold had an extra spring in his step each morning, and he wasn't the only one.

Philip Holiday and I were also beneficiaries, as we got to spar with a fighter whose deep reservoirs of knowledge were a source of wonder to us. We watched his every move: how he prepared for fights, his little rituals, his body language, the deliberate and painstaking detail that seemed to underpin everything he did, the calculated malice carried by his every punch.

Mitchell's comeback fight was scheduled for 26 November 1994 at the Sun City Resort's Superbowl Arena. He decided to set up his base there, in the heart of the gaming and amusement park capital of South Africa, with a temporary ring constructed near the popular Valley of Waves water park.

Ruddock, Philip and I were recruited as his sparring partners in what we perceived as a little corner of paradise. Our routine was to spar in the mornings and cool off on the artificial beach of the Valley of Waves each afternoon. People would flock to watch the sparring sessions, such was Mitchell's enduring mystique, even though at thirty-four he was now past his peak. There was no shortage of women amongst the throng, doubtless attracted by the chiselled shirtless bodies on display in the ultimate parade of machismo prowess. Each day that we trained, one of the PR girls from the Sun City organisation would be on hand to dish out bottled water and fresh towels. I never paid too much attention until one morning when I was ringside shadow-boxing, right next to Brian.

I turned and noticed a tall, willowy African girl in the crowd. She appeared to be staring at me. But I did a double take and looked back at her, just to make sure she was really gazing at me, rather than zeroing in on Brian, the star attraction of the impending show. She was indeed smiling coyly at me, her ivory-white teeth and pouty lips lending her the appearance of some sort of African goddess. Overcoming my innate bashfulness, I smiled back, mesmerised by her beauty.

After training that day I walked to the Valley of Waves. As I was approaching, I saw the pretty girl I had noticed earlier. Statuesque and beguiling, she was even more captivating close up. She was speaking in the Nguni tribal tongue of Xhosa to some guests and hadn't yet noticed me. When she did I smiled at her, and she returned the smile with those glistening teeth again on display.

Trying to impress her in the Xhosa language that I had mastered over the years I said with as much nonchalance as I could muster, 'Molo s'thandwa.' (Hello love.)

'Molo buti, unjani?' (Hello my brother, how are you?) she responded.

I was happy to hear her ask how I was but I needed to be more than just a brother to her.

'Ndi philile s'thandwa. Akho ngxaki,' (I'm fine my love. There is no problem at all) I said.

Before she could add anything further, I ladled on the flattery, continuing, 'Awusemhle. Uyinkwenkwezi ekhazimulayo. Yingakho namhlanje lusuku oluhle,' (You are so beautiful. You are a shining star. That's why today is such a beautiful day).

With those words uttered, she looked me in the eyes and smiled again. This time a wider, broader grin. Right there I felt a connection and something primal and powerful stirring between us.

'Enkosi kakhulu s'thandwa,' (Thank you very much my love) she replied.

She personified the old saying 'black is beautiful', with her high cheek bones, refined jaw line, hourglass curves and smooth mocha skin. I discovered subsequently, to no great surprise, she'd dabbled as a model. In my besotted state, I was in thrall of the most ravishing creature I'd ever set eyes upon. Some women can be pretty, some can be sexy. She exuded both these qualities. Our first meeting was the stuff of thunderbolts and lightning to me.

'My name is Lovemore,' I said as I extended my right hand to shake hers.

'As in "love" plus "more",' she responded, with a hint of suggestiveness in her tone, gently shaking my hand.

'Yes, exactly,' I deadpanned.

'What a beautiful name! I love it,' she said.

She then told me her English name was Florence but her Xhosa name was Nombulelo, but I could call her 'Bulie'.

Without wanting to waste any more time, I told her I would like to get to know her better and asked her if she would be gracious enough to join me for dinner.

'I would love to have dinner with you Lovemore and to get to know you more,' she replied, to my barely concealed delight.

We exchanged phone numbers. She gave me her work number and

home number. I gave her my hotel phone number. We agreed to go on a date later on that night. I then watched her walk away, my eyes lingering on her plump derrière for an indecent amount of time.

Aside from her bountiful physical attributes, I was also attracted to her clicking enunciation of her mother language. I had always found Xhosa people intriguing and their women were noted for their beauty. She was a prime example. To my enchanted ear a Xhosa woman could be spouting vulgarities and abuse and I would still be transfixed.

In fact, I subsequently discovered that Bulie's favourite chastisement when she was mad was the phrase *umnqundu wakho*. Every time she'd say it to me I would smile back and tell her I loved her more. This used to irk her further because she thought I was being a smart ass and mocking her. But the truth is I really didn't know what she meant by '*umnqundu wakho*'.

I had an inkling it was less than complimentary as she would only ever say it when she was really riled up. I only found out years later that she was in fact cussing me out every time she said that word. *Umnqundu* means anus. In most African cultures to refer to someone as an 'anus', or compare them to one, is the height of rudeness.

This woman however went on to become my best friend and confidante. She became my wife, the mother of my children, and ultimately my ex-wife. I could speak with her on matters I could never broach with anyone else. I could share anything with her. We would do everything together. We would laugh and cry together. If ever she was hurting I would share the pain, and vice versa. She let me taste and experience parenthood when she gave birth to our first child. Then a second and a third.

She introduced me to scented candles, aromatherapy essential oils, mood flames and aromatic fragrances, and many other things from the erotic to the exotic. I remember I would sometimes come home from the gym and she would fill up the bath for us with warm water. She would add some soothing, such as scented bubble bath and essential oils. She would also have some candles burning in the bathroom. In the background she would have some beautiful soft music playing. Our favourite artist was Jon Secada, with his lilting Latin rhythms and ballads. We would sit in the bath, our bodies wrapped together, for hours. The incense and candles she brought to the bedroom gave it the atmosphere of a jungle boudoir and our lovemaking was suitably untamed.

She would rub my body with oils and christened me her Shaka Zulu. She would refer to me as '*Ngonyama*' (lion) or '*Wena ka Ndlovu*' (the great elephant).

But, for all the heady and heated memories, the most beautiful gifts she gave me were our children. And for that I will always love her.

CHAPTER 13

JUSTICE FOR SALE

'At that age, it was beyond me to understand the complexities at play and that sometimes it wasn't about simply possessing an imposing physique to exert power and control over others.'

After so many false dawns and staggered starts, my boxing career was finally starting to lift off and I was gratified that the years of graft and toil were beginning to reap results. But the fallout from Christie's suicide – the trigger of which remains clouded in mystery even to this day – opened a Pandora's box of old and unpalatable memories from my own family's past.

It seemed unfathomable that somebody with her boundless life force, love of humanity and benevolent beauty would meet such an untimely fate at her own hand. Harold, consumed by a sorrow that seemed etched into his very soul, never provided any clues, and maybe he was as much in the dark as the rest of us. Or maybe he was privy to a private battle she was facing, perhaps with depression or some other inner demon. But from the outside peering in it was all just conjecture. And none of it made any sense.

The demons and scars of my own family history were in plain sight, though rarely spoken of, just like the proverbial elephant in the room. The skeletons piled high in the closet centred around my own father's attempted suicide, which I bore witness to as an eleven-year-old. It was prompted by the rape of my sister Caroline, who was just thirteen at the time.

The perpetrator hid behind the cloak of civility and respectability as the principal of Beitbridge's Dulibadzimu Primary School, the seat of learning we all attended during our three years in Zimbabwe. His name was Mr Kennedy, but everyone called him Mr Ned, and like the Catholic priests in Australia who systemically molested innocent young members of their own flocks over several decades, a complacent and complicit system of blind eyes and neglect allowed him to freely indulge his penchant for sexually abusing those in his care. He was a serial paedophile, whose heinous peccadilloes were known to many but were whitewashed by his friends in high places, once their palms had been suitably greased.

In cultures like ours, were polygyamy was rife and sexual relations with minors were not viewed as anything extraordinary, the Mr Neds of the world had virtual carte blanche to dip into their playbooks of depravity without fear of reprisal or retribution from the authorities. The age of consent in Zimbabwe was a blurred line back then, with men in their twenties or thirties marrying girls as young as twelve.

During my school days in Zimbabwe and then back in South Africa, it was common to see male teachers having exploitative sexual relationships with their female pupils. Some would even threaten to fail them in their exams if they declined to accommodate their requests for sex. If the students were subsequently impregnated the teachers would simply pay what was termed 'damage money' of about $150 Zimbabwean or 1000 rand to their families to brush the matter under the carpet.

Students would drop out of school to give birth to offspring they were in no position to raise, heaping more financial pressure on families already subsisting well below the poverty line. Multiple lives were destroyed in this manner: the mother, who was herself a child, would have to sacrifice her education to raise an illegitimate child, who would then have no father figure growing up, immersed in deprivation. Thus, the cycle of poverty and desperation was perpetuated.

In Mr Ned's case, he didn't limit his advances to his pupils; he was a serial harasser of the young teachers who came fresh from university to Beitbridge for work experience. To keep their jobs, they would have to submit to him.

The stench of his activities was all around us, particularly since he lived alone on the same street as us. He was originally from Mashonaland, in the north of Zimbabwe, where it was rumoured that he had a family. His modus operandi was to order students to come to his home to perform errands, with the vague promise of their grades benefiting as a result. It was in his lair that the monster would give full vent to his perversions and Caroline was one such pupil ordered to his home for 'domestic duties'.

I recall seeing her emerge from his house one afternoon distraught and in floods of tears. She was bleeding between her legs. My own blood boiled to see her like this, but when she told my father of her ordeal he was initially in denial about it, even questioning her own morality. I remember him raging at her, 'What were you doing going into the house of a man old enough to be your own father in the first place. Are you some sort of slut?'

His attitude only deepened her trauma and his words cut to the quick. We both explained to him that Mr Ned's activities were well known throughout the school, but he was having none of it. Insisting her talk of rape was fanciful and even malicious, he maintained that his good neighbour Mr Ned was a man of honour and integrity, who would never stoop to such acts.

Later that night I heard my parents arguing heatedly over the incident, with my appalled mother threatening to pack us all up and return to South Africa, if he didn't do anything about it. She even raised the issue of when she, too, was accosted by my father's brother, screaming at him, 'What sort of man are you if you can't protect your own family?'

My father pleaded with her, pointing out that Mr Ned was a powerful figure, with many allies in Robert Mugabe's ruling ZANU–PF party and strong ties with a corrupt and brutal police force.

'These people will kill me if I step on this man's toes, remember what happened to me two years ago when they came in our village. I almost died then.'

He also said it was no coincidence that Mr Ned had been handed his position as principal, coming as he did all the way from Mashonaland to the border country. He added that it wasn't because there was a shortage of qualified principals in Beitbridge but rather a direct result of his deep affiliation with ZANU–PF.

But my mother was not budging an inch, snapping back at him, 'I'll put up with your drinking, even though I detest it, but this I will not put up with. It's the last straw.'

It was the worst row I'd ever witnessed between my parents, and there had been a few. While I sympathised with my father's position in fearing retaliation from the authorities if he tried to expose this cowardly beast, I also had a visceral reaction similar to that of my mother.

I felt let down by the man who had always imparted on me the importance of protecting your family above all else. He'd always made it clear that as the firstborn boy, I had the responsibility to follow that mantra to the letter. I had done that by firing off those rifle shots at his brother when he'd molested my mother some two years earlier. I felt if I could do that as a callow youngster, why couldn't he as a grown man take on Mr Ned. In my mind, he wasn't practising what he preached, and to make matters worse was blaming the victim, in this case my beloved sister. He was trying to justify the injustice visited upon her, his own daughter, his own creation.

The next day, true to her word, my mother left with my siblings in tow to move in with her cousin about 5 kilometres away, leaving me to remain with my father and continue helping him with chores and the fishing enterprise which had brought extra food and money to the family.

He was still recovering from the back injury he suffered at the hands of the ZANU–PF guerrillas and was struggling to swim across the Limpopo river to set the nets. This had to be done each day, rain or shine, school day or holiday, at 5 am. It was my ritual and one of the responsibilities thrust upon me.

While the family had been splintered, the process of eking out a living had to continue. During the separation I would see my siblings at school, or when I dropped round to hand over money after my father had sold some fish, or cash generated from his regular job as a mechanic. The hardest part was attending school on a daily basis with Caroline and facing this ogre who had destroyed our family. My contempt for him knew no bounds. In my darkest daydreams I conjured many and varied ways of meting out my own personal punishment and ending his life.

He was a gnome-like figure, who barely stood five-feet tall, with sunken, hollow eyes and a habit of gesturing manically when he spoke.

Despite his lack of stature, and frail frame, he seemed to cast an all-encompassing shadow, evoking fear and blind loyalty in equal measure. Was it because he wore three-piece suits and shiny polished shoes? Or his links with powerful factions? Or his position as school principal? Either way, I couldn't comprehend how my father, with his near six feet in height and honed and toned physique couldn't simply give him the beating he so richly deserved. At that age, it was beyond me to understand the complexities at play and that sometimes it wasn't about simply possessing an imposing physique to exert power and control over others.

The respect I had for my dad was ebbing away by the day. One morning, about two weeks after the family separation, the genie escaped the bottle when my father asked me to swim out to release the anchors and free the fishing nets. Instead of complying, I point-blank refused, telling him he could do it, as I had lost all faith and belief in him.

'Why do I risk being eaten by crocodiles every day for a man who doesn't protect his family,' I barked at him. 'I almost killed my own uncle because I believed in the things you told me about taking responsibility, and then you're not man enough to practise what you've preached.'

Rather than round on me and maybe give me a beating for insolence, my father visibly crumpled in front of my eyes, tears welling and his pride punctured. The big, strong man I had always looked up to was broken, hurting and now openly weeping.

I cried too, in the emotion of the moment, and instinctively reached out to him and we held on to each other in a tight embrace which seemed to melt away all the accrued enmity and ill feeling. When we broke the hug, no further words were uttered but there was a mutual understanding between us and a fractured bond had been mended. I dived into the water and swam out to the nets. We gathered our catch of the day and headed home in a silent march.

If I imagined that some equanimity had been restored, I was sorely mistaken. My father absconded from work and spent the rest of day guzzling the home-brewed alcohol of which he'd become so fond. That evening, as the sun was starting to set, he took an axe and walked up the road to Mr Ned's house, screaming and shouting that 'he was going to kill the little rapist'.

A crowd had gathered, and Mr Ned was seen slinking down a side path and into his house through the back door. The threats of my inebriated father didn't go down well, and he was arrested and incarcerated in the local police station for the night. No charges were laid but he was told he must apologise to Mr Ned or he would be facing an attempted murder rap. He was also to never again raise the issue.

My father was not the same man after that, it was as if a vital part of his identity had been erased and, in its place, there was only a void. My parents eventually reconciled and my mother moved back in, along with the rest of my siblings.

One Saturday afternoon, my mother and sisters were off at the markets, and my father was at home, feeling the after-effects of a session sculling the locally brewed Chibuku beer at a nearby bar. Usually when he was intoxicated, he'd become irreverent and crack jokes that he was always the first to laugh at. The rest of us were normally laughing at him, rather than with him. When the mirth, and the booze ran dry he'd eventually lapse into a fitful sleep, punctuated by loud snores.

His demeanour was different on this occasion, quiet and introverted. My brothers and I were playing outside when he appeared at the doorway and handed us some coins, telling us to go and watch the Beitbridge soccer team play at the local stadium. This was highly unusual since he'd never given us money to watch games in the past.

On rare occasions he would give us some pennies to go to the Bioscope, a makeshift cinema with movies projected onto a large screen. And that only happened when he and my mother wanted to enjoy some privacy to practise their conjugal rights. I put the coins in the pocket of my shorts but before leaving we decided to change clothes as what we'd been wearing was scuffed and dirty from playing around in the street.

After arriving at the stadium about fifteen minutes later, I realised I'd left the money in my shorts and told my brothers to wait for me as I ran back to fetch the cash. When I arrived back home the front door was shut but not locked, and like every kid, I had a habit of opening doors without knocking, plus on this occasion I was in a mad rush.

So I burst in to be greeted by the sight of my father standing on a stool, there was a rope tied into a noose hanging from a timber beam supporting the ceiling. He had both hands on the rope, as if he was about to place the noose around his neck. I was frozen in disbelief, literally rooted to the spot, almost believing I'd gate crashed a horror show playing out in a parallel universe.

Ruffled by my presence, my father, breathing heavily and streaked with sweat, lost his footing, dropped the rope and tumbled off the stool. Before I could say a word, he looked up at me from his prone position on the mud floor of our home and said, 'Lovemore, you didn't see what you just saw. Understand?'

I didn't but just meekly nodded in the affirmative. He then forbade me from ever discussing or talking about what I'd just witnessed. And, true to my word, I did as I was told, maintaining my vow of silence up until he died several years later. And even then, I only ever shared it with my siblings.

The truth was he felt powerless and stripped of his manhood, and in that moment couldn't handle the shame he felt any longer.

There was to be no forgetting the deeds of Mr Ned, with my sister giving birth to a baby boy eight months later as the legacy of being raped. Born prematurely, the child died within weeks of the family moving back to South Africa, aged only ten months. The experience numbed us all, and my sister has buried it so deep it's a part of her memory bank she refuses to visit.

They say lightning doesn't strike twice, but I beg to differ because several years later, with the family back in Musina, another sister, who I don't want to name out of respect for her privacy, was also sexually assaulted with the same result: no justice for the victim. Not just once, but at least nine times, she was abused, again by a neighbour who worked as an armed guard for a security company which collected cash from banks. At first the police dismissed her complaints as frivolous, saying there must have been an element of consent, even though she was just twelve years old. But she was not a person prone to exaggeration or flights of fancy.

Even prior to its repeal in 2007, the South African sexual offences Act deemed carnal relations with a twelve-year-old to be statutory rape. For a long time the age of consent had been sixteen, though recent changes have lowered it to twelve between consenting pre-teens.

In my sister's case it was a married man in his thirties who violated her. When their first argument failed the police, with the accused's complicity, resorted to claiming the miscreant wasn't mentally fit to stand trial, hence there should be no charges laid. It wasn't their place to make such profound determinations, but instead it was the province of the courts. The police, though, didn't want the case to even go to court. A doctor's examination confirmed she had been interfered with, and the neighbour never disputed the facts but claimed she was a willing partner.

My father, at this stage his health failing following the loss of my cherished mother and his own impending kidney and liver failure, simply didn't have the energy or the will to confront this new atrocity head on. Also, as siblings we'd made the decision to shield him from the most graphic of the details, fearing it might speed his demise.

It still baffles and irks me today why, in their wisdom, the police treated the case with such contempt. Was it the cultural mores of the day? Was it sheer incompetence or were they taking bribes?

Incompetence was high on my list since it was, sad to say, rife among black cops. I'd witnessed it on many occasions, in particular with my father being stopped riding his motorcycle while drunk, or without a crash helmet. Or sometimes both. When it was put to him that he'd committed an offence, my father would all of a sudden become a lawyer. He would bamboozle his accusers by quoting fake legislation at them, as if it were set in tablets of stone.

'Do you realise that under section 133 of the Road Traffic Act I can ride a Kawasaki 500cc without a helmet, and right now you're violating my rights. if I take it up with your superior you could be out of a job,' he would state with as much gravitas as he could muster.

I believed his bluster myself until I noticed over time that the sections of his imaginary legislation kept changing. Sometimes it was section 133, then 53, then 105. But the black officers used to fall for it and would wave him on his way, sometimes even apologising for wasting his time.

The ruse worked like a charm until one day he got pulled over by a white cop, whose instant reaction to his well-worn routine was a curt, 'Moenie kak praat nie. [Don't talk shit, in Afrikaans.] You're going to jail.'

Bribing your way out of a tight spot with a traffic cop was also a worthwhile ploy, with tickets often rescinded for as little as a loaf of bread or a bottle of cold Coca Cola.

My sister's abuser never met the full force of the law and could be seen each day heading off to work proudly wearing his security uniform, as if it bestowed upon him some form of legitimacy. He did, however, one day get to feel the full force of the bullet. He was fatally shot by bandits who rammed and ambushed his armoured van one morning in Musina.

They showed him all the care and consideration he'd shown my sister. Karma is a bitch, as the saying goes.

CHAPTER 14

BEWITCHED BY THE LAND
DOWN UNDER

'I was aghast on my arrival into Sydney: all I saw was an ocean of white faces and the Aboriginals I finally did get to meet didn't, as I'd imagined, have their bodies daubed in body paint, ornaments or feathers. And they didn't speak in exotic tongues but instead chatted in perfect English.'

My face wasn't jumping off the sports pages of newspapers alongside reams of text announcing me as the next big thing in the ring, but I was at least staying busy. On 6 December 1994 I took care of business against Bheki Dlamini with a second-round knockout, and just over three months later I marked my tenth professional fight with an eye-catching victory over the experienced and wily November Ntshingila, who had a record of twenty-three wins and three losses. Two of those defeats had been for the WBC title against the Russian Anatoly Alexandrov, with the other for the South African featherweight crown. It was the biggest test of my career, and an indicator of whether I was ready for international exposure and long-craved recognition.

I out-boxed Ntshingila over six rounds at the Carousel Casino to win a split decision. Two months later, I added some lustre to my reputation as a fighter on the rise when I also overcame Jerry Ngobeni, whose record was twenty wins, three loses and a draw.

He had already come up short in a world title shot against Joey Gamache and had fought overseas in Italy and the US. I comfortably prevailed on points over six rounds, and to add to my satisfaction Brian Mitchell took me aside after the fight to tell me, 'Enjoy the moment Lovemore but there will be many more. One day you'll become a world champion.'

Such an utterance from somebody of his exalted stature and standing sent my confidence soaring. And even Harold, whose belief in me always seemed to come with a caveat, said it was time to spread my wings onto the international stage.

I was also in love. Florence and I had become an item and more than that I'd also become a father. Florence came as a package with her four-year-old daughter Maria, from a previous relationship. We moved into the two-bedroom apartment behind Harold's gym, previously occupied by the elderly white caretakers. The old man had succumbed to a heart attack and his wife had decided to go and live with one of her children.

Chance is one of life's great arbiters, and my encounter with boxing writer Pete Moscardi, who was chasing some tasty morsels after my fiery sparring session with Philip Holiday during my days of frustration, proved portentous. I didn't give him much to feast on during our first fleeting meeting, but he was omnipresent on the boxing landscape and a friendship which transcended the boundaries of apartheid's hateful separatism blossomed between the black fighter and the boxing-obsessed white writer. Over time, he became more than just a friend. He was a brother, a father and a mentor and he understood the way I viewed the world. He understood that inside this promising boxer was a fledgling political activist, not afraid to speak his mind.

In a country riven by racial fissures he was one of a tiny vanguard of white South Africans who gave me the utopian hope that one day all the factions of our country would ultimately coexist in harmony under the banner of freedom and democracy. Of Italian background but raised in the UK, he served for the British Force in Rhodesia (Zimbabwe) and as a British bobby in Her Majesty's police force. Already in his fifties when we met, he'd dabbled in boxing promotions, and his often-inflammatory articles were published in boxing publications like *Boxing News* UK, the *African Ring* and *The Fist* in Australia. He was a torchbearer for the sport in South Africa, and he helped bring my own career into the light.

While segregation permeated almost every nook and cranny of South African society, Pete and his beautiful wife Margi only saw humanity, never colour. They would open their door to my family and share a meal with us and provide a bed to sleep in if needed. He played a pivotal role in my eventual move to Australia, in search of a better life for my family. We often spoke of my desire to escape the confines, restrictions and hardships in South Africa.

I knew in my heart I'd never be anything but a bit-part card-filler with Rodney Berman's Golden Gloves Promotions. I had no contract with the company, a clear indication I was not valued as an asset. Stablemates Philip Holiday and Corrie Sanders had a set schedule of fights, and guaranteed minimum purses, privileges coveted fighters could take for granted. I was always the Cinderella figure: never knowing where my next fight and pay cheque would come from. I suspected that though I had a talent, my skin colour was always a stumbling block in reaching any great heights in South Africa.

Pete put me in touch with promoters in the UK and the US, and there was some interest in what I might have to offer. Amidst those talks of taking my career overseas, an opportunity arose for Naas Scheepers and me to make the long journey across the Pacific to fight on the undercard of the IBF super lightweight title contest between Kostya Tszyu, the Russian turned Australian, and Roger Mayweather, uncle and eventual trainer of boxing royalty Floyd Mayweather Jr.

It was Tszyu's first defence of the title he'd won six months earlier by stopping Jake Rodriguez in six rounds. My duel Down Under was scheduled for 25 June 1995 at the Newcastle Entertainment Centre.

Mayweather, known by the sobriquet of Black Mamba, was a former WBA super featherweight champion, who had also held the WBC junior welterweight and IBO welterweight belts. At the age of thirty-four, he carried the baggage of many epic battles whilst twenty-five year old Tszyu was a pocket powerhouse who was ruthlessly felling all before him.

Twelve years later I came into close orbit with Roger again when I was recruited to spar with his nephew Floyd in Las Vegas as he prepared to battle Englishman Ricky Hatton for the WBC welterweight title. Roger was Floyd's trainer and one of the few he took heed of. He recalled our meeting all those years before, and was his usual acerbic and hyperbolic self, belittling anybody outside the boxing fraternity who offered an opinion about the noble art, especially journalists.

'You don't know shit about boxing,' he'd sneer at them.

He pronounced the same judgements on trainers in the opposite corner to show his venom knew no bias. Sadly, he passed away in 2020 from diabetes; but like so many of my brethren, prior to his death he suffered with dementia, the cumulative toll his trade exacted upon him as he lingered too long in the ring.

I was scheduled to fight Australia's Indigenous brawler Cliff Samardin on the Paul Hotz promotion in Newcastle, a fighter with an impressive 22–0 record at the time. Samardin was managed by none less than Jeff Fenech (former three times world boxing champion) and was being groomed as a potential world champion in the making. Before leaving South Africa I'd been handed a book by Pete Moscardi on Fenech and his career journey. By the time I landed in Sydney I knew all I needed to know about him.

Naas and I were in the shape of our lives. He was up against Australia's Justin Rowsell in a super lightweight contest and memories of our trek together to the mysterious land of Australia have never dimmed.

It was my first time on a plane, let alone overseas, and as far as I was concerned, I might as well have been journeying to a neighbouring solar system. I'd researched the Indigenous peoples of Australia and read up on kangaroos. I expected the streets to be dusty, parched and with rogue roos hopping into your path every other step. I was aghast on my arrival into Sydney: all I saw was an ocean of white faces and the Aboriginals I finally did get to meet didn't, as I'd imagined, have their bodies daubed in body paint, ornaments or feathers. And they didn't speak in exotic tongues but instead chatted in perfect English.

They looked nothing like the late David Ngoombujarra, who played Pretty Boy Floyd in the movie *Blackfellas*. They more resembled the half-caste Aboriginal John Moore, who played Doug Dooligan, in the same movie.

I was determined to conduct my own anthropological study and ventured to the foyer of the Mercure Hotel on George Street after we'd checked in, brandishing a photo of Aboriginal people in all their tribal pomp and finery given to me by Pete. Showing the woman at the check-in desk the picture, and asking where I might find such people, she replied, with some bemusement, 'I think you might have to go to the Northern Territory for that love. But there are Aboriginal people up the road in Redfern. Why do you ask?'

I explained I was from South Africa and was intrigued to meet these people. She humoured me and explained how I could get to Redfern, suggesting it was safer by day than by night. I didn't know what she meant by that but didn't want to make even more of a fool of myself, and thanked her profusely for her help.

The next morning at breakfast, I told Harold, my voice crackling with excitement, that I'd discovered where we could find Aboriginal folk. He didn't share my enthusiasm, fixing me with a disinterested glance before intoning, 'What?'

His lukewarm response convinced me I would be on my own in my Redfern jaunt, as I sought to connect with these kindred souls. For me, it was important to meet the original landowners, whose appearance and tribal garb evoked comparisons, at least in my mind, of my own forebears.

I followed the instructions to Redfern and despite scouring the streets surrounding the grim and grimy looking blocks of flats, I saw nobody who even faintly resembled the people in the picture I carried with me. Eventually I was approached by four or five young teenagers, none of whom appeared Indigenous to my untrained eye.

'Hey, black fella, where you from?' said one.

I told him South Africa, which provoked another to ask, 'You know Nelson Mandela?'

Before I could answer, another enquired, 'Do you get to see and touch lions and tigers in Africa?'

I told him you had to go to the zoo or game reserve for that, and no touching was allowed. I added that tigers were from India, not Africa. My inquisitor insisted I was wrong about tigers, but I resisted the temptation to get into a debate about it.

As I walked away, I realised being misguided runs both ways. I did eventually chat with Aboriginal people that day, but they looked little like my picture, instead wearing the designer threads of Nike and Adidas.

Many were slumped in the street guzzling alcohol from bottles encased in brown paper bags and it reminded me of some of the downtrodden street scenes back home.

My curiosity only partially sated, it was back to the gym for light pad work and sparring. Fenech would occasionally drop by the gym to watch us, but only pleasantries were ever exchanged.

On the day before Naas and I were due to fight, South Africa was up against New Zealand in the final of the rugby World Cup at Ellis Park in Johannesburg. Harold, Naas and I headed up George Street to find a pub screening the game, and on making our entrance were greeted by swarms of Kiwis and Aussies. South Africans were conspicuous by their absence. Each time South Africa scored we'd holler and high five, while attracting some menacing-looking glares and glances from the Kiwi fans, mainly thick-set Maoris whose meaty arms were decorated with tattoos.

Harold, fearing the worst, said, 'Boys, the fight might have come a day early. If South Africa wins, I'm heading for the door.'

Naas and I discussed which ones we'd take out first, should things turn ugly. I was just bantering, but Naas was in earnest. He was never one to turn the other cheek or shy away from a brawl. His death stares harked back to an incident in Benoni earlier that year when things became heated with a group of bikies, some of whom he knocked senseless before the police arrived.

At the final whistle, South Africa had won 15–12, but we didn't have to sprint to the door because before the game had even ended some of the Aussies, and even All Blacks fans, had befriended us. We were suddenly being treated like lifelong buddies and being offered beers, which we politely declined. Harold, on the other hand, swilled down copious quantities of VB.

The next night it was rocking at the Newcastle Entertainment Centre. I was draped in all black, from my boots and shorts to my gown. I was still a bit jet-lagged but I felt an inner calm and the reservoirs of energy were running deep. The early rounds were cagey and calculated but watching the TV tapes of the fight later, featuring Fenech riding shotgun to lead commentator Alan Thomas, you'd have thought there was only one man in the ring. And it wasn't me. Fenech's connection as Samardin's manager clearly coloured his perception of what was unfolding before him. All you could hear from him was, 'Good jab by Samardin. Great body shot by Samardin.' He was blind to anything I was doing.

I realised towards the end of the second that I'd be fighting the referee, the commentators and Samardin after I was given an official warning for a low blow, despite the punch being above his waistline.

I picked up the pace in round three, contrary to Fenech eulogising over Samardin's head movement, while dismissing the twenty jabs I threw as possessing the ferocity of air kisses. I was also throwing left hooks and upper cuts which were all landing. Going into the fourth round I thought I was in control, but the judges seemed to be seeing it differently. The fifth was even and I dominated the sixth with some damaging right-hands with Samardin countering with a good right-hand which caught me on the chin towards the end of the round, stinging me momentarily.

It seemed the judges were rewarding Samardin's cameos of domination while my longer spells of sustained pressure disappeared into the ether of their minds. Thomas, during his commentary awarded me the sixth, while Fenech exercised his right to silence.

I had Samardin pinned in the ropes in the seventh, fencing him in with a flurry of combinations which threatened to tear away his defences. Thomas was again a lone voice, declaring that Samardin was hurt and in trouble. Fenech, again, said nothing.

When Samardin fought back with a counter right, Fenech regained his powers of speech, saluting 'a huge right-hand from Samardin'. We were in the centre of the ring exchanging blows with a zeal that had the crowd on their feet.

The eighth and final round didn't produce any further fireworks, and at the bell Thomas had it as a draw, Fenech had Samardin winning by a point. Two judges gave it to Samardin 77–76, and the other had it as a draw 77–77. The home crowd, abandoning the innate parochialism you'll find in any country, booed the verdict, in a transparent sign that it was a hometown decision.

Harold was proud of my performance and that's what really mattered to me and eased some of the pangs of defeat.

The next day's *Daily Telegraph* featured a stinging critique of the decision from boxing scribe Stephen Cooper, who penned the words, 'Lovemore Ndou of South Africa will go home saying "I wuz robbed" by the two judges who gave Samardin the verdict in their eight rounder. Admittedly the fight looked more like a mating session between two stick insects. But, even so, Ndou deserved a comprehensive decision.'

Naas also lost his fight to Justin Rowsell after suffering a third round TKO, and a bad cut over his right eye. After the fight I told Naas in Afrikaans, 'Een dag gaan ek daai mannetjie vir jou bliksem.' (Someday I'm going to beat up that boy for you.)

Three years later, I did exactly that, knocking out Rowsell in six rounds in one of my biggest fights ever in Australia. The ubiquitous Fenech was in his corner that night for a sprinkling of extra spice. And a dollop of relish.

Though I'd left Australia as a loser on my maiden voyage, I felt I'd discovered a wondrous new world. I'd heard all about the 'Keep Australia white policy' before my arrival, but the reception I received didn't align with that at all. Everybody saw me as a 'mate' rather than a Kaffir. I was treated with respect and as an equal, something I'd rarely experienced in my birth country.

Even though South Africa had been a democratic state for a year at that time, nothing had really changed. Racism was still deeply entrenched. You can change the laws, the rules and the system but embedded attitudes and beliefs can't simply be waved away by a magic wand. These quantum shifts take generations to solidify. Fortunately, I was one of a minority to discern that harsh reality and was not naive enough to believe all would be sweetness and light in the Rainbow Nation.

I told myself on the flight home that one day I would relocate to Australia. A love affair had just begun.

CHAPTER 15

THE LONG GOODBYE

'When you break it down into its component parts, the interaction between manager/trainer and a fighter resembles that of a hooker and a client.'

Within two months of returning to South Africa, I was in action again, this time in Eastern Cape, fighting for the national junior lightweight title against Mthobeli Mhlophe at East London's Orient Theatre. It was a familiar theme, as I dominated the majority of the twelve rounds only for the contest to be declared a draw by a hometown panel of judges. At the time, entering the arena in the Eastern Cape as an outsider was akin to fighting in a foreign land, as unfettered parochialism prospered.

The fight was beamed around the nation live on the SABC network, and those who witnessed it – other than the judges of course – were in no doubt who the real victor was. No fighter from another province would ever walk away from East London with a points decision in their favour, and I was no exception to the rule.

The Cape province had unearthed several world champions down the decades, including Vuyani Bungu, the only South African to successfully defend his world title on thirteen occasions before finally relinquishing it and moving up a division. I still wonder why he was never inducted into the international hall of fame, whereas Brian Mitchell, who defended his crown twelve times, remains the only South African to have received such exalted recognition.

My experience in East London only strengthened my resolve to move abroad, as if further motivation was required after my love-at-first-sight mission to Australia.

Meanwhile, I had found myself inducted into the corporate world, albeit on a nominal basis, after becoming a shareholder of Crane World, the manufacturing company which had become one of my sponsors. It was an unlikely alliance between me and one of its directors, boxing devote Peter Staniland. Like many businessmen of the time he'd migrated from the UK in search of the golden opportunities which dangled tantalisingly for intrepid white folks in our minerals rich land. He was a jocular figure who found humour in almost every crevice of life, and used to chuckle heartily at my jokes, even though most were politically motivated.

I used to verbally spar with him, saying, 'You might consider yourself my good friend now but once the revolution comes, I'll make sure your bags are packed because you'll be the first one on the plane back to Europe.'

He found this uproariously amusing, and each time I saw him I'd raise my right fist and holler *'Amandla!'* (power to the people) in Zulu.

At first, he didn't get the gist of what I was saying and would reciprocate by raising his own right fist, without enunciating anything. Eventually, he asked me what it meant and when I told him he added his own spin in reply, uttering earnestly, 'Power to the Black Panther.'

Those words were the genesis of the sobriquet I carried with me for the rest of my career, courtesy of his white wit. He went so far as to get me some boxing trunks with the words Black Panther emblazoned across them. Expanding on the theme, he said, 'Lovemore, it's the perfect nickname for you. You're vicious inside the ring like a panther, and outside the ring your views match those of the Black Panther party.'

He was referring to the black rights group founded by Huey P. Newton and Bobby Seale in the United States in 1966, which had fought white oppression. While Peter appreciated my attempts at political satire, he also discerned that behind the humour lurked an activist who would never shy away from a debate.

In the post-apartheid landscape, it was an imperative for white owned and run companies to have a black presence, even if it was often token.

It was a way of supporting black economic empowerment; and being an advocate of such endeavours Peter recruited me to his Crane World shareholder list. He gave me 5 per cent of the company, though I never ended up capitalising on my stake in the crane sales business.

The desire to make Australia my home was my overwhelming focus, and all else seemed to shrink into the background. My main concern over remaining in South Africa was the peril of raising a family in such a hostile and often heartless environment. I already had a step-daughter, and I couldn't countenance the prospect of nurturing her, or future sisters, in a country were a woman's worth was valued at next to nothing. I had already witnessed the fallout of such entrenched belief systems at first hand, with my own sisters the victims of sexual assault and the law failing them miserably. The prospect of my own daughters becoming targets of sexual predators and opportunists was more than I could bear. I remember promising my mother before her death that I would only ever bring children into the world if I was 100 per cent sure they would be provided with all life's opportunities, irrespective of their skin colour. I just couldn't see that utopian vision unfolding in South Africa, where the crime rate was raging and murders, whether through carjackings, house break-ins, or just random robberies or gang feuds were off the charts.

A woman being raped was viewed more as an occupational hazard than an act worthy of the deepest indignation, and life itself had little intrinsic value amongst a black population still wrestling with a sense of self-loathing instilled upon them by apartheid. Then there were the deep-seated tribal enmities which our former white rulers had cynically manipulated to their own ends.

Beyond all that, I knew I could never reach my personal potential in such an environment. Even back then I was already casting forward to beyond my boxing career. While I had the dream and desire to become a world champion, I was also contemplating life after boxing.

During my trip to Australia for the Samardin fight I'd struck up a rapport of sorts with Paul Hotz, a Jewish South African who had relocated to Sydney and was the promoter of the Tszyu–Mayweather bout. He was a successful fashion designer turned promoter, and we'd discussed my aspirations to relocate. He promised he would assist me and do whatever he could to help me further my career Down Under.

But, like almost every promoter who crossed my path, he was a Walter Mitty in disguise, spinning fairytales and whimsy. Initially, I was spellbound by his fanciful tales, believing he might be a conduit to a better life. We began corresponding, and the narrative centred around him arranging visas for me and my family and setting up a rematch with Samardin. But the words were empty, and to make matters worse he was relaying all our conversations back to Harold, as if he was playing the part of a double agent in a cloak-and-dagger drama. His deceitfulness was not appreciated, though I stood by everything I'd said to him and would have repeated it all in front of Harold. Nonetheless, my relationship with Harold was dented and things were never quite the same between us from that point on.

I appreciated that he had invested time and patience to elevate me to a certain level. But our communications had always revolved around boxing, and little else. He knew nothing of my ideals and hopes outside the ring: it was merely a manager-boxer relationship. The goal was to win a world title, and to make some money along the way. Nothing beyond that.

When you break it down into its component parts, the interaction between manager/trainer and a fighter resembles that of a hooker and a client. At the end of the transaction everybody goes their own way, without sentiment and nostalgia clouding what is purely a business arrangement. Ultimately, when a fighter's career ends, invariably so too does the relationship with his manager.

So Harold's ignorance of my long-term aims was par for the course, and he couldn't be chastised for that. I had visions of one day transplanting myself into politics or perhaps learned pursuits like psychology or the law. But the immediate agenda was all about titles.

Harold showed his displeasure at my perceived disloyalty by distancing himself from me on a day-to-day basis at the Hammer Gym, and tensions only escalated when I made it known that wherever I went Ruddock would be joining me. The atmosphere at the gym was colder than a cryogenic chamber but I knew that someday in the future he would understand my motivations. Today, he's come to that point and is proud of my achievements, inside and outside the ring. We even worked together further down the road, with my professional career ending where it had begun; under his wing.

I'd impressed upon my journalistic pal Pete Moscardi the lure of Australia and he dug into his list of contacts and came up with Brendon Smith, a Toowoomba-based boxing manager with a track record of working with South African fighters. He'd already signed up my compatriot November Ntshingila, whose career had taken on mythical status back in his homeland. We'd fawn over picture spreads in boxing magazines of his lavish Australian home and swimming pool. He had sponsors and a good job outside boxing. I'd already beaten Ntshingila, and Brendon Smith was in his corner that night, no doubt taking note.

Smith was in South Africa alongside his own fighter Gilbert Hooper, who fought Naas Scheepers on the same card that featured me and Ntshingila. Ntshingila had helped Hooper in sparring and a friendship was spawned at that point between him and Brendon. The trainer/manager from Queensland knew what I could produce and was also aware of my brother Ruddock's prowess, as he battled Moffat Mahlangu on the same bill, winning on points over four rounds.

Within a few months, Brendon had signed Ntshingila to a contract and had brought him to Australia. Pete communicated to me that both me and Ruddock were next on his list and would be sponsored through a 'distinguished talent' visa.

It was music to my ears. Meanwhile, my wife, stepdaughter and I took up the offer of living with the Moscardis while our visas were processed. They treated us with love and respect and Pete would arrange for me to train at different gyms to make sure I stayed in shape. One of our regular haunts was Norman Hlabane's gym, run by the mastermind behind the career of the great Dingaan Thobela, moulding him into one of the best fighters South Africa has ever produced.

Pete also became my self-anointed medic, though his 'skills' were self-taught. He convinced me he had a magic formula to cure myriad ailments and when a cold struck me down one week I turned to his ministrations. He ploughed his medicine cabinet, laden with capsules, potions and lotions, and fed me one remedy after another, explaining the origin of each.

'This is one we used when I served with the British army in Rhodesia,' he would wistfully recall. 'This one is my own personal concoction …'

He began to sound like an African witch doctor, with each dose followed by the ritualistic inhaling of Vicks vapours wafting from boiling water. By the time I'd finished with the treatments, I felt drained and drowsy and slept for twelve hours without stirring once. On awakening, the malaise had lifted and, to my amazement, the white African witch doctor had worked his magic.

Idiosyncratic to a fault, Pete, whose ample belly was a testament to his fondness for wining and dining, was not exactly the perfect dinner partner. If his steak was not cooked to his exact instructions, he would send flustered waiting staff off to find the manager so he could vent his displeasure voluminously. While I cringed with embarrassment, he would proceed to lecture the proprietor on the fine detail of culinary expertise and exhort them to live up to his high standards.

To compound matters, he was a serial pest, and would often return to the same establishments, which no doubt had hoped to have seen the last of him. I was always concerned about waitresses and chefs spitting in our food as a form of payback, but Pete, as if a higher power had placed a protective bubble around his plate, never batted an eyelid.

As time drifted on waiting for our visa applications to be approved, I bid my farewells in the form of 'thank yous' to those who'd helped me light the torch paper on my dreams.

The first on the list was Golden Gloves promoter Rodney Berman, who had given me my first platform in the professional arena. I also penned a resignation letter from my position as a Crane World shareholder. And I made an appearance at the offices of the ruling body, Boxing South Africa, and thanked everybody there.

While most wished me well, there were others who muttered forebodingly of the pitfalls ahead for me in Australia, insisting it was a nation with only scant boxing tradition, and I would only find oblivion and anonymity there. These same voices claimed I'd be lucky to get a job as a street sweeper, caretaker or car washer much less become a world champion. Others said I'd end up being sent home by boat, my dignity crushed beyond recognition.

But I was having none of this. Nothing, and no horror story was going to stop me from leaving. I'd already signed a two-year management agreement with Brendon Smith, and fully intended to live up to my end of the bargain.

Finally, the news came through that the visas for me and Ruddock had been approved. But my wife and stepdaughter would have to wait three more months for theirs to be rubber stamped.

The thought of leaving them behind in crime-infested South Africa wasn't my idea of marital bliss, but there was no choice. I assured them it wouldn't be long before they joined me in the great southern land across the Indian Ocean, and on 5 February 1996 my brother and I boarded our Qantas flight to Brisbane.

I knew instinctively it would be the start of a chapter in my life which would make my mother proud. And that made me all the happier as our jet left Johannesburg in its vapour trail.

CHAPTER 16

ROLLING THE DICE IN THE LUCKY COUNTRY

My second coming to Australia was a far cry from the first. After touching down in Brisbane on a blazing hot February day, Ruddock and I were greeted by Brendon Smith, sporting a big cheesy grin and hugging us both like we were his long-lost brothers. He ushered us to a waiting car, chatting incessantly about his plans for us as we settled back for the ride, the air conditioning working overtime along with his larynx.

After being seduced by the high-rises, glitter and glamour of Sydney we naively believed that our next Down Under destination, the Toowoomba suburb of Charlton, would be a close approximation of the great harbour city, thirteen hours' drive to the south.

But as Brendon set course in a westerly direction, far away from the golden beaches of Queensland's coastline, there was little sign of any hustle and bustle, much less the towering concrete and glass spires we'd been expecting. Instead, we were greeted by great expanses of farmland and the gentle slopes of the Darling Downs ranges, as we meandered inland to the sleepy town of Toowoomba and our final destination, the almost comatose suburb of Charlton, with its wide empty streets and rows of red brick bungalows and well-tended front lawns.

We were only two hours from Brisbane but light years away from how we'd envisioned the journey ending. In the days that followed, waking up each morning to a farmyard chorus of mooing cows and crowing cockerels was not something I was accustomed to, and I found it unsettling.

That feeling of unease stretched back twelve years to when I was only thirteen and both Ruddock and I had found ourselves marooned in the African bush during a visit to our maternal grandparents, who lived in the village of Folovhodwe, about 60 kilometres from Musina. It was summer in the Transvaal and by 7 am the temperature was already touching 35 degrees Celsius on its way to the mid-40s.

Ruddock and I had joined some local boys in rising early to go hunting and honey harvesting. The harvesting was actually more a case of looting what rightfully belonged to the bees and was achieved by smoking them out from their colonies sequestered amid the thick foliage of wattle trees. We gorged ourselves on our booty but the combination of a post-honey stupor and the sweltering heat brought Ruddock and I to a near standstill.

As the other boys forged and foraged ahead, we decided to make a strategic retreat back to the relative comfort of the village in search of water and shade. It was a miscalculation which almost had deadly consequences. Instead of retracing our steps, we became confused and disorientated amid the endless honey bell and thorny acacia bushes interlaced by mopane trees.

We wandered about for hours, in circles for all we knew, becoming increasingly worried, weary and thirsty as our steps took us no closer to the village we'd left that morning. We spied impalas and wild boars across the Vendaland heat haze. But there was no visible sign of human life.

Eventually we came across a baobab tree with its distinctive thick trunk and verdant network of foliage on the branches near its apex. Our father had taught us that these trees stored rainwater in hollows between branches, so we scaled the trunk in search of succour.

What we found was a shallow pool of tepid, brown-tinged liquid we surmised to be water, most likely contaminated by baboon urine and faeces. In our desperation we gulped down the rank, unpalatable concoction. It eased our thirst, but not our fears, as the blinding light of day gave way to dusk.

We'd heard the cackles and cries of hyenas nearby and knew they were not on a goodwill mission. To try and circumvent the danger they posed, we decided to spend the night in the high branches of the baobab tree. After some scrambling we found a deep cavity near its crest where we could perch. We knew staying on terra firma was not a wise option with the hyenas picking up our scent, not to mention the possibility of a close encounter with a deadly black or green mamba, or a leopard or lion looking for a midnight morsel.

Ruddock was two years my junior but not easily spooked. But, far from home and alone in this wilderness, we were way out of our depth. Sleep wasn't an option as we held on to each other, tears welling in our eyes but silence in our throats. I wondered if we'd see our grandparents again, much less our parents and siblings, and thought how angry they'd be at our foolishness when our bodies were found. If they ever were.

The hyenas had congregated close by. We couldn't see them in the dark but the foul, fetid odour they gave off was something akin to rotting meat, and proof of their presence. Their yells and yelps had the tenor of human laughter, which made our terror all the more palpable.

In African mythology hyenas are associated with witches and witchcraft. Their entrails are often used in traditional medicines and magic and in our homeland they were feared as the grim reapers of the veldt. It was said that witches would even ride upon their backs and in my fevered, teenage imagination I convinced myself that witches had sent them to fetch us with a grisly fate awaiting us at the end of it all.

Many times in the past I'd witnessed my father implore protection and salvation from our ancestors in instances of distress, and I, too, sought to tap into the power wielded by the spirits of our forebears.

He'd chant incantations like 'Rrrrr, ndzi famba hi mati. Matimba ya ngwenya i mati. A wu ndzi tati,' ('I travel by water. The strength of a crocodile is water. You don't scare me', in Tsonga), and 'Ndi mutukana wa vho-Mulidi na vho-Bileni. Athi shavhi tshithu.' ('I am the son of Mulidi and Bileni, I fear nothing,' in Venda.)

Mulidi is the name of my paternal grandfather and Bileni was his wife. She was from the neighbouring Tsonga tribe, commonly known as the Shangaan tribe, while my granddad was of Venda stock. The two tribal groups used to mix, and the couple first met in a place formerly known as Gazankulu, a neighbouring Bantustan to Vendaland. My father carried both bloodlines and thus exhorted both sets of spirits, theoretically doubling his chances of divine aid.

That night, I followed suit, channelling my father's words and phrases like a mantra. As far back as I can remember I've used these incantations to provide a courage and conviction in moments of uncertainty and distress, like when I swam across the crocodile-infested waters of the Limpopo River to tend to the fishing nets.

As we held each other close in that tree in the dead of night, the second chant changed to 'Ndi mutukana wa vho-Jachacha na vho-Mina. Athi shavhi tshithu.' ('I am the son of Jachacha and Mina and I fear nothing.')

And for an extra layer of protection I added 'Ndi mudulu wa vho-Mulidi na vho-Bileni. Athi shavhi tshithu.' ('I am the grandson of Mulidi and Bileni and I fear nothing.')

In the years that followed I'd put the protective bubble around me, shadow-boxing before fights to calm my nerves and focus my energy. In our hour of need during that long night in the wilds of Vendaland, the words gave us solace. Ruddock joined in and by the crack of dawn the hyenas had melted away and we felt a sense of liberation as we clambered down the tree, collecting some tart baobab fruits on the way down for an improvised breakfast.

We were no nearer to finding a way out of our maze until, after several hours, we came across a herd of goats who we followed for several miles as they meandered through the thorny scrub.

Eventually they led us to two boys our own age who we asked to guide us to our grandparents. They'd never heard of them but agreed to take us to the nearest village. They grabbed the teats of some of the goats and squirted the milk into our mouths to ease our thirst. The elders in the village told us we were miles from our grandparents and arranged to have us escorted to them the next morning. The experience affected me for life, and it was the last time I ever visited my grandparents in their remote home.

For some reason, the spartan terrain surrounding Charlton brought those unpleasant recollections back. To make matters worse, the glossy images of sumptuous homes with swimming pools depicted in the magazine spreads featuring fellow South African fighter and Brendon Smith acolyte November Ntshingila were conspicuous by their absence.

Ntshingila, who was a part of Brandon's stable of fighters, didn't own a fancy dwelling nor the flashy car in which he'd posed for those shoots, his toothy smile and serene expression promising a land of abundant riches. Instead, he lived at the back of the Motor Inn Caravan Park, owned by Brendon's father Brad, and drove a beaten-up old Daihatsu, which more often than not needed a push start. We were given rooms in a crumbling concrete block adjacent to the caravan park, which we shared with the long-term tenants, swarms of cockroaches and mice. We had single beds whose musty and dusty mattresses were suspended on rusting springs.

To say I was underwhelmed was putting it lightly. Had we flown around the world to live in this stalag? What would my wife and daughter think? I would have been embarrassed inviting a stray dog in for the night, let alone my kin.

I took my grievances to Brendon, recounting how I'd been told we'd have modern accommodation with a pool and a sponsor already in place. But he brushed aside my concerns, insisting all the trappings of comfort and privilege would be mine once I begun fighting. His words had a familiar refrain.

There was another sting in the tail for Ruddock and me when Brendon informed us matter-of-factly one afternoon that we would have to pay back all the money he'd invested in importing us, commodity like, into Australia, through our winnings in the ring. In our naivety, neither Ruddock nor I had fully delved into the conditions of employment in the Smith empire, blinded as we were by the promises of a life we could only imagine, far away from the hardship and degradation of our homeland.

I later discovered it was Brendon's father Brad, a hard-drinking, crimson-faced, expletive-spewing former brawler, who had financed our air tickets and paid the immigration costs. If I'd got off on the wrong foot with his progeny, it was the same story with Brad, who would saunter into the gym from time to time, beery-breathed and spouting a rhetoric which reminded us of our apartheid past.

With a tinny in one hand and fingers pointing at us with the other, he'd bark out belligerently, 'I own these fucking boys, one day they are going to make me a lot of money.'

It might have been his attempt at humour, but I had issues with it. You can own a racing dog or a horse. But boxers shouldn't be in that category, and neither Ruddock nor I had flown across the world to enter into a form of enslavement. I told Brendon I didn't appreciate his father's remarks, and he assured me it was the alcohol talking and no offence was meant.

With his tight shorts, thongs and pudgy frame, Brad looked more a like a bar fly than a brawler. But those who knew him best attested to him never taking a backward step from anybody, and a few flippant remarks aimed at a couple of wide-eyed South African imports were the least of his transgressions. He was a seasoned street fighter in his younger days with a love for guns.

He feared nobody and once meted out street justice to a serial-bully cop who'd been terrorising locals. All it took were a few well-timed punches from his granite fists and the great burly frame of the pest policeman was knocked off its hinges. On another occasion, he waited on his roof with two guns and a carton of beer for another antagonist whom he'd earlier flattened and who had vowed retribution. The problem was he got so drunk waiting for his quarry to surface that he woke up in handcuffs after falling asleep and being spied with his pistols cocked by the man he'd been lying in wait for.

These were tales told by his lifelong friend Jimmy Coleman, a greyhound trainer we called the Dog Man, who also befriended me, and years later worked in my corner as part of his passion for boxing.

Jimmy had his own peculiar peccadilloes, which surfaced one night in Sydney at a boat party thrown by one of my sponsors. Blessed with a sense of humour darker than a solar eclipse, he offered me the use of a rusty World War I pistol he called Wally, which he happened to be packing that night, to exact revenge on an innocent waiter who'd accidentally spilled red wine on my flashy white jacket. Let's say it was Aussie humour at its quirkiest. The fact he owns a gold-plated toilet seat was another statement of his unorthodox approach to life. He had a fascination with boxing and I developed a close bond with Jimmy and his wife Christine, who found his antics as bewildering and bewitching as I did.

Despite my misgivings over Brad, I discovered over time that he was more humorous than odious, and he and his jokes grew on me. His routine cussing and cursing had grated at first, until I discovered it was a trait shared by many in my new home in the backblocks of Toowoomba. My fellow pugilists in the gym, gifted fighters like Gilbert Hooper, the Shaw brothers, Mick and Matt, my compatriot November Ntshingila, Brendan Wood, Mick Thompson and Garry Weston were among them.

The swearing soon found its way into Ruddock's and my everyday discourse, as we embraced the local custom.

There was another custom embraced by the boxers at Brendon's gym that I found more troubling: the use of marijuana and methamphetamines. On weekends the routine of some of Brendon's boys was to get high and party with their girlfriends while watching porn. While neither Ruddock nor I were exactly prudes, we couldn't see how these excesses corresponded with the discipline, self-denial and sacrifice we associated with boxing.

I wanted to say something but didn't want to be accused of treachery and disloyalty to my fellow fighters. After much soul searching, I did discuss the Sodom and Gomorrah weekend scenes with the assistant trainer Glen Azar, whom I had built a friendship with, but it was agreed it would go no further than between us. It was further proof to me that I needed to find an exit strategy from Brendon and Brad's fighting factory.

I opened a dialogue with other promoters and trainers, including the great Johnny Lewis, who at the time was honing the talents of a number of accomplished fighters including Kostya Tszyu and Justin Rowsell. Johnny introduced me to Vlad Warton, who was managing Tszyu and had a promotions company. He knew who I was, after witnessing me fight Cliff Samardin on the undercard of Tszyu and Roger Mayweather on my maiden trip to Australia. He offered to promote me if I could negotiate a release from my contract with Brendon. I didn't waste time in asking him what the terms of my release might be.

Perhaps he'd seen it coming but he barely batted an eyelid, nodding wistfully before replying, 'Look Lovemore I've invested a lot of time, energy and money in you, of course I won't be willing to just let you walk away for nothing. You're gonna need to repay every cent it cost me to bring you out to Australia, plus living expenses, then I'll release you from the contract.'

I asked him to come up with a figure and had no qualms with paying him back the money he and Brad had ploughed into Ruddock and me. It ended up being around $6000, and I prepared a deed of release.

We both felt like free men again as the magnetic lure of Sydney brought us back into its welcoming orbit.

CHAPTER 17

THE GOOD, THE VLAD AND THE UGLY

The twisting terrain of Ruddock's presence in my life as a confidant, sparring partner, sometime trainer and voice of reason and responsibility took a new turn with his announcement that, for him, the Australian dream was over. Disillusioned with our fruitless and frustrating few months under Brendon Smith's boxing banner, and other personal issues, he told me his heart wasn't in it anymore and he was going home. He'd got himself enrolled in college in Johannesburg in an IT course, which would be a stepping stone to a university degree. Graduating from boxing's academy of disappointments and chicanery was no longer for him.

With no time for rumination I was headed for the Newtown Police Boys Club, the famed fighting faculty in Sydney's inner west where the learned trainer Johnny Lewis was the governor. No sooner had I arrived than I was thrust straight into a sparring session with Kostya Tszyu, who was preparing to defend his IBF light welterweight world title belt against America's Corey Johnson.

Another on Tszyu's roster of sparring partners was Mexican-born, California-raised Hector Lopez. Dynamic inside the ropes, he was laidback in between sessions and could often be found puffing on a joint in his downtime. But when the gloves were on he was all business: focused, fast with his fists and an elusive target. He was gone in a puff of smoke, you might say. Tragically, he died aged only forty-four after suffering a heart attack from an apparent drug overdose in 2011.

I took an immediate liking to Johnny Lewis. He was quietly spoken and exuded a serene calmness amid the hectoring and hollering of the gym. He was taller than I'd imagined, and his spaghetti-thin legs were on show in a pair of shorts as he issued instructions in his measured, authoritative way to the boxers in his thrall.

Also there that day was singlet-wearing rugby league fanatic and Wests Tigers' number-one fan Laurie Nichols. The silver-haired extrovert would patrol the touchline at every home game at Leichhardt Oval, firing up his fellow fans and the team with his shadow-boxing routine.

It was my second encounter with him, after a first brush during my initial trip to Australia when I fought Cliff Samardin in Newcastle. He'd stood out in the crowd during the weigh-in because he was the only one wearing a singlet on a cold winter's day. Strutting about, as if walking on hot coals, he would punctuate his movements with the shadow-boxing routine with which he became synonymous. I remember Harold Volbrecht, Naas Scheepers and I looking at him aghast, and agreeing he'd need to keep the phantom upper cuts and jabs coming all day to ward off the chill.

After my controversial loss the following night, Laurie strode into my dressing room and proclaimed loudly, 'Killmore, they robbed you. You won that fight.'

His quirky intrusion caused an outbreak of laughter, lifting the morose mood in the room.

On his second coming into my life, he was still wearing his trademark Tigers' singlet and still calling me 'Killmore'.

'Welcome back Killmore, Johnny will get you ready and you will kill Samardin this time,' he boomed out in his rasping voice as he gave me a suffocating bear hug. His words reminded me of another reason I'd come back to Australia.

I'd discussed a Samardin rematch with Vlad Warton and badly wanted that redemption shot to be my first fight back on Australian soil. Vlad Warton was also at the gym that day keeping an eye on his prize asset, Kostya Tszyu. But he still found time to pull me aside and regale me with his well-worn and polished promoter speak.

'I've got big fights being discussed for you,' he said. 'I'm going to take your career to the next level. You've had the wrong people around you before. But don't worry, you're going to make up for lost time now.

Don't be surprised if you're fighting for a world title in a year.'

He'd given me the same spiel in our previous phone conversations but wanted to hammer home the mantra.

As sizeable in stature as he was in self-regard, the wide expanse of Vlad's bald pate was lathered in sweat as he trotted out his sales jargon in a monotone stream of consciousness. His words seemed as hollow as the beads of perspiration specking his head. A one-time used-car salesman, Vlad was a master of manipulation and mind games. But while scepticism had become my default reaction to promoters by now, his association with Tszyu did lend him a measure of credibility amid the snake oil.

After being subjected to the full force of Vlad's hurricane-strength personality, he signed off by saying he'd arranged for me to base myself at the grandly named Agincourt Hotel near the centre of Sydney. It was located on George Street, opposite the Mercure Hotel, where I'd stayed on my first trip to town. It was more a run-down, moth-eaten pub than a hotel, with most of its dusty, dingy rooms occupied by drunks, drug users and those simply down on their luck. It has since been renovated and looks a lot better now. Back then music blared out at the weekends and its motley-looking clientele seemed to idle away their days pouring schooners down their throats and money into the pokies. But needs must and, as it turned out, it was Laurie, not Vlad, who had taken care of my accommodation, with the latter seeking to take the credit for putting a roof over my head.

Laurie would come by each Monday and we'd have breakfast together. He became a trusted and valued friend until he sadly passed away aged seventy-nine in 2000, a departure from the stage which was greeted by many Tigers' fans like a death in the family. To me it was the loss of a man whose eccentricities made him all the more lovable. He was a legend who touched many hearts and souls, and there's a passageway outside Leichhardt Oval renamed 'Laurie's Lane' in his honour.

Unfortunately, Laurie and I never got that opportunity to 'kill' Samardin. All attempts to secure a rematch were unsuccessful. In fact, it turned out that after our fight he had just one more before, as Australians put it, he went 'walkabout'. The term, for those unfamiliar with Strine, refers to a mysterious journey taken by an Indigenous Australian into the outback to live in the time-honoured traditional way. He simply vanished off the boxing map, and today Samardin remains one of the sport's enigmatic figures. It's one of those 'what if?' stories. He had so much talent and I believe the potential to have won a world title. I have no knowledge or wisdom as to why he chose to quit the ring. But I do know that one reason many boxers bail out is the deceit, dishonesty and double dealing they encounter from those they take into their trust along the way; and some they don't. It could be a contractual dispute, or threats from mafia-type figures and assorted hardcore crooks. There are many unseen reasons why boxers beat a premature retreat. In Samardin's case it left us all wondering what might have been.

I had my first return fight in Australia on the undercard of the Vlad Warton promotion featuring Tszyu versus Johnson at the Sydney Entertainment Centre on 24 May 1996. My opponent was Filipino Antonio Tunacao whom I stopped in three rounds. But in truth it wasn't my best performance. I was ring rusty, having not seen action in almost ten months. I knew I'd have to up my game significantly if I was to win fans in Australia and carve out a credible future in a country I saw as my new long-term home.

There was also the matter of at the time being on a temporary distinguished talent visa, which meant I needed to prove that I had something special about me if I was to convince the Department of Immigration to grant me permanent residency.

Earnings from that first fight allowed me to fly over my wife and step-daughter for a long-awaited reunion. But the Agincourt, where bloody discarded syringes were often spotted in the communal toilets and showers, was hardly the ideal venue for my daughter. I couldn't afford anywhere more salubrious and Vlad, who was duty-bound by the immigration services to cover my living expenses and accommodation, wasn't interested in upgrading me to less down-at-heel digs. I couldn't complain because if I did, and he took umbrage, he could pull out as my sponsor and my visa would have been immediately cancelled.

The notion of returning to Africa didn't bother me in theory. It was more about going home as a failure that prevented me from entertaining the notion. But the angels – in the form of Johnny Lewis and his Fijian born wife Sita – were smiling on me, and they offered to take in our daughter while my wife and I looked for a more suitable long-term home. It was a gesture which still touches me. To this day I look at Johnny as a father or a brother and Sita as a mother or sister. While some pay lip service to being anti-racist and non-discriminatory, Johnny has always lived and breathed those beliefs through his actions. They even refused offers of money to cover the costs when I finally started to earn a little.

A few weeks after my wife's arrival, Johnny was able to get me a job with the poker machine company, Olympic Video Gaming. Fellow fighter Justin Rowsell, who was a stablemate and sparring partner, was also involved with the company. Due to the terms of my visa I was limited in any work I might be able to do, so the company agreed to become a sponsor, but instead of paying my fees directly, the money went to Vlad who would then pass it on to me.

At least that was the plan. The trouble was that Vlad often elected not to keep up his side of the bargain, forgetting to pay or simply withholding the money I needed to cover my living expenses.

Johnny arranged for me to lease a room at the house of fellow trainer Frank Keane, which was a step up from the Agincourt. But financial woes were a constant and unwelcome companion, and I was always behind with my rent.

I had to wait four months before I fought again on another Tszyu undercard. While he took on the explosive South African knockout specialist Jan Bergman in another title defence, I was up against another Filipino, Teofilo Tunacao. I am not sure if he was related to the previous Tunacao I fought. This time it was a unanimous points decision and I was happy with the win.

While it was good exposure to feature on a Tszyu promotion, financially it was far from a ticket to riches. A world champion can afford to fight every six months and reap a big pay day, but as an up-and-comer I needed to be active.

My mistrust of Warton was fermenting fast. His constant promises of fights on the horizon, or an imminent rise up the rankings with the governing bodies, were lies. And the breaking point came after I found myself unable to pay a doctor's bill after our daughter had fallen ill. The hot temper of my youth had given way to a calmer demeanour as I'd matured. But the humiliation of not being able to come up with the $50 I needed to pay the doctor, as a non-Medicare card holder, was the last straw. To compound matters I was also being faced with eviction from my new apartment for non-payment of rent and my fledgling marriage was beginning to suffer.

Vlad had my sponsorship money but wasn't returning any of my calls. Patience and I had parted company and I was willing to jeopardise my visa and my boxing future by righting this wrong. I was sick of Vlad and his deceptions.

I'd found out he lived in the St George area in Sydney's south and I headed out there with only one thing on my mind: to retrieve what was mine. Fortunately, my wife had taken note of my vengeful mood and had followed me out there. Had she not, I suspect something bad might have happened

After finding his house I knocked on the door. But those knocks had to turn into kicks before it opened. It was midday, and a sheepish and startled looking Vlad was clad in a white robe, the sort you get in the half-decent hotels. I thought, for a moment, he must have knocked it off, but I had more important things to worry about.

'Lovemore, what brings you here? Great to see you … I was going to come to the gym later and discuss some plans,' he drawled. 'Sorry to leave you waiting. I was taking a rest and didn't hear you knocking. I've been under the weather and the medication has got me so drowsy …'

And so he went on. Let's just say the rest is history. Vlad waved his wand and my rental arrears disappeared and I got paid the money he owed me.

Vlad went on to be front and centre of one of Australia's biggest boxing scandals in 2013 when he borrowed $500,000 from Jeff Fenech to try and rescue the match-up he was promoting between 'Sugar' Shane Mosley and Anthony Mundine at Sydney's Crown Casino. The fight was called off when Mosley flew back to the US on its eve and Fenech never got his cash back either, with Warton ultimately setting up shop in America.

His life ended prematurely in 2018 when he was found dead in a lift in his hotel in China after a night out in a karaoke bar during a business trip. Vlad wasn't all bad and could be a charmer when he wanted. If they ever made a movie of his life you'd have to entitle it, The Good, the Vlad and the Ugly.

I told Johnny of my troubles with Vlad, but while he sympathised, there was nothing he could do. But one afternoon after training he pulled me aside and suggested that I link up with rival promoter Bill Mordey, who he said would be highly likely to take me under his wing. He couldn't speak to him on my behalf because of a bitter feud between Mordey and Tszyu, whom the former was in the process of suing for breach of contract. Mordey had issues with anybody in any way aligned to Tszyu.

Johnny, guilty by association, passed me Mordey's number, and I decided to give the man dubbed 'Break Even Bill' a call. I'd first become aware of him when reading a book on Jeff Fenech, whom he promoted to three world titles. He'd also masterminded the career of Aussie brawler Jeff Harding and was responsible for bringing Russian-born and raised Tszyu to Australia as an immigrant. But their relationship had curdled into bitterness and rancour, and Mordey was seeking compensation from Tszyu after he'd unilaterally signed a three-year contract with the pay-TV Sky channel.

Mordey was victorious in that legal bout and Tszyu and Sky were forced to cough up $7 million. Mordey's antagonism towards Tszyu ran so deep that he couldn't bring himself to even utter his name, referring to him instead as 'the Russian'. After a few schooners it quickly changed to 'the fucking Russian'.

I made contact with Mordey and he was receptive to say the least, telling me, 'Mate, I've seen you fight. You've got talent. You just need someone to give you water and proper advice in your corner. No fighter in your division in the country can beat you.'

He was right about that because, other than the disputed loss to Samardin in my first foray Down Under, no Australian-born fighter ever beat me.

The thought of severing ties with Johnny didn't sit well with me. I loved the man for his grace, humility and the knowledge he imparted in his gentle way. We had a strong trainer-fighter relationship and understood and respected each other.

I asked Mordey to give me three days to think about my future. I had no idea how to broach the subject with Johnny and tell him of the caveat in Mordey's offer to me. I went to the gym the next day, and at the end of the session Johnny asked me if I'd made that call to Mordey. I lied, telling him, 'No Johnny, but I will soon.'

'You need to do it mate,' he replied. 'He's a good man. He can be a prick sometimes but he's a good promoter.'

I made a swift exit from the gym to avoid any further questioning, musing as I went that after my first conversation with 'Break Even Bill' I concurred that he could certainly be one hell of a prick. And I hadn't even met him in the flesh yet.

I went home stressed and worked up, and I couldn't even engage in my normal playful chit-chat with my chatterbox daughter. My wife could see something was amiss, and in bed that night, whilst trying to massage away my worries, she quizzed me over what was bugging me.

When I told her she said Johnny would never have given me Bill Mordey's number in the first place if he hadn't had my best long-term interests at heart. 'Go and talk to Johnny and everything will be fine,' she added. 'He will understand.'

The next day after training I plucked up to the courage to tell Johnny and without hesitation he told me I had his blessings, adding that if I didn't take the offer he would personally 'knock me out'.

'If ever you need anything, I'll always be here for you son, I love you,' he added to reiterate the message that I was free to go.

The next day I called Mordey and gave him the news. He summoned me to his office in Surry Hills, saying the contract would be waiting for me. I expected to meet a bull of a man, on the basis of his hoarse, raspy voice, but when the door of his office swung open I was assailed by a wafer-thin figure who looked like Mr Burns, the odious owner of the Springfield nuclear power plant from *The Simpsons* TV show. His son Craig, a younger facsimile, was there, along with the sports commentator and matchmaker Ray Connolly.

The way Mordey spoke to me differed from Vlad's 'promise the world' approach, and was a lot more circumspect. He pledged only to keep me busy, match me judiciously and pay me accordingly.

'The rest is up to you kid,' he said. 'If you are ready to move up the rankings and fight for the world title I will make it happen. I'll work on your residency and make sure you can stay here permanently. But you have to keep winning.'

I was impressed with his frankness and signed the contract there and then.

year-old Lovemore in 1985 training at the Musina per Mine gym.

Representing the copper mine team against the local army team in an amateur bout in Musina in 1985, age 14.

ining at the Musina Copper Mine gym in 1985, 14.

In school uniform in Musina in 1986, aged 15.

From left, Roger Mayweather's trainer, Lovemore Ndou, Roger Mayweather and Ross Thompson in 1995 at t Newcastle Entertainment Centre during a press conference.

During training with Cassius Baloyi (left) in Malamulele, Giyani in 1986.

At Tshakhuma, Venda sitting on a tree Lovemore chopped down as part of his strength training, 1986.

Lovemore's wife Florence in 1995 in South Africa.

Lovemore's mother and siblings. From left, Lovemore's mother Minah Emmah Ndou holding his sister Gertrude, Patience, Moffat and Ruddock.

Second from left, Justin Rowsell, the late Hector Lopez, the late Vlad Warton, Lovemore, Kostya Tszyu and an unknown person (right) on Sydney Harbour in 1996.

Above: Lovemore (right) training with his brother Ruddock in 1996.

Left: At Brendon Smith's gym in Charlton, Toowoomba in 1996, imitating former world champion, Chris Eubank.

Below: Lovemore showing off his muscles at Brendon Smith's gym in Charlton, Toowoomba in February 1996.

year-old Lovemore in Musina in 1987 with one of many deadly weapons he owned at the time.

Ruddock (front left) with a boxing team from Musina in 1989.

ovemore (left) and his brother Ruddock in 1994 at e Valley of Waves in Sun City, South Africa following raining session.

Training at the Hammer gym in New Modder, Benoni, 1994.

With trainer Harold Volbrecht in 1994 at the Valley of Waves in Sun City, South Africa.

Training at the Hammer gym in New Modder, Benoni, 1994.

Sparring against Brian Mitchell at Sun City, South Africa in 1994.

In action during the Transvaal Championships.

Norman Hlabane's gym in 1995.

...emore (left) with the late Jacob 'Baby Jake' Matlala at the King Korn boxing awards in South Africa in 1995.

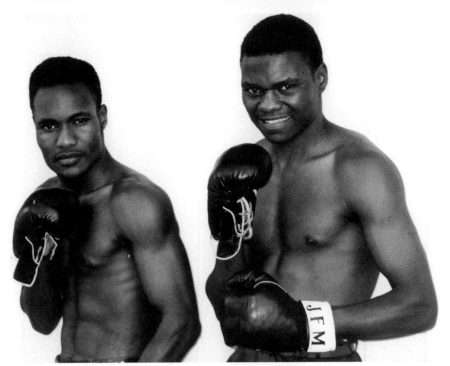

Lovemore (left) and Ruddock (right) photographed by the late Pete Moscardi in Johannesburg, South Africa in 1995.

Kostya Tszyu and Lovemore at the Newtown Police Boys Club in 1996 following a sparring session.

From left, Ruddock Ndou and Lovemore Ndou in 19 at Brendon Smith's gym in Charlton, Toowoomba.

CHAPTER 18

FIGHTING TALK AND FIREWORKS
FROM TEAM FENECH

'I'll get you, you black cunt, I'll fucking kill you.'

Bill Mordey delivered on his pledges and kept me busy, beginning with my first fight under his banner against local scrapper Simon Maidment, which was aired live on Fox Sports TV. I ended Maidment's night in the eighth round in a bout scheduled for ten, as he withered under the relentless onslaught of my punches. I was pleased with my performance, as was Mordey and the Fox Sports production team, who adopted me as a regular on their boxing broadcasts.

Mordey had almost monthly shows on the channel, and when I wasn't fighting I was co-commentating, as I explored an evolving gig as a fight analyst. It was nice to watch other people getting hit for a change as I observed and pontificated from the safety of my ringside seat.

For the first time in my life I was beginning to feel the financial noose loosening from around my neck as I was able to secure a number of sponsors, that drip fed me the cash I needed to keep myself and my family comfortable, and allowed me the luxury of focusing fully on the build-up to each fight without having the bills mounting on the doorstep.

Another boxer in Mordey's stable back then was the Wollongong wild child Shannan Taylor, who would join me as the other headline act on fight nights on alternate months. Shannan was a solid performer inside the ropes but his fondness for illicit substances outside the ring was a drain on his mental and physical wellbeing.

That first year under Mordey's wing I fought four international opponents and won all four of them by knockout. The first was against Ian Fajardo who I stopped in four rounds.

A week before my next duel against Lauro Wilton tragedy struck the Ndou family when 'The Great Elephant', my father Freddy, finally succumbed to the excesses which had pervaded his life since the passing of my beloved mother years earlier. He had never come to terms with her death and guzzled ever-increasing doses of home-brewed wines and spirits to anaesthetise the grief. We all knew where it was heading and I suspect he was beyond caring. Years of poisoning his body with cheap and toxic concoctions had finally caught up with him and he perished from kidney and liver failure.

I couldn't fly home to attend the funeral for two reasons. Firstly, it was a week before the fight and I'd convinced myself that he'd have wanted me to continue with my career and make him proud that way. Secondly, I was only a few months away from obtaining my permanent residency in Australia and it was a statutory requirement that I remained in the country for a minimum of two years. Failure to do so would have jeopardised my chances of being allowed to ever return. All I could do was send enough money home to ensure he was given a proper and decent burial in a plot at Musina cemetery next to the wife he had mourned for five soul-eroding years. I wanted them to be together again, so he could rest in peace

The following year, 1998, was a breakout year for me. In March I stopped Johar Abu Lashin, who had an impressive record of twenty-one wins, four losses and one draw. He'd had enough of the sustained beating I was handing out after eight rounds of a fight scheduled for ten. It was meant to have been the toughest test of my career to date. He was bigger than me, a full-blown welterweight matching up against a lightweight. But I wasn't looking at anything other than the man in front of me and caught him with left jabs and piercing body punches in every round, and in the eighth floored him with a left body rip. Winded and wounded, he failed to beat the count.

The victory propelled me up the WBC rankings and Mordey, who to this point had delivered everything he'd promised, told me I was ready to fight for a world title and he was going to make it happen.

Three weeks later another Ndou entered the world when my first biological child was born. We named her Maxine Emmah Ndou. Emmah was one of my mother's names and I felt it befitting to pass that on to my child.

This was a period of rejoicing for the Ndou clan and my brother Ruddock, back in South Africa, had followed his dream of going to university, where I happily covered his fees and living expenses. He went on to graduate with a Bachelor's degree in Computer Science, a Graduate Diploma in Public Management and Master's degree in Public Management.

I followed up the win over Lashin with two more victories over accomplished fighters, Isander Lacen and David Armstrong. Then came my rematch with my compatriot Jeremiah Malinga, the first man to have beaten me as a professional. It was a different story this time. I didn't have to drain myself to make the weight, and weaken my system, as had been the case in South Africa four years earlier. As a result, I was fresh and full of dark intent, stopping Malinga in four rounds with an array of body punches which left him doubled up.

Avenging the loss felt, to me, like winning a world title. And that's what I thought I'd soon be fighting for with Mordey telling me beforehand that if I won convincingly my next fight would be for the WBC or IBF belts.

At the time I was ranked number eight lightweight contender for the WBC title held by Mexico's Cesar Bazan. The great Shane Mosley held the IBF title. He'd won the crown by beating my former stablemate in South Africa Philip Holiday, and was also very much on my radar. But Bazan would have been a more suitable choice at the time because Mosley was in his pomp, and going to the US to take the belt from him would have also pitted me against judges and a referee likely to be sympathetic to the champion on home soil. Next to Roy Jones Jr, back then, Mosley was one of boxing's most marketable and talked about talents.

History has shown that it normally takes a knockout to win a decision over a celebrated champion, especially in their own backyard. Having witnessed Sugar Ray Leonard's hugely controversial points win over Marvin Hagler back in 1987, as he returned from a three-year boxing absence to beat the middleweight champion, I knew all about how the fates too often favour the beauties over the beasts in boxing. Another glaring example came in 2002 when Floyd Mayweather, whom I know all about after hours spent as his sparring partner years later, got incredibly lucky with a unanimous points verdict in Las Vegas to take the WBC lightweight title from Mexico's Joe Luis Castillo, who according to everyone but the judges clearly won the fight. Had justice been done it would have been the only blemish on Mayweather's unbeaten career. A loss for Hagler and Castillo, but a win for the money men, namely the promoters.

Facing Bazan would also have suited me stylistically. He was a one-dimensional fighter and I think my fast hands, accuracy and timing would have tied him up in knots. Mordey's promise hung in the air like an alluring perfume, teasing my senses.

While my career was blossoming under Mordey's banner another lightweight in the country, Justin Rowsell, was also climbing up the IBF rankings. The previous year Mordey had promoted Rowsell for two fights, on the proviso that he didn't have Johnny Lewis in his corner on fight night, in light of his ongoing feud with Rowsell's former promoter Vlad Warton and his star fighter Kostya Tszyu.

Like me, Rowsell had tired of Warton's deceit and deceptions and needed a new promoter to guide him. But after just two bouts with Mordey calling the promotional shots, Rowsell had a change of heart and returned to long-time trainer and mentor Johnny Lewis. It was a show of loyalty and trust atypical in the cutthroat and opportunistic boxing landscape. Hence my undying respect for Rowsell, whose star would have shone even more brightly during his nine years as a pro fighter had his punches carried greater ferocity. In terms of craft and guile he was right up there with the best lightweights of his era.

His conduct bucked a boxing trend in which fighters blithely turn their backs on those who've got them to where they are for more lucrative opportunities. They're like politicians, switching camps and knifing colleagues in pursuit of a bigger and better payday.

In my new life as a lawyer, the more things change the more they stay the same. Clients praise their legal representatives as miracle workers one day, only to drop them summarily to take up with the next solicitor or barrister who comes along offering a couple of dollars discount on their fees.

Rowsell's career hit a fallow patch after quitting the Mordey camp and he was out of action for almost eight months before linking with Jeff Fenech, whose decorated career in the ring had given way to a new incarnation as a trainer-cum-manager and promoter. Fenech's decision to finally hang up his gloves had been hastened by his devastating second-round loss to my compatriot Philip Holiday in Melbourne.

Fighters were throwing themselves into the gravitational field of Team Fenech, hoping that some of the stardust of his incredible feats in the ring would somehow rub off on them. Not to mention his contacts across the globe, and the promise of being matched in world title bouts and securing lucrative sponsorships. Almost overnight, Fenech became a threat to just about every promoter and manager in the country, including Bill Mordey.

The tension between the pair was palpable, with Fenech a very real threat to Mordey's lucrative TV deal with Fox Sports. Rumour had it that Fenech approached Fox Sports offering to telecast his boxing shows for a quarter of whatever Fox Sports was paying Mordey at the time. This fuelled the feud between the former fighter and the promoter.

It didn't take long for both Rowsell and I to get caught up in the unfolding drama. At the time, we were the leading lightweights in Australia. Rowsell was ranked number three by the IBF, while I was sitting at number eight with the WBC. We were seemingly heading in different directions with Rowsell chasing Mosley's crown while I had my sights set on dethroning Bazan.

It would have been boxing business nirvana for Rowsell and I to win those respective titles and perhaps meet in a title-unifying fight in Australia. It would have been the sort of fight which would have set both of us, and our families, up for life. But, unfortunately, the rampant egos of Fenech and Mordey put paid to such fanciful musings.

Fenech was keen for me to join the flow of fighters to his camp. But I had a binding deal with Mordey and didn't want to be placed in the same situation as Tszyu and have to pay Mordey millions for breaching our agreement. I liked the idea of working under Fenech's umbrella, and liked what he was trying to do, but there was no way out for me.

I'd often head to Fenech's gym in Alexandria to spar with some of his fighters, including Rowsell. At the time I was trained by Shannan Taylor's mentor Bill Corbett, who was mainly based in Wollongong, and it was a trek to get there; hence my decision to use Fenech's gym as an occasional base. It didn't escape me that each time I sparred with one of Fenech's troupe he'd goad them into turning the session into a mini-war, telling them I was open to a right-hand and could easily be picked off that way

'Sit on your back foot and throw the right-hand and you'll catch him,' he'd screech at them.

I was slick and quick on my feet, and much as they tried, their right-hands were making contact with clear air, as I glided away from trouble, much to Fenech's annoyance.

Out of frustration, Fenech decided one day to hop into the ring and show his boys how it should be done. It had been two years since his retirement in 1996, and he was sluggish, slow and out of shape. His mind might have been willing but his body wasn't.

For four rounds he hunted me around the ring, looking to unload that fabled right-hand but it wasn't landing. Finally, breathless and frustrated, he jumped out of the ring.

That evening I received a call from Mordey, who screamed down the phone, 'Mate, what are you doing sparring with Fenech?

'He's probably a light heavyweight right now with all the pounds he's packed on. I'm working on a world title shot for you and don't want you suffering any unnecessary injuries. That little mongrel will do anything to derail your career. All he cares about is hogging all the limelight. He was pissed off when Jeff Harding won a world title and can't stand it when he's not the centre of attention.'

Harding was an Australian warrior at light heavyweight level, whose life spiralled into an alcohol-induced haze of self-destruction after his retirement.

Mordey explained that Fenech had pulled the same sparring session stunt with 'the Russian', but it had backfired with Tszyu almost breaking his ribs as the punches flew. I was never able to ascertain if this rumour had substance. But it wouldn't have surprised me if it were true.

Mordey added that Fenech had also called him, boasting that he'd 'punched the shit' out of me during our four-round interchange and that he believed his charge, Rowsell, would 'eat me up for breakfast' if we were ever to fight. Bemused, I told Mordey that it wasn't quite how things had gone down, chuckling down the phone at the impudence of Fenech's fanciful assertions.

Before hanging up I told Mordey that I was prepared to fight Rowsell if the conditions and compensation suited us and that I would wipe the floor with him. I added the caveat that it wasn't an ideal scenario because Rowsell and I were former teammates and workmates who had built a friendship forged on mutual respect. But it was more than that, I saw him as almost a brother.

In the days and weeks that followed I started receiving phone calls from Fenech telling me pointedly, without so much as a hello, that I was 'no good' as a fighter and was in over my head.

It was the beginning of a very uncivil war between the pair of us, with Fenech going on the offensive. I wasn't sure if it was his way of trying to goad me into fighting Rowsell, even though word was already out there that Rowsell's title challenge against Mosley would be confirmed for early the next year.

Meanwhile, Mordey was close to locking in a WBC title tilt for me against Bazan. Or so he claimed. At the same time, Mordey was also in favour of a duel between me and Rowsell, even though the career of the loser would have been seriously derailed. He told me he'd spoken with Justin and he'd said he was up for it and had boasted he would 'beat me up'.

'Think of it this way Lovemore,' he spruiked, 'if you beat Rowsell you've beaten the best lightweight in the country. Then you're guaranteed permanent residence and are in a position to take on Mosley or Bazan, depending on who offers the most money.'

I told Mordey that I would only fight Rowsell if I heard it from his own lips that he wanted the bout.

Meanwhile, the calls kept coming from Fenech and they were becoming abusive and threatening. He would ring my number and hand the phone to Con Spyropoulos, a kid with Down syndrome, or some of his fighters, and they would taunt me and hang up. Years later some of the fighters came forward and personally apologised to me.

At first I thought it was all just an infantile ploy hatched by Fenech's febrile mind. But it eventually got out of hand. One night I got home from training with my wife and daughters in tow and the red light on the answering machine was flashing. My daughter pressed the play button, and the stream of invective that boomed out in Fenech's unmistakable high-pitched drawl was enough to peel the paint from the walls.

'I'll get you, you black cunt, I'll fucking kill you,' he taunted.

It wasn't the sort of homecoming I'd been expecting and things were about to get even uglier.

CHAPTER 19

WHEN FRIENDS BECOME FOES: THE UNCIVIL WAR

'Racism is a disease that can make you think less of yourself. It diminishes you right to the core and shatters your self-esteem. Being told you're a worthless Kaffir ultimately undermines you, no matter how resilient you might be.'

Taunting and trolling your rivals is part of boxing's lexicon. Insults, insinuations, character assassination, slurs and slights, they're all intrinsic to the theatre of the sport, especially when you're trying to sell tickets and pay-per-views. Call me a 'bitch', a coward or an excuse for a fighter. Almost anything goes when you're trying to promote a bout. But I draw the line at racial abuse, and that's what was spewing from Jeff Fenech's mouth.

Where I came from people were killed for racial putdowns, and escaping race hate was one of the main motivators behind my exit from South Africa. I wanted to make sure my children were never exposed to such ignorance and stereotyping. Racism is a disease that can make you think less of yourself. It diminishes you right to the core and shatters your self-esteem. Being told you're a worthless Kaffir ultimately undermines you, no matter how resilient you might be. I didn't actually realise I was a man of worth and value until I came to Australia. All my life I'd been treated more like a savage.

It was just when that esteem began germinating inside me that the fragile shoots were scythed off by none other than a guy whom I respected immensely as a fighter, and as a person. I'd read a book on his life story and had been inspired by how he'd used boxing to fight his way out of poverty and a life of crime.

He'd always shown me respect each time I'd visited his gym, until that sparring session when he'd sought to show the fighters in his stable how vulnerable he thought I was to a right-hand by stepping inside the ropes to take me on. For me, it was a routine few minutes which never got out of hand. Even afterwards, Fenech was firing off advice as he departed the scene. Just as he did on every other occasion I visited his gym. His largesse towards me had even extended to Fenech taking me to a sports equipment store, probably owned by one of his sponsors, where he loaded me up with free handouts of Asics boxing gear.

Then, weeks later, he's talking about killing me. Something must have triggered his rage towards me, but I was scratching my head looking for answers. His behaviour made me question his state of mind. Maybe he was bipolar? I'd been told people with such traits are unpredictable and can swing like a pendulum. Was this the case? Or was this all about coercing me into a showdown with Rowsell? Perhaps he was just being smart and simply pressing all the right buttons to make the fight happen. If that's what he wanted then the fight would happen. And not only that, through his egregious comments he had just secured a serious beating for Rowsell, the friend who was about to become a foe.

My eight-year-old daughter broke down in floods of tears after listening to Fenech's voice message, wailing, 'Why does that man want to kill you Daddy?'

I reassured her that nobody was going to kill me, and that he'd just been pranking me. But she wasn't swallowing it.

'It doesn't sound like he's joking. He sounds very angry,' she responded.

While I reassured her he was just play-acting, the reality was I was worried, angry and concerned for the safety of my family. But needed to stay calm and measured. My wife, who had overheard some of Fenech's jibes over the previous few weeks, wasn't buying any of it. 'You call the police now, or I will,' she said.

I told her I'd talk to a lawyer the next day and take it from there. But she wasn't backing down and picked up the phone and began dialling 000. I wasn't surprised by her reaction because where we came from you never make idle threats about killing someone, unless you intend to carry it out.

The police showed up, and after listening to the message, didn't hear anything but malice cracking down the line. 'That's a threat to kill you … we can go and arrest him now if you press charges,' said one of the officers.

I told him I didn't want to press charges and just wanted him to stop. 'He's messing with my family, and upsetting my wife and daughter,' I intoned.

They told me I could alternatively take out an apprehended violence order against him, which would force him to cut out the threats, or face being arrested and charged for breaching the order. So that's what I settled for.

The next day at the offices of Olympic Video Gaming, where both Rowsell and I had our part-time day jobs, I confronted him.

'Is It true you want to fight me. That's what I'm being told.'

He appeared surprised and denied any willingness to take me on, with both of us agreeing the timing was not ideal and we had other targets in mind, Shane Mosley in Justin's case and Cesar Bazan in mine.

I was stunned later that night, while watching the news, when an item featuring Justin and Jeff Fenech popped up. There they were, standing together, with Justin calling me out. Minutes later Bill Mordey was on the line, growling, 'Mate, did you just watch the news? Justin just told the whole nation he wants to fight you.'

My disappointment in Justin prompted a snap decision. 'Just make the fight happen,' I replied.

The media had picked up on the AVO taken out against Fenech and put it to him. He manned up and admitted leaving the threatening voice mail, but tried to pass it off as a joke, going as far as to make a public apology. But at the same time, he challenged me to a fight, with the stipulation that Rowsell would take care of business first by knocking me out. He added that I was a nobody who didn't belong at this level. An imposter who was about to be unmasked.

Having sparred countless rounds with Rowsell, I thought Fenech's bravado was misplaced, and was convinced he didn't have the firepower to floor me. I'd always viewed him as a slick, slippery fighter but soft around the edges. I'd also noticed that since he'd joined Fenech's circle of fighters he'd become less of a boxer and more of a brawler. That was Fenech's trademark trait during his career, and he sought to bring out the inner street fighter in his students. Brawling didn't suit Rowsell, and I knew if he adopted that approach against me I'd cut him apart with my jabs, and ultimately knock him out.

Screw it, I thought to myself, I would execute the promise I'd made to my former stablemate and friend Naas Scheepers that I would one day avenge the loss he'd suffered against Rowsell. This was the opportunity to do that.

Mordey was busy salivating over the fight, and how much he stood to make. He got busy promoting it in the press, dubbing it 'The Uncivil War'.

But the media seemed more preoccupied by the protection order placed on Fenech than in the fight itself. They made it sound more like Ndou versus Fenech, rather than Rowsell. The bout was scheduled for 14 December 1998 at the Sydney Entertainment Centre, and as far as I was concerned it would determine who the best lightweight in the country was. I also saw it as a chance to secure a world title shot, and as another plus, my Australian residency.

I ramped up my training, picking bigger and heavier sparring partners, like Shannan Taylor, who would basically try and brawl me, pin me to the ropes and fire off body shots. I knew if I could handle him, I would be perfectly prepared for anything Rowsell planned to throw at me. My riposte would be about popping the left jabs, followed by combinations, using the angles, staying away from the ropes, and targeting his eyes. I planned to have them almost welded shut within a few rounds. I'd never been fitter. I'd run a half and full marathon that year, plus Sydney's City to Surf race.

The impending collision had created divisions at our workplace, with some of our colleagues barracking for me and others for Rowsell. Others remained neutral. Justin and I decided to take extended leave, to focus on training and avoid running into each other at work.

His proposed fight against Mosley, meanwhile, had already been confirmed on the undercard of Roy Jones Jr's fight against New York cop turned fighter Richard Frazier on 9 January 1999 in Pensacola, Florida. But he needed to beat me first, just three weeks earlier.

It was hardly the ideal timeline for Rowsell but he couldn't get out of the fight because a cast-iron agreement was in place with the notoriously litigious Bill Mordey. No opposing fighter or promoter was game to renege on a Mordey contract after he'd taken Vlad Warton and Kostya Tszyu to the cleaners.

Rowsell took his training camp to Queensland's Gold Coast under the guidance of trainer Ray Giles, who to my mind was the godfather of boxing. He was famed for his rigorous and disciplined approach, and never allowing his fighters to take short cuts. He was both intelligent and no-nonsense, as I experienced first-hand years later working under his wing. He'd keep close tabs on his fighters, to the extent of having them stay at his home while preparing for a bout. There would be no carousing with the ubiquitous procession of willing women who floated around the boxing fraternity. Not on Ray's watch. He'd wake you up at 5 am to make sure you were doing your road work and would even prepare your meals to ensure you were sticking to the right diet. That said, when I was under his wing I'd sneak in the odd chocolate bar, procured by his beautiful wife Lynne, to break up the culinary tedium.

I dubbed Ray 'Snoop' in reference to the rap artist Snoop Dogg. Not that he resembled him in any way. He looked more like Dr Hannibal Lecter in the 1991 hit movie, *The Silence of the Lambs.* Like Lecter, he has all the traits of a brilliant man, refined tastes in music and cuisine, and a disdain for bad manners and rudeness. I never used to see him smile much. He appeared careworn and devoid of mirth until one afternoon when he walked into my room to collect my training bag before we headed to the gym.

I was playing one of Snoop Dogg's X-rated music videos. Ray had never heard of Snoop Dogg and I feared he'd chastise me for watching such lewd and loud material, as opposed to pouring over boxing videos. To my surprise, Ray was hooked on the TV screen and mesmerised by the beautiful half-naked models flaunted in the video, shaking their butts to the beats. Ray always wanted us to arrive first at the gym but that afternoon he was happy to sit back, enjoy Snoop's music videos and arrive late for a change.

'Who is this fellow? he asked, his mouth agape. 'I'd love to trade places for a day and be surrounded by all those beautiful women.'

From that instant on he was known to me simply as 'Snoop'.

I had no doubt that Ray would have whipped Rowsell into mint condition, before sending him back to Sydney a week out to finalise his preparations. Although I'd been caught up in the media circus surrounding my spat with Fenech, I had to keep focus and reinforce the fact that it was actually Rowsell whom I was fighting. I knew Fenech could mess with my mind and I needed to keep my objectives clear, or risk paying the price in the ring.

I've always been an advocate of reverse psychology, and so I decided to play along to the extent that I'd keep tossing verbal hand grenades at Fenech, in the expectation that Rowsell would be the one to lose sight of the big picture and subliminally believe that Fenech was my real target. The script went off flawlessly. In every pre-fight interview Fenech would berate me as a fake fighter, whom he'd personally relish knocking out. There wasn't too much coming from Rowsell. I performed my role, boasting that after I beat Rowsell I'd go after Fenech and shut his gob for good.

Feelings were running high as the clock ticked down to fight night. I deliberately arrived late to the pre-bout press conference to piss off the Fenech camp, dressed to the nines in designer threads and putting on a show of haughty swagger and bravado. All eyes and cameras were on me as I sauntered into the room. It had the desired effect, with Fenech telling the assembled throng I was a fraud and a phony.

'He might look the part but he's a wolf dressed in sheep's clothing,' he blustered, insisting that beneath the suit sat a man of no boxing substance who would be exposed as a myth of his own making by Rowsell. I just kept smiling as Fenech ranted on, challenging me to come and box him in the gym later that day.

'If you do that I guarantee you won't be getting in the ring with Justin later in the week,' he mocked.

I told him I'd fight him in a big arena for nothing, or for charity, and let the public make their own minds up.

The burlesque show took another twist when one of Fenech's entourage, one-time triple fly-weight champion Peter Mitrevski got in on the act.

'I'll fight you too, step outside now and I'll knock you out,' he goaded.

I looked him in the eye and countered that he probably needed to grow a few more inches before he could contemplate fighting a real man. Peter, for all his boxing smarts, looked more like a jockey than a pugilist and my jibe set off ripples of laughter in the room.

The Fenech-Mitrevski relationship is instructive. They were once best buddies, so tight that Peter would have killed for Fenech. But sometime in 2009, the bromance of thirty years soured badly. Nobody knows exactly what happened but there was talk of a feud over some cheap diamonds which allegedly resulted in Fenech king-hitting his erstwhile pal, who lost a tooth in the process. Fenech has always denied any incident ever took place, but even to this day he continues to publicly ridicule his former ally. His putdowns include the line that Mitrevski became an Australian champion by beating the same guy on three occasions.

Another of Fenech's crew, a lawyer named Theo Onisforou, asked me if I would retire if I was KO'ed by Rowsell. My trainer Bill Corbett intervened, and next thing Fenech was inviting him outside so he could knock him out.

Bill didn't appreciate it, and nor did my sparring partner Shannan Taylor, who was also in the room and up until this point minding his own business. Suddenly he was kicking off his thongs (flip-flops) and shaping up to some of Fenech's hangers-on.

I stayed seated, amused by the bizarre turn of events, but resolved to not becoming involved in what had degenerated into more of a pantomime than a press conference.

Another idiot in the crowd started yelling he was going out to his car to get his gun, and later, on the evening news, there was vision of a man in the throng grabbing a glass in preparation to play his part if an all-in brawl erupted. He wasn't the smartest of souls, with police later identifying him as a suspect in an ongoing murder inquiry.

As a consequence of a media event considered unseemly, even viewed through a wide lens of pre-fight histrionics expected by both punters and press, Fenech, Rowsell and I were summoned before the NSW Boxing Authority to explain what had occurred. I wasn't quite sure why I had been implicated in what went down, as I had remained seated, just a trace of a smile crossing my lips, throughout the entire charade.

When the dust finally settled, Fenech came up with a new ploy by challenging me to turn the fight with Rowsell into a winner-takes-all event. I replied that Rowsell had a family to support and I wasn't willing to take food from the mouths of his children. This wasn't bombast because I truly believed I had his measure and he was heading for a knockout.

The drama surrounding what had descended into a circus was unending, with the Fenech camp insisting that the weigh-in should, in contravention of existing rules and regulations, take place the day before the fight, rather than on the day itself. It was an imbroglio which almost led to the whole thing being called off.

In those days, weigh-ins a day prior were only permitted in title fights, or eliminators. Any other time it was 10 am on the day, and our fight was a non-title contest scheduled for ten rounds.

Fenech was persistent in his requests, but I point blank refused to comply, telling him to abide by the rules. I learned the reason for Fenech's persistence just a day out from the fight, as ticket sales slowed and doubts grew that it would actually happen. It turned out Fenech was looking for a ruse to ensure Rowsell could extricate himself from the fight without formally breaching his contract with Bill Mordey. If the fight was canned over the weigh-in squabble Rowsell would not technically have flouted the terms of the deal and would be free to parachute straight into his world title shot against Mosley in the following weeks. I was an inconvenient obstacle standing in the way.

I only learned of Fenech's plot when I received calls from US boxing promoter Cedric Kushner and a reporter from the States asking me if the fight with Rowsell was going ahead. Kushner was also offering me a tilt at Mosley's title, if I beat Rowsell and subsequently signed with him.

At the time Mosley was in his stable and I informed Kushner of my binding deal with Mordey but suggested maybe they could team up to forge some sort of agreement. After the conversation with Kushner, it made perfect sense why Fenech was playing his game of brinkmanship because Rowsell would have been set up financially for life were he to fight Mosley. I decided that whatever eventuated, even if Rowsell weighed in 10 kilograms over the limit ahead of time, I was going ahead with the fight, especially now with the carrot of Mosley dangled before me.

On the evening before the fight, Fenech invited the media to witness Rowsell's weigh-in on a pair of bathroom scales in the kitchen of his Sydney home. It was unsupervised, with Rowsell weighing in right on the limit. Fenech was hoping the stunt would prompt the NSW Boxing Authority to cancel the fight. But all he achieved was mentally messing with his own fighter, who was banking in bypassing me and heading to the United States for the biggest purse of his career.

At the official weigh-in, I told everybody the fight was on, which caught Fenech by surprise. Rowsell was 5 kilograms over the limit, while I was just under. During the face-off for the cameras I could see fear and confusion in Rowsell's eyes, and knew right there I'd already won the battle of the minds.

I told Mordey, without any sense of false bravado, that the fight wouldn't go beyond seven rounds, and that I was going to end Rowsell's career. After the protracted and heated build up, I was feeling surprisingly mellow, as if was an observer in the story but somehow divorced from it.

When the time finally arrived Justin 'The Cowboy' Rowsell, resplendent in silver trunks and a silver robe trimmed in black, entered the ring first. The dominant feature of his get-up was an outsized cowboy hat, synonymous with his nickname. He entered the arena to a thumping country music backing track booming out from the speaker system. He was escorted into the ring by his brother Daniel and the Fenech camp. I could see it all from the TV monitor in my dressing room. But outfits and big entrances don't win fights.

My entrance was accompanied by my usual musical mix: the roaring of a panther, in homage to my nickname, the sounds of glass smashing followed by Survivor's 'Eye of the Tiger'. Each time I heard those beats I felt untouchable, almost in another realm. I was decked in gold trunks, with matching robe and boxing boots. The atmosphere felt electric, and I stopped momentarily en route to the ring to kiss my ten-month old daughter Maxine, who was sitting ringside with her beautiful mother and sister.

I stepped through the ropes and sauntered around the ring and past my opponent. It felt like it was my jungle out there, and he was invading my space. I headed to my corner, kneeling to pray and ask God to protect my opponent and me, but allow me to whoop his ass. I looked around the crowd and my wife and kids were blowing kisses. This is what I was fighting for, my family. To give them a better life and a future in Australia.

Ring announcer Andy Raymond announced us, the national anthem came and went and as the referee called us together in the middle of the ring my gaze was blazing at Rowsell, but he was avoiding eye contact. He was looking at the referee and not me as we received our final instructions. I interpreted that as a sign of fear, and my already sky-high confidence was ratcheted up another notch.

When the bell rang Rowsell, as I'd expected, came charging after me in an effort to force a quick finish, and maybe erase a few of his own doubts. I took evasive measures and shot out jabs to the head and body. He kept pressing, while I kept jabbing and then hooking off the jab. He countered with straight rights but they were only finding air.

It was this punch, the right counter, which Fenech felt I was so vulnerable to, that had started the whole thing. But there it was: swishing aimlessly into a void as I danced away. I could still hear Fenech's voice from those sparring sessions buzzing in my ears 'sit on your right foot, throw a counter and you'll catch him'. Those words had never felt so hollow.

Meanwhile, my punches were landing. I was aiming for his eyes. At one stage I blasted out a huge right, missed and spun around. Rowsell tried to take advantage of the momentary lapse, pinning me to the ropes with a volley of body punches. I responded in kind and spun away.

At 70 kilograms by fight time, he had a decided weight advantage and I knew I had to stay on my toes. I finished the round with a flurry of punches, including a big right-hand. I was happy with the round and his left eye was starting to swell, which is exactly what I wanted.

Bill Corbett was not happy with the big right I'd thrown and missed with, and he told me to double up on my jabs and left hooks. I listened intently. I liked and respected him and knew how well he could read a fight. Just keep it simple was his main message.

That's what I did in the second: sending out the jab like a jackhammer and following up with left hooks.

I could hear my wife and daughter shouting the words '*hlali imbambo*', which means 'stay on the ribs' in Xhosa. They had become accustomed to me knocking down opponents with left body rips and felt I was in need of a reminder. But I had my instructions from Corbett to keep things simple, so I inwardly apologised to my family, and kept firing off the jabs and quick combinations.

It was working well but Rowsell wasn't taking a backward step, much to the detriment of that left eye of his which was growing bloated with all the jabs I'd been feeding it.

The third round followed the same pattern until the midway point when I caught him with a thumping right-hand which dropped him for a count of eight. I was not surprised that I dropped him with the right counter. Often fighters spend too much time on perfecting a punch but forget working on also defending against the same punch. I have no doubt that Rowsell spent many hours working on perfecting his right-hand counter because his camp believed I was susceptible to the punch – but they forgot to teach him to defend himself against the same weapon.

I thought he'd take a step back, chastened by the experience, but he did the opposite, which laid him bare to more punishment. He walked into a thicket of upper cuts, as he tried to pummel me with body shots. I decided to return the compliment, and for the first time in the fight I had him in retreat, if only briefly. As the bell sounded for the end of the round, I fired off a glancing right-hand, for which I apologised to referee Gary Dean.

In the fourth, Rowsell kept up the remorseless forward march and he caught me with a good left hook. He was throwing plenty of bombs but most were missing, and when I countered, I caught him.

As commentator John Casey put it, 'Rowsell threw the quantity of punches in the round, but Ndou threw the quality.'

Round five was a copy of the fourth, and Corbett berated me for spending too much time on the ropes.

'Come on mate, first minute of the fucking round and you win the last thirty seconds,' he scolded.

In the heat of the moment, I misunderstood him. And believed he wanted me to go out and end it in the first minute of the sixth. If that's what he wanted, that's what I'd do, I decided. I trusted him and thought he'd seen something I hadn't. I came out unloading five successive jabs and a right-hand that missed. I did it again, five jabs, followed by the right-hand. But this time it connected, and stung Rowsell.

He kept coming forward and I followed with a combination of upper cuts and left hooks. Down he went. He was back on his feet after an eight count but I was waiting to inflict more pain in the form of more than ten unanswered punches as his resistance caved in. He was trapped in the corner. Gary Dean had seen enough and after forty-seven seconds of round six it was over.

Amid the cacophony of crowd noise, I looked around: in Rowsell's corner his brother Daniel was crying. I embraced Rowsell and told him I loved and respected him and hoped we could remain friends. I knew, though, that this was no ordinary defeat – if such a thing exists – and had effectively ended his career.

He didn't say anything, maybe just stunned, not so much by the punches but the implications of his first loss in thirty-one fights. He'd previously easily beaten twenty-nine of those opponents and to suffer such a devastating blow would be difficult to reverse, mentally more than physically.

I knew he'd never be the same fighter because at twenty-six he was too old to change deeply ingrained traits, beliefs and habits. A loss for an up-and-coming fighter, on the other hand, should be something to embrace and harness as part of dealing with adversities looming in the future. It's much easier to process and move on from a loss when you're still wet behind the ears.

I've witnessed many boxers over the years painstakingly construct long unbeaten records only to slide into deep decline after encountering the first defeat. The opposite can be said for fighters like the enduring Bernard Hopkins, who lost his first professional bout but went on to become one of the ring's master craftsman. When he fell to his second defeat five years after the first, against the pound-for-pound potentate Roy Jones Jr, he was able to bounce back and win an array of world titles.

The other side of the ledger is littered with the skeletons of some big names. Mike Tyson, the fearsome fighting machine who struck terror into the heavyweight ranks in knocking out thirty-four opponents in thirty-seven wins, was a shell of his former self after being stopped by Buster Douglas in 1990. Though he went on to beat Britain's Frank Bruno for the WBC title and Bruce Seldon for the WBA belt, he couldn't cope with the pressure applied by the likes of Evander Holyfield, once he no longer carried that aura of infallibility.

The infamous occasion when he chowed down on a chunk out Holyfield's left ear back in 1997 was testament to his inability to deal with the frustration which boiled inside him. The notorious bout was renamed the bite fight, with Tyson disqualified in the third round and transported to eternal infamy. Had he fought Holyfield earlier, while in full indestructible mode, he would likely have beaten a fighter who was in effect a pumped-up light heavyweight. But once the seed of doubt had been sewn, it was a different story.

Tyson, of course, had other issues outside the ring, like habitual drug use and imprisonment for rape, which he strenuously denies and maintains his innocence even to this day.

Another example is Orzubek Nazarov, the southpaw lightweight from Kyrgyzstan. He went unbeaten over twenty-six fights in eight years, winning the WBA title along the way and successfully defending it six times. But his first defeat at the hands of Jean-Baptiste Mendy was also his last, because he never fought again. Rumour has it he retired due to eye problems, but I believe it was more about his inability to deal with the crushing aftermath of that maiden loss.

You could say something similar about Fenech, who having racked up twenty-six wins and a draw, was forever shell-shocked by his KO loss to Azumah Nelson, with whom he had earlier drawn. The likes of Calvin Grove and Philip Holiday wouldn't have been able to live with Fenech prior to the loss to Nelson. But once the veneer of vulnerability had been exposed, he was a flawed fighter living on borrowed time.

Floyd Mayweather, my one-time sparring partner, has had a couple of close calls but remains unbeaten. A loss at any point would have seen him hang up his gloves but he's never been able to resist the mega-deals on the table to keep prolonging his career.

The point is: it takes a special type of fighter, and man, to rise again after a devastating defeat, and I knew that Rowsell wouldn't be making that improbable journey. He had six more fights following that night at the Sydney Entertainment Centre, winning four of them against very ordinary opponents, drawing one and being stopped in the second round by future world champion Ricky Hatton. The truth is, Rowsell should have left the ring for good after our meeting. Today, he's a sad story, his mind muddled and his words slurred in another possible case of early onset pugilistic dementia.

In a change of heart, I reached out to Fenech in the moments after the fight, shaking his hand and announcing that I would drop the interim AVO against him. Life is all about forgiveness. I had proved my point and I told the crowd and live TV audience that perhaps he would no longer question my boxing prowess.

Fenech, for his part, did grant me respect from that night on, never again belittling my ability. Ironically, he trained me years later, and helped in many ways with my career. He was loyal and honourable with his fighters and would do his utmost to provide the best opponents and purses he could.

When I fought Junior Witter, for example, the bout almost never happened after a post weigh-in dispute over money and the bout agreement. Yet Fenech actually doubled my purse. Whenever he told me he would get me a sponsor he'd come up with one. Whenever he said he'd have me moved up the rankings he would deliver.

In my heart, I don't believe the man is racist; in fact he's far from it. He said something in the heat of the moment, which he subsequently regretted. At the time I was hyper-attuned to racism having just left a country torn apart by discrimination, even to this day. I've seen Fenech mingle and train with people from Aboriginal, African and Pacific Islander backgrounds and treat then all with respect. His closest pal is African American Mike Tyson.

He ultimately introduced me to Iron Mike after my loss to Witter in 2005 while we were in Los Angeles. We met him for dinner at the famed Mr Chow restaurant in Beverly Hills. Tyson brought along an entourage of six burly buddies, and there were five of us, all piling into a private room. We were treated like royalty, ordering all the prime delicacies and the most expensive spirits and champagnes on the menu. At the conclusion of the feast, some of us reached into pockets to pull out our wallets to chip in. But somebody told us to wait for Tyson to speak to the maître d', and when he did that we should all just get up and head to our cars.

At first I didn't twig what was going on, until it was explained to me that such establishments always expected somebody from Tyson's crew to settle the bill, rather than the man himself. It turned out, surprise surprise, that something sneaky was going down and it was Fenech who got left holding the baby. It was he who had phoned earlier from our hotel to make the reservation and he'd unwittingly left his number.

Later that night, somebody from Mr Chow's called Fenech's room demanding he pay the bill. The figure was in the thousands and Jeff paid up. Suffice to say he had a face like thunder when we met for breakfast in the hotel lobby the next morning.

CHAPTER 20

ROCKY RIDE ON THE MORDEY MONEY TRAIN

'You're going to fight or I'll pull your application for residency at the Department of Immigration and put you on the first plane back to South Africa.'

The elation of beating Justin Rowsell was of a magnitude I'd never experienced before, and I believed the pathway was now clear for me to fulfil the dreams first hatched back in Musina, as a boy with an imagination that stretched far beyond my humble origins.

I wasn't the only one who felt that way, be it the media, the fans or just about anybody who'd watched that fight. I'd delivered when it mattered and I could see no impediment to a shot at one of the world championship belts.

Writing in Sydney's *Daily Telegraph,* respected boxing scribe, the late Terry Smith, put it like this: 'Ndou won the mind games in the lead up to the bout and was simply too classy when the pair got into the ring. The former South African will almost certainly get a chance to bid for Mexican Cesar Bazan's WBC lightweight crown early in March at Sydney Entertainment Centre.'

Another boxing writer, Hall of Famer Grantlee Kieza, said the win had capped off 'boxing's week of shame', referring to the histrionics of the Fenech camp.

As he bluntly put it in the *Sunday Telegraph:* 'Justin Rowsell should think seriously about those responsible for his horrific crash from the world boxing ratings. The admirable Lovemore Ndou, despite giving away 5 kilograms, courageously kept his word and did the job he had promised by stopping Rowsell in the sixth round.'

Kieza questioned what Rowsell, with a world title shot on the agenda, was doing tempting fate against a 'hungry panther like Ndou in the first place'.

He also queried why a fighter with 'a magnificent left-hand and superlative footwork had suddenly turned into a slugger. 'He was so easy to hit with a straight left that Ndou must have thought Christmas had come two weeks early,' he opined.

'How must Rowsell have felt on the biggest day of his life, not knowing whether he was going to fight Ndou or whether his chest-thumping trainer would be fighting him instead. Most of all, it's unwise to rile an opponent like Ndou, a Venda warrior from a tribe which has been fighting oppression for centuries.'

In the aftermath of the carnage that befell Rowsell and Fenech, I shared Kieza's sentiments.

He concluded: 'Having had dealings with the meat works [Rowsell had worked at an abattoir in Casino in northern NSW], he must know what it's like being led to the slaughter. Those responsible (i.e. Fenech) should hang their heads in shame.'

Rowsell never had a hope against me. After all, he was pitched against a fighter who like him was also hunting a global belt and had the added incentive of seeking to secure permanent residency in Australia.

As Kieza summarised, 'Fenech's abusive and threatening phone calls, which became the subject of an interim AVO, only served to spur on Ndou.'

I was so wound up, I'd have been even money against Mike Tyson on the night. It wasn't in my DNA to try and do more damage than was necessary to an opponent but Rowsell was on the cusp of being badly hurt. Fortunately for him the referee stepped in and stopped it.

It was the perfect end to the year, and I was utterly convinced that my next fight would see me battle, at long last, for a world title. But, one evening early in January 1999, less than a month after the Rowsell fight, I received a call which brought my world crashing down.

'Hi Lovemore, happy New Year to you and your family, Bill wants to talk to you.' The voice on the line belonged to Gwenda, Bill Mordey's wife.

I'd become accustomed to receiving calls from Mordey at night, and half the time he'd be inebriated. He never called during the day, even if the matter was pressing. He'd lived up in the wine producing Hunter region, two hours north of Sydney, and his son Craig used to manage the Sydney office in Surry Hills. Years of heavy smoking and excessive drinking, be it beer, spirits or vino, appeared to be slowly catching up with him, and I suspected that he got Gwenda to call me because he was too drunk to remember, or even dial my number. Even then there were invariably long silences before he could get it together to muster a single word. There would just be muffled, wheezy breathing and a shuffling sound echoing down the line followed by heavy coughing. On this occasion, though, he was straight to the point.

'Hello mate, I've good news and bad news for you,' he croaked in his familiar rusty cadence.

'The good news is we will fight for the world title, the bad news is it won't be anytime soon. The reality is no champion wants to fight you after the way you disposed of Rowsell. Nobody wants to risk it against you. You're too friggin' dangerous.'

I was at a loss how to react, not least to the good news and bad news part. To me, it was all bad news. I couldn't believe, let alone digest, what I'd just heard. I'd not missed a beat since the Rowsell fight, clocking up the hours in the gym over the festive season, convinced a defining fight that would set me and my family up for life was just around the corner. Mordey had told me prior to the Rowsell fight that a meeting with Cesar Bazan was a done deal, explaining that he had agreed to come to Sydney in March. I blithely believed him, and didn't question him either when he told me that were I to beat Rowsell I could choose between Bazan or Mosley for the IBF title.

The US promoter Cedric Kushner had also promised Mosley, on the condition he was granted an option to co-promote my first three title defences, should I take his crown. My mind froze, and an anger welled as Mordey continued to talk.

'Meantime, I'm going to keep you busy,' he spluttered. 'You'll be headlining a show in March in Sydney against an international opponent.'

What he didn't know was that two days earlier I'd spoken with Kushner, who had described Mordey, with undisguised scorn, as 'an arrogant Aussie piece of shit'. The two were at loggerheads over co-promoting the Mosley fight, with Kushner saying that Mordey wouldn't agree to any sort of deal, no matter how advantageous it was to him.

Kushner, who promoted Mosley, wanted a mandatory option written in for a re-match with his man, which was entirely logical. He informed me, before Mordey's fateful phone call, that the Bazan fight was off the agenda, as the Mexican had a stitched up a re-match against Stevie Johnston at the end of February.

'Mordey's been bullshitting you,' he told me. 'He's giving you the run-around. The guy doesn't give a fuck about you.'

I didn't want to believe it but reality hit hard as Mordey lingered on the line, his deceit and deception exposed as he spun his lies through a haze of inebriation, his words barely fully formed.

I had learned from my father never to speak your mind when you're truly upset because you may say things you later regret. 'Words hurt more than swords,' he would say. 'Wait till you calm down and then speak.' I've carried that mantra throughout my life and found it to be beneficial. When I'm really angry I go silent … when I'm still talking and shouting back at you then I'm not anywhere near upset. It's when the words dry up that you should worry. Logic tells you that when you're apoplectic you can't think clearly.

Speaking calmly and clearly, I cut the conversation short, telling Mordey, 'Look, I'll call you back another time and we will continue this discussion. Have a good night.' Click.

I was devastated by Mordey's lies, but at the same time I needed him because he held the key to my hopes of finally being granted Australian residency, and the aspiration of citizenship beyond that. An atomic-sized explosion would jeopardise or destroy those dreams, and I'd have to pack my bags and go back to South Africa. Either that, or find another credible sponsor, which would have been far from easy.

When the new world rankings were published, to my horror, I

discovered I'd not moved up a single spot, despite having beaten such a formidable opponent. I remained the WBC number eight, and it took me three more fights to ultimately hit the number-three ranking.

I'd go on to beat Mexican Arturo Urena on 12 March 1999 with a third round KO, Puerto Rican Hector Arroyo in the fourth with another KO on 13 June 1999, and very tricky Thai Daomai Sithkodom, who was third ranked by the WBC, on 20 August of the same year to cement my rise. He came into the fight with a daunting record of sixty wins for only eight losses, but I won a unanimous decision after ten strength-sapping rounds to supplant him in the ratings.

Following the fight, Mordey – to my dismay – decided to activate a clause in our contract which enabled him to extend our promotional agreement for a further two years. When I'd signed the deal, foresight had not been my strongest suit, and I had no legal way of wriggling out of it. In tandem with my tortuous rise up the WBC totem pole, I'd also not shifted in the IBF pecking order, despite beating their third-ranked fighter. Mordey's explanation was another deception, designed to make me despise a man who today I count as a dear friend, and a man who ultimately helped me secure a shot at the IBF super lightweight world title, which I went on to win.

'Mate, Ray Wheatley doesn't like you for some reason,' he grandly intoned with all the conviction he could conjure. 'I reckon he doesn't consider you a real Australian and won't vouch for you to get a shot at the IBF title. I'm not saying he's a racist but the guy's xenophobic and he's got it in for you.'

Wheatley, at the time, was vice-president of the IBF ratings committee. He went on to be voted the organisation's overall vice-president in 2000 and held the position for some years. He was also a former Golden Gloves champion, and Australian heavyweight contender. Today he's an Australian Hall of Famer, and all-round doyen of the sport. And yet I'd been led into loathing him, on the say-so of a promoter whose own agenda was working overtime.

I'd met Wheatley a few times prior to these accusations, and he'd actually refereed my fight against Lauro Wilton. I had no idea why he'd have an issue with me, but foolishly I bought Mordey's make-believe and for years I carried a grudge against Wheatley. I studiously ignored him when we ran into each other on fight nights, and I simmered with indignation towards the man.

On the world title radar at the same time was another Australian lightweight, Renato Cornett. I never believed him to be anything special as a fighter but he was leaping up the IBF rankings, which only strengthened the theory espoused by Mordey that Wheatley was out to hinder my progress at all costs. Here was a fighter who I didn't categorise in my class, on an upward curve while I flatlined. He ultimately got a shot at the IBF title before I did.

After eight successful defences of the lightweight title Shane Mosley vacated the belt, allowing Pennsylvania's Paul Spadafora to take the vacant mantle, defeating Israel Cardona over twelve rounds.

Spadafora's first defence was against none other than Cornett, winning by TKO in round eleven. I was incredulous that Cornett had managed to get a title shot since, at the time, I was the best lightweight contender in Australia, if not the world. What made even less sense was that Spadafora, back then, was promoted by Mordey's US-based international matchmaker and agent Mike Accri. He was responsible for all the international opponents I had faced under the Mordey banner.

Logically, it would have been easier for Mordey to negotiate a world title fight for me with Accri in his corner. But instead, I continued to toil around the RSL fight circuit while Cornett was up in lights with a world title tilt. It made me question whether Mordey ever had a genuine desire to get me on the global stage, or simply viewed me as a regular pay-cheque on the home front.

In October 1999 I beat Argentinian Gustavo Fabian Cuello on points and was informed by Mordey that he'd reached an agreement with Mike Accri whereby I would fight Cornett. If I beat him convincingly I'd get a shot at Spadafora's IBF title.

'Look mate, you beat Cornett, and then you and Spadafora share a common denominator of beating the same man,' he said. 'It's attractive to the TV networks and the fight will sell. Mike Accri has already informed me it's a done deal. You could also fight Stevie Johnston for the WBC title.'

Johnston had just regained his crown in a rematch with Bazan. This time, I challenged Mordey's line of bullshit, replying, 'But Bill, you told me the same thing after I beat Rowsell.'

Ever-adept at thinking on his feet, he dredged up the Wheatley line. 'Lovemore, I've already told you that Wheatley doesn't like you. That's why you didn't get a shot to move up the IBF rankings. The man has no scruples'

But I wasn't to be silenced on this occasion, firing back, 'No mate, I didn't get a shot at Mosley's title because you refused to do a deal with Kushner. So please stop feeding me the bullshit.'

It was the beginning of the long deterioration of our relationship, which ended up with me eventually refusing to speak to him and not even attending his funeral when he passed away a couple of years later.

I subsequently discovered that the accusation that Wheatley was antagonistic towards me was a classic Mordey fabrication. The truth was that Wheatley rated me highly and had campaigned behind the scenes to put me in the frame for the IBF title. It turned out he'd approached Mordey about me battling it out for the crown ahead of Cornett because he thought I had a better chance of success. But his offer had been rejected by Mordey, who also rebuffed the opportunity for me to fight for the vacant IBF Pan-Pacific title. Wheatley informed me he wasn't willing to pay the $5000 sanctioning fee. It was only then that Cornett got his chance. After I escaped Mordey's gravitational field I eventually took the route suggested by Wheatley and ended up winning the IBF super lightweight crown.

Today, Wheatley remains a loyal friend who I love dearly. We speak on a weekly basis and catch up for lunches. Such camaraderie is rare in boxing, where so-called friends more often than not vanish into thin air after a fighter retires. But Wheatley is cut from a different cloth. The man even remembers my birthday.

I was tiring of Mordey's mysterious ways. Boxing is a short life. You get few opportunities and you need to get in, make some money and get out of the sport before it consumes you. The man who was supposed to have my best interest at heart was only looking after himself.

Heading into the Cornett fight on 17 March 2000 I was confused as to how to approach it. If I went out there and demolished him I might get some other lame excuse from Mordey claiming the champion didn't want to fight me because he feared for his health. If I gave a lacklustre performance then the TV networks might not be interested in screening any of my future flights. Either way, I had no doubt I'd win. This wasn't an underestimation of Cornett. It was just an intrinsic belief that he wasn't at my level. He'd already challenged for two world titles and lost both.

The fight venue was a world away from the glamour of a Las Vegas or a New York. Western Sydney's prosaic Merrylands RSL, a pie-and-pokies venue situated slap-bang in the middle of Cornett's home turf, isn't the sort of place where grandiose dreams are forged. As expected, I was loudly booed by the locals as I entered the ring by Cornett's cheer squad. In my corner that night was former Australian middleweight champion Vito Gaudiosi, and my eccentric pal Jimmy Coleman.

My plan was to end it in the seventh round. The first three rounds were uneventful. Cornett kept charging forward and I kept him at bay with straight punches, eventually opening up a gash above his right eye.

I picked up the pace in the fourth and fifth rounds, concentrating on body punches to hasten the erosion I had already begun to see in him. But Gaudiosi wasn't overly impressed, telling me curtly before the sixth, 'If you want to be a champion you'll need to work harder brother. You've got to dictate. Don't just throw one jab and stare at him. You've got better hand speed. Use it and get on the front foot mate.'

I took his advice to heart and thirty-one seconds before the end of the round I dropped Cornett for an eight count with a left-handed body rip. He survived the round but at the mid-point of the seventh a three-punch combination appeared set to prove my pre-fight prophesy correct.

A left hook to the head, the body, and back to the head wobbled him. I followed up with repeat combinations. He was ready to go, but with the tape on my left glove coming off the referee halted the barrage and walked me to my corner to have the tape malfunction addressed. A relieved but badly shaken Cornett survived the round, albeit with the cut above his eye now oozing more blood.

He also made it through the eighth. He was almost a sitting duck in the ninth and was badly stung by a big right-hand. Trapped in the neutral corner, a volley of uppercuts left him dazed and defenceless. The referee had seen enough and stopped the fight.

While Cornett announced his retirement in the ring afterwards, I crowed to the crowd that I'd be the next world champion.

On the same day, Johnston successfully defended his WBC title against Julio Alvarez in Denver, Colorado and then announced his next defence would be against Mexico's Jose Luis Castillo. Despite Mordey's promises there was no mention of a showdown with a certain Lovemore Ndou. Nor was there any mention of Spadafora fighting me next. He, instead, was scheduled to defend his belt against Mike Griffith.

As usual Mordey had an excuse at the ready when I confronted him over the latest discrepancies to matching words with deeds.

'Listen mate, I know it's not what you want to hear but they're asking for too much money to come and defend their titles in Australia. It's not viable,' he said.

'I'll travel anywhere in the world, anytime, to take them on in their own backyards,' I responded, barely concealing my contempt.

'That's not an issue for me, you know that. Trust me mate, give me some time, and I'll bring one of these champions here to fight you,' was his unconvincing reply.

By this stage it had become crystal clear that Mordey, for all his bravado, never had any intention of giving me a shot at a world title. Financially, the numbers didn't stack up for him. Between me and Shannan Taylor we were providing him with a hefty monthly cash infusion through his Fox Sports TV deal. It was a bonanza he didn't want to forsake. He also pocketed gate takings and sponsorship dollars, just to sweeten the cocktail. If, God forbid, I was to win a world title he'd have to pay me more, and that wasn't part of his business model. He was in a comfort zone, and also perhaps feared that were I to become a global champion I'd likely move on with bigger and better promoters.

Rumour had it that Mordey was in hock to the Australian Taxation Office, and that most of the windfall from his Kostya Tszyu lawsuit had gone towards repaying that debt. He was also known to have a heavy gambling habit, which wouldn't have helped.

Despite my plight, I was tied to him for two more years. A seeming eternity in terms of my career aspirations. So desperate was I to extricate myself from his clutches that I offered to buy myself out of my contract.

Adding insult to injury, Mordey refused. He needed me and Taylor in his stable in order to keep shaking the Fox Sports money tree.

The contract only required him to keep me busy and 'endeavour' to secure a world title bout. He was careful not to breach those terms. I was told my next fight would be against Guillermo Mosquera on 30 June 2000. About three weeks into the build-up I noticed something unusual, and unwanted, going on with my health. I began to feel drained and lethargic. At first I thought I was over-training and needed to wind back a bit. But when I began suffering fevers and headaches, muscle pains and a sore throat I realised it was more than a simple case of fatigue from training overload. I went to see renowned boxing medic Dr Lou Lewis. He ran a battery of blood tests and I was diagnosed with glandular fever. It was a fight-ending finding in the eyes of the physician.

'Mate, you're going to have to pull out of the contest,' he said. 'It's that simple. You need three months of total rest before you can even contemplate training again. This isn't something you can mess with.'

I told him I'd inform Mordey of the situation, and my short-term prognosis. I had a feeling it wouldn't go down well. Our relationship was already on the skids, and Mordey knew I wanted out of the contract. His response was, as I'd feared, more confrontational than compassionate.

'Forget about taking a rest,' he barked back when I broached the matter. 'You're going to fight or I'll pull your application for residency at the Department of Immigration and put you on the first plane back to South Africa. I'll also sue you for every cent that I stand to lose if this promotion falls through.'

He didn't care that I had a medical certificate. As far as he was concerned it was fake news. 'You don't look sick Lovemore. It's going to be business as usual,' he added.

That day I saw a side of Mordey that shocked even me: it was far from the caring, irreverent image he'd cultivated for media consumption. There was a darkness and coldness deep inside and from that day on I viewed him as a toxic presence in my life

Back in the gym I was spent and exhausted after three rounds of sparring. Even shadow-boxing left me gasping for air and feeling dizzy. Yet Mordey wanted me to fight. I had a big decision to make. Not fight and risk getting sent back to South Africa along with a possible lawsuit.

Or fight, get badly beaten and tumble down the rankings. I'd worked so hard to come this far and I was in a muddle over which way to turn. A loss, I realised, was to Mordey's advantage because he wouldn't have to pretend any more that he was trying to get me a world title fight.

I opted to continue on, regardless, at least until I'd been granted my residency. And only then walk away from Mordey and face the consequences. Maybe even give up boxing.

On fight night nothing could lift the weariness and weakness which had taken hold of me. Not even the exuberance of Fox Sports' charismatic ring announcer Andy Raymond could erase my malaise.

'In the blue corner, hailing from south Sydney with a record of 27–2–1, he's the WBC number two and tonight weighing in at a slim, trim, lean, mean, ripped, chiselled and buffed 62.8 kilograms: Ladies and gentlemen, the Black Panther, Lovemore Ndou,' he boomed.

But his oratory acrobatics barely registered as I sleepwalked into the fight. Forget the Black Panther I was about as threatening as the Pink Panther. The gloves felt like concrete blocks on my arms, I couldn't stop yawning and every step was like wading through treacle. My corner knew I was in for a torrid night. I told them that no matter what happened not to throw in the towel, and that I'd fight to the end. Even if it meant being stretchered out of the ring.

As expected, after the first three rounds I was spent and felt glued to my seat in the corner, struggling to maintain the illusion of menace to an opponent who must have thought the hype that had built up around me was devoid of all substance.

How I managed to struggle and stagger through the ten rounds still baffles me to this day. Needless to say I was never in any danger of winning and the judges' verdict was a unanimous points loss. I was just glad to make it through without suffering serious bodily damage. My reputation, though, did take a pretty big hit. It was my first loss in eighteen fights since arriving in Australia. But I was too debilitated to care.

CHAPTER 21

RISKING IT ALL FOR A TASTE OF FREEDOM

'It's that or I'm not fighting for you ever again. Sue me if you want. I don't care.'

After my loss to Mosquera and the poisonous turn in my relationship with Mordey, I knew it was time to engage legal help to provide some clarity on my promotional contract and the perilous state of my permanent residency application. I spoke with a few and the consensus was there wasn't a loophole to be found and my only course of action was to see it through to the bitter end. The thought of almost two more years of marching to Mordey's drum was, in itself, enough to have me heading to the airport. But I thought better of it.

In the midst of this stalemate, my fortunes took a turn for the better one afternoon during what was an otherwise humdrum workout at the Sydney Football Stadium gymnasium, where I used to go several days a week for my strength work. As I went about my business in the weights room, I noticed a guy who bore a remarkable resemblance to harassed and hen-pecked TV sitcom husband Al Bundy, of *Married with Children* renown. The tall figure was hunched over, throwing mistimed haymakers at a punching bag, sweat gushing off his brow and his breathing laboured.

It's not my natural inclination to engage in chat-chat while ploughing through my routine, preferring to tune out distractions and concentrate on each set of exercises in a single-minded solace. But after numerous sightings of this uncoordinated character pawing the punching bag with all the venom of a newborn lamb, I decided to intervene. I just couldn't stand to witness the egregious misuse of the gloves any longer.

'Hey, brother I think I can help you with your timing here,' I interceded.

Startled, the man who I later dubbed Stevie, looked my way, a quizzical expression creasing his features.

'Sure, why not. Don't tell me: you're probably a pro boxer,' he chortled.

'You might say that,' I replied.

It was the start of a beautiful friendship which continues to this day.

He couldn't throw much of a punch in the gym but Steven Arthur Lang, as it turned out, was a heavy hitter in the business world and had a legal background to boot. He may have been a dead ringer for Al Bundy (played with enduring downtrodden stoicism by Ed O'Neill) but he was far from the born loser we saw on screen. Stevie had a sharp tongue, an attuned mind, and was a former law partner turned investor who is today in the beverages business.

His lack of coordination brought out the coach in me and I began to tutor him in the art of punching correctly, and as our friendship evolved he went on to become my business advisor and manager. This turn of events heightened tensions between me and Mordey, who didn't approve of any of his fighters having a personal manager. For obvious reasons. When I told him, his reaction was a cutting, 'You don't fucking need a manager.'

The truth was I didn't just need a manager: I needed a miracle worker to release me from Mordey's clutches. Mordey took the same uncompromising approach with Kostya Tszyu. The moment he installed Vlad Warton as his agent, their relationship imploded.

With all the uncertainty clouding my status in Australia I eventually consulted an immigration specialist named Adrian Joel, who came highly recommended. He also had the appearance of a sitcom star, in this instance Richard Kind of *Mad About You* and *Spin City* fame.

At our first meeting I thought I'd stumbled onto the set of his own one-man show, as he talked incessantly and earnestly. Mainly about boxing. It turned out he was a ring fanatic, and former would-be pugilist who had followed every twist and turn of my career since I'd arrived in Australia.

His opening line sounded like a symphony to me, as he declared with unwavering certainty, 'Oh Lovemore that loss to Mosquera isn't going to stop you getting your residency. Not a bit of it. You're a great fighter and you just had an off night. Simple as that.'

I immediately cast him as a clairvoyant. How else could he know of my concerns that the defeat might end my hopes of settling in Australia? I hadn't discussed the specific reasons for booking the appointment with his receptionist.

Before I had a chance to break his stream of consciousness, he'd already reached into a drawer and extracted a copy of *The Fighter* magazine, flicking through the pages to find the world rankings columns and where I was placed in the pecking order. I sat dumbfounded as he went on to discuss and dissect several of my previous fights in forensic detail.

As the clock ticked in his office, I wondered to myself whether this guy had an off switch, not that I objected to his subject matter. In fact, the more he talked, the more I liked him. He knew boxing inside out: his knowledge was encyclopaedic. Be it Tyson, Hagler, Hearns, Sugar Ray Leonard, Lennox Lewis. You name it.

Just when I thought he'd never stop. There was an abrupt silence, followed by the words: 'Okay then, what can I do for you Lovemore? What brings you here?'

I outlined my concerns regarding my tenuous situation and the threats Mordey had been making. Smiling broadly, he settled back further into his chair and pronounced, 'No worries Lovemore, I'll make sure your residency is approved. Unfortunately, people try to take advantage of this type of situation. It happens all the time. I deal with these sorts of matters on a daily basis and it is common for people such as you to have issues with their sponsors. Rest easy, I'll get this moving and we'll meet again in a few weeks.'

Grateful, and fortified with a new hope I enquired about his fee schedule. His gaze narrowed, as if I'd insulted him, before he snapped back, 'Fees? It's on the house Lovemore. I've enjoyed watching you fight for a while now. It's given me pleasure. The least I can do is help you stay here. We need some more Aussie world champions, and I think that's where you're headed.'

I grew up believing that lawyers were all about self-interest and milking as much money out of clients as possible. But here was a living, breathing exception to the rule. I promised to send him tickets to my fights but he wasn't looking for any freebies and his offer was non-negotiable.

I later discovered this altruistic boxing devotee had a deep history in the sport, despite coming from a privileged background seemingly worlds apart from the gristle and grunt of boxing gyms. It turned out that he had strayed into a boxing gym at the age of fourteen one afternoon, still wearing his uniform and straw boater from his day at a top-end-of-town private school. He was the proverbial fish out of water amid the sweat-soaked din of sparring sessions, shadow-boxers, rope skippers, trainers and nefarious characters coming and going.

It turned out the gym was a front for a gambling syndicate and the only reason he wasn't tossed out on his ear was because the boss happened to be there and was so amused by this out-of-place waif from another world that he decided to indulge him. An unlikely friendship was born between the gangster and the rich kid, with the former becoming an influential figure in the teenager's life.

This middle-class white boy was given a glimpse into a world where the rules of gentility didn't necessary apply. Yet there was a code of ethics within this parallel universe of bailed criminals, chancers, Aboriginals looking for a pathway out of poverty and assorted hangers on. He wasn't just an observer: he also laced on the gloves and ultimately had, in his own words 'eight low quality amateur fights' before getting smashed by Rocky St Clair at Blacktown RSL in Sydney's west at the age of twenty-two.

Fortunately, he had never entertained any serious aspirations of a career in the ring and his law studies were already well advanced. So he walked away but retained a love for the sport. Rocky St Clair went on to turn pro, eventually winning a New South Wales heavyweight title.

Having learned a little of his background, I understood were his ardour was coming from. While his ring prowess was found wanting, he's gone on to become one of Australia's foremost immigration lawyers because he never gives up fighting for his clients, no matter how lost the cause might appear to be.

He's also been a champion against the human trafficking of children and was an influential figure in the class action brought by Australia's lost and stolen generation against those government agencies which perpetrated such grave injustices against Australia's Indigenous people.

After several more meetings, he called me one morning to give me the news I'd longed to hear.

'You're now an Australian resident,' he told me. 'Your application has been approved. In two years' time you can apply for citizenship, if you like.'

As his words washed over me, I felt euphoria mingled with relief, and decided at that instant it was over between Mordey and me. I decided I'd rack up a few more wins under his promotional banner, and then call it a day. Contract or no contract.

On 25 August 2000, exactly two months after by misfire against Mosquera, and with my health much restored, I stopped Juan Angel Macias in one round of a fight scheduled for ten. Eight weeks later I beat battle-hardened Argentinian Victor Hugo Paz with a unanimous decision, and on 25 February 2001 I stopped Chile's Carlos Uribe in the fifth round.

The loss to Mosquera hadn't affected my ranking and I remained the WBC number two. But, surprise surprise, there was no hint of any world title bout on the horizon from Mordey. Our relationship had reached such a low point that we were barely speaking. After the Uribe fight I called Mordey and once again offered to buy myself out of the contract. He declined.

'Mate, you either release me from the contract or let me buy myself out,' I insisted. 'It's that or I'm not fighting for you ever again. Sue me if you want. I don't care.'

Before he had time to react, I hung up the line. It was the last time we ever spoke.

CHAPTER 22

THE RETURN OF THE BLACK PANTHER

'Son, when you get hurt in boxing hold on to your opponent like you want to fornicate with him. Turn him into your lover. One you never want to lose or let go of.'

Walking away from my disintegrating relationship with Bill Mordey wasn't a decision I took lightly. But after much reflection I felt I had no choice but to sever ties – even if it meant prematurely ending my boxing career.

I was already weary of all the bullshit that permeated almost every sector of the sport. But most of all I was tired of Mordey playing God with my life, career and future. I also knew that at some point boxing would no longer be my be-all and end-all. It's a short-time career and, unless you are a sucker for punishment and willing to heighten the already high risk of brain injury, it's not something you can do forever.

I began dwelling on what my long-term future might hold. I'd always harboured ambitions of one day sampling the world of academia, no matter how fanciful that might have seemed in light of my turbulent and disadvantaged upbringing. I'd always valued education, right back to the days of pouring through books, seated on the dusty street outside our home in Musina, while the other kids played games and fooled around a few yards away. My parents always drummed into us the importance of education, and while the message got lost at times it eventually stuck.

One of those times when the message got messed up was when as a naive and foolish pre-teen, I joined my younger brother Ruddock in perpetrating an act neither of us are proud of. Right up to this day it's something I'm ashamed of. On the night our mother told us we'd be moving back from Zimbabwe to South Africa the very next morning, we did the unthinkable. Out of bravado and sheer stupidity we slipped out while our mother slept to pay a visit to the local primary school where we'd been students up until that day. Like demented fools, we roamed from classroom to classroom smashing windows and stealing books. We valued the education system in Zimbabwe far above the Bantu indoctrination of South Africa and wanted to take some of the knowledge with us. We just went about it in completely the wrong way.

While we later regretted the wanton vandalism, we wanted to keep the books to further our education. But our plans were thwarted by our maternal grandmother, who stumbled across our ill-gotten gains among our belongings when we returned home across the border. She thought the books might fall into the wrong hands and land us in deep trouble with South Africa's apartheid masters, as they differed in their interpretation of history from the version being taught in Musina schools, particularly at a time when Ian Smith's whites only government had just been deposed in Zimbabwe. Her solution, much to our dismay, was to burn them. I remember shedding tears when they were thrown, one by one, into a bonfire. All that knowledge being consumed by the flames was heartbreaking for us.

The whole episode, whilst hardly showing Ruddock and I as apostles of righteousness, gave us clarity over how we wanted our lives to ultimately unfold. And being academics of some sort was part of that plan. Today, we can proudly say that we're the only ones from both the paternal and maternal sides of our family to have embraced such a path. The only ones to have accumulated Bachelor's and Master's degrees: in my case as a lawyer and in Ruddock's as an IT manager.

But none of that has erased the guilt of what we did. By way of recompense, when I started making money in the ring I became a sponsor of the school, donating cash for computers, desks, chairs and books. It was one way of erasing the shame. I never told the school's governors my motives and they never asked.

After the decision to renege on what I considered my servitude to Mordey, I resigned myself to being out of the ring for fourteen months while the contract ran its course. I resolved not to just sit around waiting for the clock to tick down and decided to study, and then study some more. The problem was I was anything but computer literate, and all the assignments needed to be completed online. I enrolled into a computer course at TAFE and took tips from my computer-savvy eleven-year-old daughter along the way. We made a deal: if she wanted me to take her to the movies or on shopping trips she'd have to teach me. The arrangement worked out well and following that I enrolled in a communications course at UTS. I was initially interested in journalism as I thought it would provide a pathway into exposing corrupt promoters and politicians. But the more I studied, the more I realised I wanted to be a lawyer. My dealings with boxing promoters, managers, the police and the legal system in South Africa had me focused on becoming a champion for justice. I foresaw one day replacing upper cuts with affidavits.

It took a comment from one of my lecturers, a wonderful woman called Roselyn Turner, to cement that ambition in my mind. I'd penned an essay about the injustices and unequal distribution of national resources in South Africa, and after she'd read and marked it she pulled me side.

'What a great piece Lovemore,' she told me. 'You should consider becoming a lawyer or a politician. Maybe both. You could right a lot of wrongs.'

I took her words to heart. During my time at UTS I also wrote, directed and produced a short film as part of a group presentation. I graduated with a certificate IV in communication and was also awarded a prize for general proficiency. It was the stepping stone to my acceptance into a double degree in law and communication at the University of Western Sydney.

Things were moving with my family also and on 22 October 2001 my wife and I were blessed with a second baby girl, whom we named Marion Minah-Romanah Ndou. We thought it fitting that she should have my mother's first name Minah as part of her middle name. Her birth was one of the happiest days of my life, even though I didn't quite see it that way at the time.

I'd always wanted a big family, and having come from one myself had seen the benefits and camaraderie it can bring, despite the financial burdens. Growing up in Musina, despite the daily hazards and difficulties, we'd always managed to find positives amid the pitfalls and together we thought we could face and overcome any challenges. We were always there to listen to each other and provide a shoulder to lean on. That's not to suggest we didn't have our differences and there were many times we wanted to tear each other apart, sibling rivalry being what it is. My relationship with Ruddock encompasses all these highs and hiccups. He's the only one I can truly open up to when I'm going through a bad time and vice versa. But we've also been at each other's throats more times than I care to recall.

Being bestowed with three daughters was a gift. But I'd always also nurtured hopes of a son, and when Marion was born a big part of me was hoping for a boy. When the doctor announced the arrival of a girl I couldn't hide the disappointment on my face.

'Cheer up Dad, she's beautiful,' said the doctor, noticing my less than ecstatic expression.

I turned to look at my wife and she was laughing. She'd already forewarned the doctors and nurses to keep an eye on my reaction. She'd known the sex of the child from when she was six months pregnant but had kept it a closely guarded secret, even hinting cryptically that we were having a son. I guess the joke was on me; I should have just been happy without putting any caveats on my delight. I blame my upbringing in a culture where sons were more highly prized than daughters for a number of reasons, not least that a son carries on the family name. Today, I find that reasoning misguided and wrong in every sense. I love, value and respect women so much. Without them there is no life cycle. They carry and nurture our futures and anybody who doesn't respect that needs a self-check. To me, a woman is the next thing to God and today my daughters and I share the most unbreakable of bonds.

Seventeen months after Marion's birth God blessed us with a tall, handsome boy, whom we named Lovemore Ray Ndou Jr.

Despite the continuing uncertainty over my boxing career I remained in prime condition, sweating and punching my way through countless gym sessions and liaising with other promoters over what might lie ahead when I returned to the ring. One of those interested in signing me up when I became a free agent was US-based Goosen-Tutor Promotions, run by the late Dan Goosen and Ronald Tutor. But talks were only preliminary and we were all playing a waiting game.

My ring sabbatical allowed me more time to spend with my growing family. I'd always been a hands-on dad but now I had the time and opportunity to become a full-time carer. There's nothing more beautiful than watching your kids progress from crawling to walking to running and hearing them utter their first words.

Finally, after fourteen months of inactivity, my contract with Mordey ran its course and I was a free man. Soon afterwards Goosen-Tutor Promotions forwarded me an agreement but this time I went through it with a fine-tooth comb, with the aid of expert legal advice. I made sure there was an escape clause should there be a fallout between boxer and promoter. The offer made to me was close to an insult in its stinginess, considering I'd been ranked number two in the world by the WBC before the Mordey row derailed my career. It was almost like I was a novice starting out all over again. But I had little choice but to accept. My bargaining chips were few and my world ranking had dropped through the floor. I signed the contract and was told my comeback fight would be on 7 April 2002 in California. To add salt to the wound, Goosen told me they would cover my three-night stay in Los Angeles but I'd have to pay my own travel expenses from Sydney. That was confirmation, if any were needed, how far I'd dropped down boxing's pecking order. I was told my opponent, Mexican-born Jose Luis Juarez, would provide only modest opposition as I sought to brush away the cobwebs of my long absence.

'He's not up to much,' breezed Dan Goosen down the line from LA. 'He's had nine wins, two losses and a draw but his punches don't carry any venom. He's never knocked anybody out and I reckon he'd struggle to deck my grandmother.'

The venue was the Soboba Casino in San Jacinto, and the duel was to be beamed back to Australia on Fox Sports. I found out on fight night that I'd been badly misled by Goosen, whose rehashing of Juarez's record was somewhat miscued. He, in fact, had twenty-three wins, and twenty of those by knockout, plus four losses and a draw. And those defeats were disputed defeats against great warriors like Vivian Harris and Alex Trujillo. Goosen could get away with smudging the figures because, unlike today when you can simply log into Boxec.com, you had to rely on the promoter's word. Never a good scenario for anybody seeking the truth.

Not that any of this truly bothered me. I just wanted to get active again and knew I had the sort of busy, go-forward style which made me easy on the eye and likely to light up fights. Win or lose I felt that once the American networks and public got to see me, they would want me back.

Dan Goosen informed me he'd have his brother Joe work my corner to save me the cost of flying my trainer over. None of it worried me and I packed my bags for the USA, boxing's spiritual home.

On touching down at LAX airport, I was picked up by a designated driver who had my misspelled name 'Nadou' scrawled in magic marker on a battered looking piece of cardboard. The driver, his hair unkempt, his eyes cloudy and sunken and his complexion swarthy, looked like he'd just crawled out of bed.

He introduced himself as Eli, from parts unknown somewhere in the Middle East, and he was about as likeable as the LA smog. He joked about Aboriginal people boxing like kangaroos and African people riding on ostrich backs. But he wasn't tapping my funny bone. I don't know what movies he had been watching but I told him to keep his eyes on the road and give his mouth a rest. Instead, he cranked up some Arabian music as we headed out into the notorious peak hour LA traffic in silence for the ninety-minute crawl to our destination some 35 kilometres away.

I wasn't expecting the Beverly Wilshire but my heart sank when we came to a stop outside a dilapidated looking three-storey motel straight out of one of the seedier scenes from *The Rockford Files*. It was about as welcoming as a trip to the clink, with a couple of crack addicts loitering around the dingy reception area, and hookers coming and going with clients while I checked in in the smoke-filled reception area. After declining the offer to buy a line of coke from the guy who hopped in the lift with me to the second floor, I finally made it to my living quarters for the next ten days.

I'd decided to fly over early to acclimatise but after less than three hours in the country I was beginning to question the wisdom of my decision. I thought, at the very least, Goosen would have lined up digs in the three-star and above class, especially as he was only paying for three nights. But I was sadly misguided. My digs were more a no-star, one-stop shop for quickies and low-level drug deals than a place to get some shut eye in relative peace and tranquillity. The walls were wafer thin, and every manufactured moan and tortured grunt from the hookers and their clients was all too audible, day and night, as I tossed and turned on my prison-issue mattress trying to sleep.

The endless moans and groans were interspersed by slamming doors, and shrieks and shouts as one dude or another decided the sex wasn't up to scratch and like hell was he going to pay up. Welcome to the land of the brave, I mused, my head buried in the moth-eaten pillow, trying to drown out the din.

Three days before the fight I was still 3 kilograms over the lightweight limit. I'd been starving myself and taking in less fluids in an effort to trim down but it was a torturous process. During my long layoff I'd packed on muscle at the gym and, now in my thirties, I had a bigger frame. In the end, I made the cut but feared a repeat of what happened the last time I'd raced to shed the kilos, my first loss as a pro fighter to Jerry Malinga.

It wasn't just the weight issue; after fourteen months out of action I had the fluidity of the Tin Man, and the last thing I needed after such a long absence was a seasoned and downright dangerous opponent. I'd never been knocked down in my life, whether in the ring or a street brawl, but that all changed in the third round when I got caught with a left hook and touched the canvass with my knee.

Referee Marty Denkin gave me a count, which was the right thing to do. Sensing I was there for the taking Juarez kept up the pressure and bashed my eardrum in the same round. That knocked me off balance, quite literally, but I managed to soldier on, blood oozing from my ear. Up to that point I was ahead, but such are the vagaries of the untameable beast that is boxing.

Things got worse in the ninth when I was floored by a punch I never imagined coming, let alone saw. I'm told it was delivered with timing and accuracy by the hand of a fighter with an executioner's instincts. I was only able to verify that description on seeing the tapes at a later date. All I recall is a voice counting 'seven, eight … are you okay?'

'Yeah, I'm fine,' I responded to the referee's enquiry.

The truth was far from that. My legs were shaking, and I didn't know where I was. Was it a bad dream? What was I even doing here?

When some semblance of cognition kicked in, I remembered what my old amateur trainer Divas Chirwa had told me back in 1986: 'Son, when you get hurt in boxing hold on to your opponent like you want to fornicate with him. Turn him into your lover. One you never want to lose or let go of.'

I took those words to heart, holding onto Juarez like I was glued to him.

I was trying to buy time, in the knowledge that a referee won't disqualify you for holding. He'll step in and try and separate you like a zealous parent who's caught his daughter in a compromising position, and he might even give you a warning. You're still winning precious seconds of recovery time. Filling the lungs and staving off the light-headedness which has robbed you of your composure. So that's what I did, and I survived the round. It's a message I pass onto younger fighters. Like the saying goes: you have to know when to hold 'em and when to fold 'em. And I prefer the former.

I saw out the final round but lost by a majority decision. I wasn't unhappy with the verdict. I'd lost the fight but had won a few new friends, and maybe even admirers. Not many boxers would have come back from such a devastating knock down to battle as hard as I did in the final round.

For a first comeback fight, it wasn't a disaster and it showed fans that I had a chin made of rock. I'm often asked who of the sixty-four opponents I've faced in my career was the most fearsome, and despite having fought some of the most vicious punchers in the sport like Miguel Cotto, Kermit Cintron and Saul Canelo Alvarez, my answer is always the same: Jose Luis Juarez. Nobody has ever come close to knocking me down like that Mexican kid did. I'd lost the battle but a bruised and battered Black Panther was back in business.

CHAPTER 23

WELCOME TO MISSISSIPPI

'Life is undeniably what you make it.'

With the chains of the Mordey years cast aside, I felt a surge of optimism spring forth. The air – even in the urban sprawl of Sydney's south where I'd set up home – smelled sweeter and the morning light seemed to shine brighter. The first order of business was to find a new manager-agent.

Six years earlier I'd met an American boxing agent named Mike Marchionte at Jupiter's Casino on the Gold Coast. Little did I know then that he would become the man to guide and steer my career. At the time he was riding shotgun with Hector Arroyo, whom I had fought under the Mordey banner. We struck up a rapport and I took note. He was fast talking but thoughtful and seemed to possess a genuine sincerity beneath the patter. I later discovered he'd worked with ring luminaries like Naseem Hamed, Jermain Taylor, Brian Viloria and Ike Quartey, just to name a few.

We kept in touch in the intervening years and we met again three days prior to my loss against Mexican-American Jose Luis Juarez in California. He told me at the time I was walking into a trap, saying dolefully, 'Lovemore, they've brought you here to get beaten. It's a set-up. This Mexican kid is tough as fuck. It's not the right comeback fight for you.'

He, of course, was proven right.

He was a straight shooter, minus the deceit, and I liked him. Back then he was in cahoots with one of the leading US promoters Lou Dibella, and told me he could hitch me a ride on that bandwagon if I put my faith in him.

'Globalisation,' he said. 'You've wasted too much time being used up by Mordey. You need some big money fights.'

The 'Globalisation' moniker was lifted from the voice mail message on my mobile phone where a heavy Jamaican twang drawls out the greeting: 'Hey man, do so global mobilisation. You can't meet conversation with Lovemore Ndou man … but no consternation just leave bookalisation after audio notification. Man, it's just me leave a message after the beep.'

He took a liking to the message, and henceforth, to him at least, I was known and referred to simply as Globalisation.

It's an apt representation because he was responsible for helping me go global in the ensuing years, with fights across the world, taking up the challenge at all points possible around the atlas.

He was good to his word on purses too, lining me up for a plethora of decent paydays in stark contrast to Mordey's treadmill of servitude. Through him I crossed paths with prime-cut promoters and powerbrokers like Al Haymon – the mastermind behind money machine Floyd Mayweather Jr, DiBella and world champion turned matchmaker Oscar De La Hoya. And I stepped into the ring with accomplished fighters like Paulie Malignaggi, Kermit Cintron and Saul Canelo Alvarez, just to mention a few.

My first fight under his wing was against Filipino Jun Gorres on a Lou DiBella/Tom Moffat promotion in Honolulu, Hawaii. He was no pushover, with an intimidating record of twenty-five wins – twenty-two of which were by KOs – two losses and one draw. But I wasn't concerned in the least. I'd already dusted off the ring rust and was ready to take on all comers.

The fight was scheduled for 17 May 2002 at Honolulu's Blaisdell Center Arena but it almost didn't happen. On my first night there after arriving eight days earlier to acclimatise to the local conditions I came down with a nasty bout of food poisoning from a suspicious fish dinner consumed at a Denny's diner. Within hours I was throwing up nonstop and doubled up with diarrhoea to make it a perfect storm of digestive distress. I was holed up in my hotel bed for three days, sweating and cramping between dashes to the toilet. There were no worries about making weight for the fight after my crash course in fluid loss but I needed to regain my strength, which fortunately came back quickly as my body cleansed itself of whatever bacterial toxins I'd played host to.

By the time the fight arrived I was in near pristine shape and I made light work of Gorres, knocking him out with a big left hook in the second round. I was back in the zone and felt ready to take on the world. As a tragic postscript to the fight, Gorres was stabbed to death a month later back in the Philippines in circumstances I'm not privy to.

For the next eighteen months I remained active, winning the IBF Pan Pacific welterweight title along the way and successfully defending it on a number of occasions.

There was also another chance to appear on the Fox Sports Network in the US, this time at the Silver Star Casino in Choctaw, Mississippi. I was up against slick southpaw Damien Fuller, who was 21–2 at the time and not a boxer to be taken lightly.

For the first time in my career I sustained a cut above my right eye, an injury which as anyone in the sport knows can have grave implications for a fighter's ring longevity. Should you get punched again on the same spot there's a tendency to reopen old wounds, and prematurely end careers. Any trainer worth his salt will research the cuts history of an opponent and get you to aim blows at that vulnerable area of scar tissue in a grisly strategy to open the old wound. It came off an accidental head clash in the eighth round and left me with blood seeping from a deep gash above my right eye, which later required five stitches.

I won the fight – after the ringside doctor abandoned it – as at the time I was leading on all three judges' score cards. I'd dropped Fuller with a sharp right-hand in the seventh and he'd been lucky to survive the round after I followed up the knockdown with a barrage of damaging blows. But with the oozing blood affecting my vision as it flowed around my eye socket, the doctor had little option but to instruct the referee to call a halt.

During this trip I stumbled across a man whose positivity in the face of great adversity changed my perspective of my own life. His name was

Antonio V. Wright, and he made me realise life is undeniably what you make it. He was an African-American bull of a man, with a rippling upper body and an energy and attitude that screamed out that almost anything was possible.

Being bound to a wheelchair – the result of a spinal injury suffered in a dreadful car accident – was treated as a minor hiccup by this force of nature, whose career as an all-star football player at Jackson State University was cut short by the injury which left him paralysed from the upper thighs down. His disarming smile would have melted glass, and was forever painted across his lips. He also had a wicked humour which broke the sombre, funeral-like atmosphere in my dressing room as I was stitched up by the doctor post-fight.

Wheeling himself into the room, he manoeuvred himself next to me and congratulated me on the win. Within a few seconds the jokes were coming thick and fast and the twelve or so others in the room were in the palm of his hands.

He sensed that I was brooding over the cut and its possible implications. He then fixed me with his gaze and said with a honey-smooth purr, 'Hey Lovemore, I'll tell you what I do when I'm stressed about something.'

'Yes, go ahead. Tell me,' I replied.

'Well, I pick a spot on the wall and I keep focusing on that spot,' he said in almost a whisper. 'I focus, and focus and focus on that tiny spot, my mind making it the centre of my universe …'

Everybody in the room was hypnotised. We felt like the privileged few about to receive some sort of revelation from a fountain of wisdom. After a brief pause, during which we all remained rapt, the resonance of his voice rose a notch and he said, 'And then …'

The anticipation was palpable.

'… I bang my head on that spot and go "fuck, fuck, fuck".'

The room convulsed into laughter, including the doctor. And all thoughts of cuts and career threats were blown to smithereens.

In truth, his story is inspirational. He didn't let his devastating circumstances stop him chasing new dreams after the old had been extinguished. He excelled at wheelchair basketball, swimming, power lifting and went on to coach gridiron. He lived life on his terms, ignoring the nuisance of physical limitations. Each of us in the room that night was deeply touched by this immense fun-loving figure of forbearance. Far from content with simply helping himself, he sought to impart to others the special qualities distilled within him.

In 2011 he founded an organisation called MACE – Metro Area Community Empowerment – which championed the cause of disabled athletes, showing what can be accomplished no matter what the impediments. He also published an inspiring autobiography entitled *From a Label to a Brand*.

He wasn't the only memorable person I encountered on my mission to Mississippi. There were two others, in the form of Shaun and Nicole Seales, who became like an extended family to me to the extent that I'm a godfather to their son Sultan Rahsool, whose third name is Ndou, in reference to yours truly.

The relationship with both didn't begin promisingly, in fact quite the reverse. Brother Shaun, as he's known, is a devout Muslim who owns a limousine car service. He was the designated driver for the duration of my stay in Jackson. I arrived from the gruelling twenty-two hour journey from Sydney in the expectation that a driver would be there to ferry me to my hotel. What could possibly go wrong?

As I hauled out my bags, I called the fight promoter who said the chauffeur was already there waiting for me at the arrivals hall. I expected to see a man holding aloft a cardboard sign with my name on it, but there was nobody there announcing their presence.

People were coming and going and I made my way to the main entrance to await my ride, my frustration gradually building. I was tired, jet-lagged and needed a hot shower and some shut eye. I never sleep on flights, which is maybe down to this feeling I have that if the plane crashes I want to be awake for my final moments. During my long wait, as I watched enviously as friends and family were reunited and on their way, I'd noticed a tall African American guy in a dark blazer and grey pants stride in and out of the arrivals hall on several occasions, walking right past me without any hint of acknowledgement or even a quizzical look. So, it didn't cross my mind that he could be my driver

I called the promoter again, pleading with him to solve the situation. He replied that the driver had been there two hours and said there was no sign of me. I asked what the chauffeur looked like. He didn't know but told me he was black. That didn't narrow the field down much, since the place was packed with African Americans. He said he'd call him to pinpoint his exact location and told me to stay where I was by the entrance.

Within a few seconds, the tall, thick guy who'd been walking in and out passed me for the umpteenth time. As he did his cell phone rang. I heard him answer, his voice laden with exasperation.

'I've been here for two hours now,' he bemoaned. 'I'm telling you man, there's no African Australian here. Are you sure he even made the flight?'

African Australian? What was this idiot thinking? Was he expecting an Aboriginal? Maybe half-naked and brandishing a spear and full tribal and face and body paint. Or maybe he thought Shaka Zulu was about to enter Mississippi.

I approached him while he was still on the line and enquired with all the equanimity I could muster, 'Are you here to pick me up?'

'I am if your name is Lovermore,' he answered, butchering my name.

That only served to ratchet up my smouldering annoyance. I fixed him with a cold gaze, before retorting, 'The name is Lovemore, not Lovermore.'

He told the promoter he'd found me, before turning to me and adding, 'Sorry brother. I saw you there but didn't think you were the person I was supposed to be picking up. You look nothing like an African Australian. You look, and dress, more like one of the local knuckle-heads around here.'

He didn't just say that, I thought to myself.

'Did you expect to see me running around, half naked like your forefathers when they first came to this country as slaves?' I jabbed back.

His face creased into a wide smile and a throaty burst of laughter as he reached out to shake my hand, introducing himself as Brother Shaun. Although initially offended by his comments, not to mention his inability to bother holding up a card with my name on it, I realised I shouldn't be judgemental. I recalled my first trip to Australia when I had visualised Aboriginal people through the same caricatured lens.

During the drive back to the hotel we hit it off. He was a staunch family man and I liked that about him. In dropping me off he gave me his cell and home numbers and told me to call him night or day if I needed to get anywhere. He also offered to show me around town.

The next morning, after completing my morning road run to shake off the cobwebs, I decided I wanted to see the Jackson County Court House. I'd always had a fascination for such places in an inkling of the direction my life might take post-boxing. And I'm not talking about being in the dock here! I saw myself as more a defender of those who were. So I called Shaun's cell number. It went to voicemail, so I tried his landline.

After a couple of rings a female voice answered, 'Hello, this is the Seale residence. Can I help you?'

'Yes ma'am,' I replied. 'Can I please speak to Brother Shaun?'

'He ain't home at the moment. May I ask who is calling?' she responded.

Feeling in a mischievous mood, I told her it was 'Shaka Zulu' on the line, knowing he'd remember our airport discourse on the matter of African Australians. 'Would you kindly ask him to phone me at the hotel?' I continued.

The line went quiet, before she said softly, 'Shaka Zulu did you say?'

'Yes ma'am,' I reiterated.

Without even replying she hung up, leaving me somewhat perplexed.

About ten minutes later I received a call from Shaun. He got straight to the point.

'Brother Lovemore,' he enquired, 'what did you say to my wife?'

I told him I'd called asking for him.

'Did you tell her your name was Shaka Zulu?' he queried.

'Yes I did.'

'Oh Brother Lovemore you're going to get me killed,' he said.

'Look, we have a local male stripper here who goes by that name. He's well known. Now my wife thinks I'm driving him around, or I might even be a stripper too. All these late-night calls I receive and working such long hours … she's getting the wrong idea.'

I couldn't contain my mirth but at the same time could tell it wasn't a laughing matter for him. He was serious. I told him I'd call her back and clear the matter up.

'You can do better than that,' he snapped back. 'I'm coming around to pick you up right now and you're coming to my house to explain.'

It was the beginning of a beautiful relationship.

CHAPTER 24

FROM WEDLOCK TO DEADLOCK

'Some people react to challenging times by sinking into depression and hopelessness. I'm the polar opposite. When difficulties strike, I dig deep, work tirelessly and turn anger into positive energy.'

My boxing career was finally on a consistent upward arc but my personal life was heading the other way, as tiny cracks in my marriage turned into giant fissures. Communications between Florence and me were becoming more fractured and fractious and each day we seemed to be a little further apart.

I don't know how it started; maybe my constant training and travelling had taken its toll or perhaps the natural lifespan of our relationship had run its course. It's a question I couldn't clearly answer but I did know that I was slowly facing up to the fact I was losing the woman I considered my first true love.

The notion of our children growing up in a broken family was not something I'd ever entertained and was anathema to me, especially as I was raised to believe that a man never walks away from his family no matter how dire the circumstances. But as time wore on, I'd also begun to believe that some things are best left behind you, particularly as I began to see fragments of Florence's character which troubled me.

In truth, they'd always been there, right back to our heady times together at the dawn of our relationship, after our first chance meeting at the Sun City Casino some twelve years earlier. Of course I'd chosen to ignore those little signs because the love I had for her was all-consuming.

I use the word 'chose' because that's truly what it was. Sometimes we see warning signs flashing all over the foreheads of those we date and even marry but ignore them because we're blinded by infatuation and love.

That said I'm reluctant to speak ill of the mother of my children despite what she put me through towards the end of our time as a couple. If anything, I continue to respect and thank her for the beautiful children she gave me. They remain the joy of my life. Each time I look at them part of me pays a silent tribute to Florence and the gifts she bestowed upon me.

The words of my father also ring in my mind; from my time as a teenager he told me portentously in one of his father-son moments, 'Son, never speak badly about the person you are dating or were dating. Or the woman you are married to or were married to because it reflects badly on you. There's a saying it takes two to tango and if you're telling people that she's crazy, or was crazy, that means you were, or are crazy too. Remember: birds of a feather flock together.'

I've always carried those words with me and endeavour never to speak badly of any woman I've been with, let alone been married to.

The final straw of our doomed relationship came in the form of unsubstantiated allegations she made against me, and her threats to destroy my career whenever I plucked up the resolve to tell her I was contemplating leaving the marriage. I didn't say those words to her lightly but, for the good of my mental health, I knew I had to leave. It was just a matter of when.

Out of respect for my children I won't divulge the full details of a number of incidents which took place during a toxic episode in both our lives. But there are some facts worth recalling to provide a flavour of what unfolded and also some clarity. More importantly, they provided ultimate proof that I needed to extricate myself from a marriage gone badly sour. On coming to this realisation, I needed to make sure I had a future with my children and was able to continue with my career. They were my overriding priorities.

It was a Thursday afternoon and I'd just returned home from the gym. All too quickly yet another heated argument erupted from what had become a simmering unease between us and I went into the bedroom to pack my bags so I could leave. The atmosphere had become so poisonous that I felt I'd succumb to the venom if I stayed any longer.

Within minutes, I heard voices and noises in the next room and the bedroom door burst open with police officers, guns drawn, telling me to drop everything. It was like a scene from an action flick where the cops have just descended en masse on a drug den or were intercepting a serial killer.

It turned out Florence had called them, claiming I'd assaulted her and the kids, and threatened to kill her and the children. What made it worse was the children had to witness the whole traumatic incident.

Looking back though, I see that day as a blessing in disguise because it made me realise that sometimes a man should walk away, if it's ultimately in the best interests of the children, who should never be exposed to any form of family violence.

Despite protesting my innocence I was hauled off to Kogarah police station in Sydney's south and told I'd be spending at least the night there, as the police had denied me bail.

'Mate, the charges are too serious, you're not going anywhere right now,' a sergeant told me after I'd asked to be allowed to go. You'll have to go before a magistrate first thing tomorrow morning and make an application. This is no small matter,' he added gravely.

Wracking my brains, I recalled my budding friendship with a rookie lawyer and part-time DJ named Danny Bazzi and decided to reach out for his help.

Danny was fonder of music than he was the law but I was in no position to be picky as I settled in for an unwanted and unwarranted night of internment. Danny used to mix some tunes for me as backing tracks to my training sessions, while I was returning the favour by helping him shed some kilos in the gym. Danny had a big booming voice to match his pudgy frame and was a larger than life presence. I dubbed him the Lebanese Suge Knight, the roly-poly former record producer and manager of the rapper Tupac, who is currently incarcerated for manslaughter. On the body mass index alone there was an uncanny resemblance. The manner in which he trimmed his beard even resembled that of huge Suge. I placed a call to him, telling him of my predicament.

'Don't sweat it Lovemore,' he hollered down the line. 'Sit tight man, I'll be there in the morning to make sure you're bailed out. Should be a piece of cake. Rest easy.'

After a sleepless night in the stark surrounds of the holding cell, Danny arrived, fresh-faced and bouncing with vigour, first thing in the morning. I was due to appear before a magistrate at 9.30 that day.

'You'll be fine champ, we'll make bail,' he reiterated. 'You've got no prior convictions and that will help.'

It all sounded perfectly logical and I was anticipating a quick end to my predicament. The magistrate, however, didn't quite see it that way. I won't quickly forget my brief appearance before him and to this day still berate Danny about it.

He was fresh out of law school and rawer than sashimi. Standing next to him in court, it dawned on me that I perhaps should have sourced a more senior counsel considering the gravity of the charges. An allegation to kill your wife and children is not something the courts take lightly, and Danny – for all his confidence and swagger – was still wet behind the ears. But I was still confident I would walk free because of my unblemished record. I couldn't have been more wrong.

'Is there a bail application?' the magistrate said matter-of-factly.

'Yes, your honour,' Danny replied.

'Then what say you,' said the magistrate.

'Your honour, my client does not have a prior criminal record and these charges will be defended vigorously,' he spouted, putting great stress on the word vigorously.

'Is that all?' the magistrate intoned incredulously.

'Yes, your honour,' Danny responded in a tone which suggested he had presented a glowing and unimpeachable argument, sure to secure my speedy release from the shackles of injustice.

Without pause for further thought, the magistrate fixed Danny with a withering stare before pronouncing: 'OK, bail denied. The matter will be adjourned for two weeks.'

Danny and I exchanged glances, his conveying a sense of disbelief, mine more along the lines of 'what the fuck'.

'These charges will be defended vigorously, are you kidding me Danny,' I thought to myself. Why didn't you at least offer a sum of money as security or propose some bail conditions including reporting to the police station. Or propose any other stringent bail conditions including a curfew. Or maybe a cash deal to mitigate any concerns the court might have regarding any bail risks, I screamed to myself.

I was studying a law course myself back then and even I knew you had to tell the court more than just the charges would be defended vigorously. I was furious, and Danny was embarrassed. Later he came to the holding cell, sheepish and apologetic. I think he wanted to cheer me up but I could see he needed solace more than I did. I sensed he expected me to blast him with a fusillade of expletives while demeaning his competence to run any sort of case, let alone one with such grave implications. Such an outpouring of vitriol is the normal reaction from aggrieved clients who don't make bail.

'Champ, I'm so sorry … you couldn't have got a worse magistrate,' he spluttered. 'I'm going to find you a top barrister to get you out of here. I'm thinking of Avni Djemal. He won't let them keep you here, guaranteed.'

He was struggling to make eye contact and his shoulders were slumped, his omnipresent smile replaced by a frown. He was taking the setback personally, a pitfall I became familiar with myself years later when I began practising law. You can't do that in the law game if you want to have a long career because it will eat you alive. You have to be phlegmatic about such situations and acknowledge that you're always going to win some and lose some. To behold the grim expression on Danny's face, it looked like he'd been the one denied bail rather than me.

The mood needed lifting, and I took the matter in hand. Chuckling, l looked him in the eye and snorted, 'These charges will be defended vigorously …'

When he realised I could see a dark humour in the situation, the tension seemed to drain from him and the colour returned to his cheeks.

I spent the weekend in a holding cell in Surry Hills before being transferred to Silverwater Correctional Centre in Sydney's west. There I spent the next two weeks while Danny made it his mission to find me a more seasoned counsel. He was unable to secure the prolific Avni Djemal, as he'd promised, because he was in the midst of a trial. But he did land leading barrister Rick O'Gorman-Hughes who went on to become my long-term counsel, friend and mentor in my life of litigation beyond boxing. Not only did he get me out on bail, he also successfully defended the allegations against me and I was found not guilty at the subsequent hearing.

While being denied your liberty and holed up surrounded by individuals of highly questionable character might be most people's idea of a living hell, I wasn't bothered in the slightest. I'd been in far worse prisons in South Africa as a minor and Silverwater, by comparison, was like a luxury resort.

My adaption to the surroundings wasn't shared by my cellmate, a haunted and haggard fifty-something, with more creases on his face than vintage linen. He tossed and turned at night, waking up from nightmares and vowing to kill himself in the morning. For his wellbeing – and certainly mine – he was transferred elsewhere within a few days and I was left on my own.

Most of the guards and fellow inmates knew who I was and I was treated with respect all round. Being locked up allowed me time to reflect on my future, and that of my children. Did I want them to grow up without a father while I was caged over unfounded allegations, I asked myself rhetorically? I made up my mind: Florence and I were, from that moment on, history. There would be no going back, no misty-eyed reconciliations and hugs of forgiveness.

If I believed that the entire episode was simply an aberration, I was sadly misguided. Rather than the end, it was just the beginning of a compendium of wild accusations levelled against me.

The battlelines had been drawn for the custody of our children. I was prepared to lose a wife but under no circumstances the kids. My world centred around them and everything I did was for their benefit. Florence knew the only way to break me down was to take them away but that was a fight I wasn't prepared to lose.

By the time this unseemly chapter in my life had played out I'd been charged on no less than twenty-three occasions, without a single conviction. It cost me dearly financially but I had no other choice but to jump through the hoops placed in front of me, however vexatious the litigation.

Another lowlight on the list of incidents came long after we were separated and had joint custody of the kids. I'd booked a holiday with the kids and was expecting her to drop them off, as per the court orders. Instead, she told me on the phone she was sick and I should come over and pick them up. When I arrived, I immediately got the feeling that something was amiss. Things didn't add up. She looked anything but sick and seemed in no hurry for me to leave, asking that while I was there could I help her fix the TV, which she said was playing up. Reluctantly, and against my better judgement, I stepped inside the apartment.

She was keen to give me a knife to tinker with the TV. I asked myself why I would need one and declined the offer. On taking a look at the set, I realised all was well with it other than the fact the antenna cord at the back had been disconnected.

While I was fiddling about she'd surreptitiously headed out to my car, where two of my kids were already waiting for me. Our eldest daughter Maxine remained inside with me. Unbeknown to me at the time, she had placed the knife under the driver's seat while I was otherwise engaged. On reappearing, she told me to hang on a few minutes while she packed some clothes for the children. I told her not to worry but she was persistent about it.

I headed off to wait in the car, within seconds of me shutting the door, the road outside her unit was filled with not one, or two, but six police cars, in another scene from a cinematic crime epic. Before I'd had a chance to collect my thoughts the officers were banging on my door, guns drawn, ordering me out. The siren of an approaching ambulance could also be heard as it joined the throng.

I didn't hesitate to respond, raising my hands as I exited the vehicle to be restrained and told I was under arrest. This time the allegation from Florence was that I'd come to her home and stabbed her and that I had a knife with me in the car. My kids watched on incredulously as the scene unfolded. They were too young to fathom what was going on but they were clearly distressed.

Before I knew it, one of the officers was rummaging around in my car and he emerged clutching a kitchen knife.

'Is this yours? he demanded.

'No it's not,' I fired back.

'I think it is and you've stabbed your ex-wife with it,' he accused.

Before he could go on, both kids chimed in, telling him, 'No Dad didn't, Mum put the knife there.'

To give her story credence, Florence had actually inflicted some wounds on herself, and showed the police and ambulance officers puncture marks on the back of her head.

But after my eldest daughter confirmed she'd been with me in the unit when the supposed attack had taken place, the police quickly came to the conclusion that I'd been set up. They asked me if I wanted to press charges against Florence but I decided against it and to just let the matter go, mainly for the sake of the kids.

Despite the ramifications of such episodes, Florence was undeterred, and there was another incident when I picked up the kids only for Florence to call the police after my departure claiming I'd threatened her. As a result, the police took an apprehended violence order out against me. The very same day she called police again to allege I'd left the kids at home alone. Twice police came to make welfare checks and twice they left satisfied.

She took it upon herself to come calling and while I was downstairs in the garage the children buzzed her up. They say once bitten twice shy and after the previous dramas with Florence I'd had cameras installed in both my house and car as a sort of insurance policy for moments exactly like this. After I'd got over the shock of seeing her there, she launched into a tirade, telling me I should forget about continuing my boxing career, or ever becoming a lawyer because she was going to ruin my prospects. With that, she started scratching herself, her talons ripping at her own flesh, tearing up her own clothes. Then, in a blind fury she called the police on her mobile. I sat there impassively, after telling the kids to go to their rooms, as the self-harm session unfolded. With the cameras I'd had installed rolling, I knew she would only incriminate herself rather than her desired outcome of painting me as the villain yet again. She also shrieked down the phone that I had guns in the house and was involved with the mafia. On this occasion, the police outdid themselves, with probably ten gun-toting cops showing up at my home.

I calmly told them what had happened and invited them to watch the CCTV footage of Florence ripping at her clothes and placing a knife on the table, which she also claimed I'd threatened her with.

After some deliberation they decided to send her to hospital for mental assessment. Despite these interventions, the allegations were never-ending. On another occasion, after my son had fallen off a stationary bike and scratched himself while I trained at Sydney University Gym she reported me for assault when I dropped him home. I was actually charged with assault occasioning bodily harm in a matter that rumbled along for months before being dismissed. The kids had to testify in court where they told the judge I'd done nothing and they'd been coached to lie by their mother.

It was hard for them to be put through all this as Florence sought to build a case in the family court which would potentially exclude me from having any sort of future access to the kids. Each time I travelled overseas, she'd call customs and tell them I was a drug dealer and had been convicted back in South Africa. It got so bad that wherever I went I got stopped and had to go to the lengths of getting a police clearance form which I carried with me at all times on my travels.

It was hard standing up in court and hearing her spouting all these lies about me, thinking all the while this was the woman I married, the mother of my children. What is she doing trying to destroy me? How has it come to this?

Her tactics backfired badly with the Family Court ultimately reaching the conclusion that she was unstable and prohibiting her from contacting the children. I decided though to allow her to see them because I always felt that, no matter what, it was in their best interests to have a relationship with their mother. I would always regret it afterwards because she would use the opportunity to try and turn the children against me, instead of spending quality time with them. She would badmouth me to the kids, placing unwarranted blame and criticism for the breakdown of our marriage upon me. She would coach the children to call the police on me and make unsubstantiated allegations. It continued for years.

I've since forgiven her. In my own small way, I've tried to follow the example of Nelson Mandela, who on his release from twenty-seven years caged on Robben Island found it in his heart to forgive his captors. He said at the time he had to put his bitterness and hatred behind him, or otherwise remain in jail. Like him I've learned the art of forgiveness and Florence has subsequently apologised for her actions. The most important thing is that she ultimately recognised she was in the wrong. We didn't speak for many years, and in the intervening period she married twice as her life took a new course. She contacted me out of the blue after the death of her second husband and I helped her make the burial arrangements.

My kids sometimes still ask me why I'm so open to communication with her after all that has passed between us and I tell them simply, 'Well, she's your mother and I respect her for that. She gave me you guys after all. If it wasn't for her I wouldn't have you.'

Despite all that they still find it perplexing I've reached such a place of peace regarding the trauma of those times. The scars were evident for a long time, with my traumatised kids clinging on to me and crying every time they saw a police officer in the street, or heard a siren, in the fear they'd come to take me away again.

Looking back down the time tunnel, I've reached a point where I thank her for what she put me through because it turned me into the person I am today. Some people react to challenging times by sinking into depression and hopelessness. I'm the polar opposite. When difficulties strike I dig deep, work tirelessly and turn anger into positive energy.

Amidst these upheavals, I went on to win world titles, graduated from university with degrees and today I'm an inductee into Australian boxing's Hall of Fame. I am also running a successful law practice.

I look back and thank Florence because but for those harrowing times I doubt I'd have achieved these things. I still don't know why she did what she did but I will always love and respect her and wish her the best in life. She was there for me in the beginning when we were fighting the injustices in our country and I was struggling to fight my way out of poverty. We barely had a roof over our heads and were just starting to make our way together. She was there and I respect her for that.

When we separated, our kids were young. My son was only a few months old, Marion was in day care and Maxine had just started school. Taking full custody was a huge responsibility, especially since I had no family in Australia to offer help and support. On top of that I was a boxer full time and was studying for a double degree. Today, on reflection, I don't quite know how I managed it. But I did.

It was a daily test but the fact I came through shows that, with the right mindset and tools, anybody can. It was not easy at all. There were times where I would be angry at myself for a failed marriage. There were times where I felt sad, played the blame game, and felt sorry for my children for having to be raised by a single parent considering I was raised by two parents. I come from a tribe that upholds the sanctity of marriage. A tribe that believes that marriage is not disposable. I, however, eventually came to realise and accept that what I was going through at the time was normal following a marriage breakdown. It is through this experience that I came to acknowledge that single parents do a heroic job.

It is hard for children, in particular girls, to be raised without a mother. Girls need a female role model in their lives, just as boys need a male role model. I recall when my daughter had her period for the first time I was lost and didn't know what to do. I still remember that day like yesterday. I was in my study room preparing for my law exams and Maxine walked in holding onto her stomach.

'Dad, I'm bleeding down there,' she said.

'What did you do to yourself?' was my response.

'I didn't do anything. I have my period,' she said.

'So, what do we do?' I asked her.

'What do you mean what do we do? You are the parent,' she retorted angrily.

'Okay I will call an ambulance,' I said.

'Oh, you are an idiot,' she said as she walked out of the study room.

I truly didn't know what to do. At that moment I really wished Florence was there to handle the situation. Daughters need their mothers at a time like this. The parenting courses I'd undertaken to prepare for the trials ahead had never tackled such tough subject matter. So, I ran and knocked on the neighbour's door. Luckily, I had a good neighbour.

'Relax,' she said to me. 'It's not a big deal. I will take care of it for you.'

She came to my place and spoke to my daughter and gave her lessons on what to do during a situation like that.

Studies also show that teenage daughters raised by a single parent are prone to teen pregnancy. I can say without shame that I was not spared from this. My daughter fell pregnant at age sixteen. This is why it is important for parents to continue working as a team when it comes to parenting their children, even following separation. Like the old African proverb says, 'When elephants fight it is the grass that suffers'. When parents fight it is the children who suffer.

I've always believed that tough times toughen you up. The world works in strange ways and it's gratifying to me that the lawyers who assisted me during those turbulent times went on to assist me as my own fledgling legal career began to evolve in the ensuing years.

Rick O'Gorman-Hughes became a mentor and I did my placement under his guidance while Danny Bazzi, who to this day remains a dear friend, got me started as a lawyer. He supervised my first two years as a solicitor, which is a requirement by the Law Society. We worked in tandem until he moved onto his first love – a career in the music business as a top-notch promoter. I still believe that notorious bail incident had him so traumatised that he never again dabbled in criminal law.

My Vigorous Friend, as I refer to him today, wasn't averse to anything but point-blank refused to touch criminal law. Ironically, that became one of my domains. I'm a sucker for the underdog, and get a kick assisting clients who've been through the same sort of travails as myself. I'll take on cases some of my brethren are reluctant to touch, where, for example, there have been serious allegations of family violence. The fact I've been through the mill myself has taught me to delve deeply into each case before prematurely judging clients.

To illustrate this the case of one of my clients who was an international student comes to mind. He was a kid who turned up at my offices one day, with enough demerit points and fines on his international license to fund a small country. He was a victim of the now jailed former deputy mayor of Auburn, Salim Mehajer. Mehajer and his cohorts had somehow gotten hold of his licence and used it with impunity, racking up speeding, parking and multifarious other traffic offences across Sydney in his name.

The kid's licence was eventually suspended by the authorities and he'd been to various lawyers around town looking for a way out of the mess he'd unwittingly found himself in. He also needed his licence to supplement his earnings as an Uber driver. Nobody was keen to touch the matter because of Mehajer's status at the time as an influential politician and property developer. Speed cameras had logged countless images of Porches, BMWs and Mercedes with the SM numberplate of Salim Mehajer. But it was the student who was taking the rap for the actions of Salim, who was eventually banged up for twenty-one months for electoral fraud.

His excesses reached their pinnacle when his extravagant wedding to fiancée Aysha illegally blocked off streets, while hired helicopters ferrying him and his entourage hovered overhead. He later boasted that 'Mayweather's got nothing on me'. These capers put him in the spotlight – and not in a good way – leading to the police investigations which ultimately sealed his downfall.

The kid in question was simply collateral damage along the way. I looked at his case, and I decided to help because such grievances were the reason I'd gravitated to the law in the first place. My overriding goal was to assist people. We identified all the cars, we got Channel 7 involved and ultimately he got his licence back and Mehajer was charged. Not only did we get justice for my client, the case also sped up Mehajer's fall from grace as his labyrinth of lies and deceit began to be exposed.

For me, it's all about justice and I'm happy to take on a case pro bono if I see a person has been a victim of wrongdoing. Without my own personal history of being the one on the receiving end perhaps I wouldn't see things with the clarity I do today.

It takes me back to my encounter with Adrian Joel, the boxing tragic who helped me become an Australian citizen. He refused to charge me a cent for his life-changing help. As far as I'm concerned, I'm just spreading the love.

CHAPTER 25

THE FIRST SHOT AT THE
WORLD TITLE

*'The ones who promise you the world and a lifestyle doused
in glitter and glamour are most likely to be charlatans who
will use you up and dispense with you before you know what's
happened.'*

The fights were stacking up nicely and so were the wins as I
dispatched Damien Fuller, and Argentinians Cesar Alberto Leiva
and Carlos Rios in quick succession. There was also a pretty straight-
forward victory over Kenyan-born Australia-based Fred Kinuthia. I
wasn't displeased with life but still hankered after a marquee match-up.

Those aspirations took a favourable turn when I received an early
morning wake-up call at 3.30 am out of the blue from Tom Browne,
the matchmaker for Goosen-Tutor promotions.

Before I had the chance to rub the sleep from my eyes, he was hollering
down the line, 'Hey buddy would you take on a fight with Sharmba
Mitchell in Atlantic City for the interim IBF light welterweight world
title? The only issue is that the fight's in a week's time and I don't know
what sort of condition you're in? It's short notice but it's an opportunity
for you to showcase yourself on one of the major TV networks in
America and earn some good money for your trouble.'

I repeated what he said back, almost word for word, just to make sure this wasn't some type of prank call. 'For the interim world title?' I queried.

'Yes,' he clarified.

'Against Sharmba Mitchell?'

'Correct, Sharmba Mitchell,' he affirmed.

'In a week's time? I double-checked.

'That's right, in nine days to be specific,' he said.

'Send me the contract,' I replied without further ado.

'Aren't you going to ask what the purse is?' he continued.

'I heard you say it was an opportunity to make good money, so send me the paperwork,' I responded.

In all my dealings with Goosen-Tutor promotions, Tom Browne and Craig Goosen, the son of the co-owner Dan Goosen, were the two people from the organisation who could be counted on not to be telling porkies.

Tom was Dan Goosen's brother-in-law and honest to the core. I sometimes wondered how such an upstanding and scrupulous operator had ended up in a business populated by cutthroats and shonks who'd sell their own mothers for the right price.

The more time I'd spent in the land of the free and the home of the brave, the more I realised that the majority of promoters were either out-and-out miscreants looking for some semblance of legitimacy and reflected glory, or were former or current lawyers, in most cases in the practice of criminal law. The dividing line between the two is blurred and shrouded in ambiguity; they both deal with proceeds of crime, the only difference being the latter is licensed by the law society and is Teflon-coated.

Boxing has for eons been used by the criminally inclined as a vehicle to launder ill-gotten gains. Underworld figures and boxing promoters forge unholy alliances and are effectively partners in crime. I'm not claiming all promoters and lawyers are crooked – I'm a lawyer myself these days – but there is a significant infestation in both industries. The ones who promise you the world and a lifestyle doused in glitter and glamour are most likely to be charlatans who will use you up and dispense with you before you know what's happened.

The former lawyers have their own sales pitch, pulling you aside to warn you of the shady motives of others while swearing on the Bible to protect you from wrongdoing and exploitation. They are wolves in sheep's clothing whose conniving minds are far too agile for trusting and naive fighters whose best mental moves are reserved for between the ropes.

I have more respect for a loud and proud ex-con like Don King, who doesn't hide behind a camouflage of propriety. With King, you know he's either going to rob you or make both you and him rich. There are plenty of tales from fighters alleging that the tall-haired one screwed them over financially but I'm going to buck the trend and defend him.

Of all those earning a living in this grimy, slimy game, King is probably the most transparent. His life, warts and all, is an open book. Everybody knows he's a former jailbird and a connoisseur among con artists. But his charm has somehow overridden it all. Who else would have been able to convince two of the world's most despised dictators – Libya's Colonel Gadaffi and Zaire's President Mobutu Sese Seko – into funding the historic 1973 Rumble in the Jungle between Muhammad Ali and George Foreman? He somehow managed to secure $US10 million from the two despots to cover the fighters' purses, which in today's money would be worth more like $100 million. That takes con artistry to genius levels.

The truth is that many of the fighters who claim King fleeced them are being disingenuous. Mike Tyson, for example, made over $US200 million through his collaboration with King back in the 1990s. That's more like $1 billion in today's financial lingo. If King says he'll make you $10 million for a fight and happens to make another $90 million for himself on top then he hasn't actually robbed you, assuming you signed the contract for the stipulated amount. He kept his side of the bargain, so don't fret too much about how much he milked from the deal. If you're looking to apportion blame anywhere, maybe look at your advisers or yourself for signing the contract in the first place.

My opportunity for a world title shot was ironically created by fellow Australian Kostya Tszyu, who had pulled out of his scheduled fight with Mitchell because of a shoulder injury.

Mitchell was a mandatory challenger for Tszyu's crown and I was ranked number nine. The two shared the ring three years earlier with Tszyu claiming Mitchell's WBA title after he retired in the seventh round, claiming a knee injury. With no definite date set for Tszyu's ring return, the IBF had decided to sanction an interim title fight. While it was short notice – nine days to be specific – it was the sort of chance I'd been waiting for and wasn't going to pass up.

I was in great shape because, unlike some fighters, I was a ubiquitous presence at the gym whether I had a fight scheduled or not. I trained up to six hours a day, six days a week. I saw it as my responsibility to put in the hours and to be ready for anything. My trainers at the time were Roy Alexander and Marco Furia. I'd first crossed paths with Roy years earlier when he was in Renato Cornett's corner when I knocked him out.

I was also being assisted by Stuart Duncan, a canny businessman turned boxing manager. He was more of an adviser than anything and our friendship continues till this day with Stu now a leading international matchmaker. Stu quickly assembled a team for our mission to America. It consisted of sparring partner Gary Comer, my trainers Roy and Marco, Dave Hitchcock and Stu. It was the same team I'd travelled to Mississippi with for the Fuller fight.

The fight was scheduled for 7 February 2004 at Bally's Park Place Hotel and Casino at Atlantic City in New Jersey. It was still freezing on America's east coast and the air was thick with falling snowflakes. I'd never seen snow before except on TV. After getting some needed sleep after the eighteen-hour flight, I decided to hit the streets outside the casino for an early morning run. As I stepped out of the main foyer onto the driveway I felt a blast of wind so cold it would have snap frozen an emperor penguin. I swiftly retreated back into the welcoming embrace of the casino. There was no way I was going jogging in those Arctic conditions, not unless I was intent on catching pneumonia.

It reminded me of a scene from the movie *Cool Runnings* where the Jamaican bobsled team arrive for the Winter Games in Canada and empty their bags of all their clothes and frantically throw them on after arriving into a whiteout scene of sub-zero temperatures.

I settled for a treadmill instead but being unable to venture out for a run wasn't my only problem: we'd been unable to find a gym nearby where I could train. I'd brought my sparring partner along and I needed to get a few rounds in. The prospect of facing one of the best fighters on the planet, a former WBA champion to boot, without sparring as part of the preparation would be like jumping out of a plane at 6000 feet without a parachute.

The only gym we located declined to accommodate us because the manager wasn't available. When he was, we were told that without gym insurance we wouldn't be allowed in. In my travels and training around the world I'd never heard of such a stipulation. The whole thing smacked of a charade, possibly engineered by the Mitchell camp, to frustrate and thwart my preparations. As if he didn't have enough weighing in his favour already.

With necessity being the mother of invention, I decided to transform my hotel room at the casino into a makeshift gym. We moved the furniture around, turning the bed and mattress up against the wall to create enough room to work in. The gloves were laced and we went about the business of tuning up for the fight, skipping, shadow-boxing and ab work all included. That was the routine for the next six days and I was ready to show that lack of preparation time wouldn't be a hindrance to my hopes.

Mitchell and his team knew I was a credible opponent but were banking on the lack of notice leaving me vulnerable to a quick capitulation. That seemed at least to be the game plan when the bell sounded in the grand ballroom at Bally's. Mitchell, normally as evasive and elusive as a rare bird, was immediately on the front foot, charging forward with the intent to bring matters to a swift conclusion. But I was ready, mentally and physically. If he thought he could tire me with an early onslaught he was wrong and I resisted the temptation to brawl, firing off shots from long range and matching him for speed.

In the second round, I turned the tables taking the fight to him, using my jab and speed to shift him off balance. A minute into the round I landed a blurring right-cross left-hook combination which he stood up to, and he answered back with a few combinations of his own. The first two rounds were about even.

I was again on the offensive in the third, and within the first minute I landed a big right-hand flush on Mitchell's face. It brought an audible roar from the crowd. Mitchell was rocked and held onto me to buy time, before the referee moved in to separate us. Two minutes into the round I caught him with another big right. He smiled back at me with a mocking grin, and I knew I'd hurt him.

When fighters smile after being hit it's usually a tacit form of acknowledgement while simultaneously attempting to brush it away as if the blow were nothing more than a gnat bite. He knew, by now, I wasn't going to roll over for him and he came back with some combinations but they were all missing as I weaved and twisted away from danger. I finished the round strongly and could hear the ringside commentators offering their approval. The judges, all three of whom were American, were coming to their own conclusions, and I knew coming into the fight I'd need to do something spectacular for them to rule in my favour.

I could hear somebody in his corner screeching, 'You better move baby.' I knew at that moment I had his number. His team were getting worried and I finished the round with another telling right-hand. I knew I'd won that round.

Mitchell sought to redress the balance in the fourth, using his southpaw stance, but nothing was getting through. I switched stance from orthodox to southpaw and started jabbing with my right hand. This seemed to confuse him further, and I was landing blows easily, following up with short-left crosses. The reality is most southpaws don't know how to handle another one and he seemed bewildered.

After my victory over Carlos Rios some two months prior I'd been diagnosed with articular cartilage damage to my left elbow, a legacy of the injuries I'd suffered as a sixteen-year-old during my encounter with the brute force of the South African police. The exact same injury which had almost ended my career before it had even begun was coming back to haunt me some sixteen years later.

During my preparation for the Rios fight, I started noticing some inflammation and stiffness of my left elbow. It was a nagging, niggling pain and my left arm wasn't moving as freely and easily as it should. An MRI scan confirmed the doctors' suspicions and they warned me that if I were to continue boxing the condition and the degeneration would inevitably get worse. They said the wear and tear over the years had already caused irreparable damage to the joint and to continue boxing was like playing Russian roulette. Some surgical options were noted but only on the proviso that I quit boxing for good. Otherwise, I was told, they would only paper over the cracks and would essentially be a waste of time and money on the road into full-blown osteoarthritis.

The news was as unwelcome as the New Jersey weather, and whatever the medicos said I wasn't going to quit boxing. The issue was that my left arm was my most damaging weapon, particularly with the power and penetration of my jabs and body rips. You take that away from me and you take away 50 per cent of my potency.

Instead of hanging up my gloves I decided to change my boxing stance from orthodox to southpaw to alleviate the forces and pressure in the joint and to buy me some precious time in the ring. Whenever I felt the gnawing pain and stiffness creep up on me I'd switch to leading with my right hand for a few rounds, until my left arm had sufficiently calmed down. That was the genesis of my journey to becoming a switch-hitter and the more I practised in the gym the more proficient I became. It didn't take long before I was as accurate with my rights as I was with my left and my sparring partners were often left in a state of befuddlement and confusion.

The truth is, when I fought the likes of Canelo Alvarez and Kell Brooks towards the end of my career I was effectively a one-handed fighter, with incessant pain radiating around my left elbow as the arm almost seized up. Pride, blind courage and a determination which bordered on foolhardy carried me through those battles and allowed me to go the distance. I kept my own counsel over my troubles, telling only my trusted brother Ruddock of the grave diagnosis. And only then on the understanding he wouldn't breathe a word to anybody. After the Brooks fight, Ruddock didn't pull his punches. Hugging me in the dressing room, with tears forming in his eyes, and telling me, 'It's time to call it a day brother – you've got nothing left to prove. If you don't stop you'll end up getting badly hurt one day.'

Using my southpaw stance, I was jabbing with precision and purpose in the fifth, and also landing some stinging right hooks. I felt myself in the ascendancy and the confidence was flowing. Mitchell's sweat-smeared face was a picture of exasperation as he absorbed short punches to the body and head. We exchanged combinations before the bell and at the end of the round I felt I was ahead by as many as three rounds.

I was being driven on by the prospect of facing Kostya Tszyu back in Australia as a reward for beating Mitchell. I imagined it was his face and not Mitchell's gazing back at me as I unloaded my shots in the sixth. I'd always wanted to take on Tszyu, my appetite only lubricated by the countless rounds we'd sparred together training under Johnny Lewis.

The sixth round was a classic to and fro but I was still landing the most telling blows, particularly with my overarm left.

Bernard Fernandez from the *Philadelphia Daily News* had me ahead 48–47 going into the seventh, while Stephanie Ragusa from Eastsideboxing. com placed me in front at 49–46 with the New York *Daily News*'s Tim Smith scoring it 48–47 in my favour.

I switched back to orthodox in the seventh and started the round throwing some sharp jabs. It became a jabbing duel as Mitchell reciprocated with his featherlight flicks glancing off me. The round finished with a toe-to-toe exchange and it was a better one for Mitchell.

I stalked him in the eighth, now and again catching him with counter rights and looping hooks as he left himself open to body shots. But he kept throwing punches, the majority of which landed on my arms.

I charged forward in the ninth, switching from orthodox to southpaw, as Mitchell sought to keep out of range. But I was scoring almost at will, my right-hand leads, followed by left hooks were getting through his defences and at times he seemed to lose his balance as I hunted him down. It was an even round, depending on whether you had an appreciation for clubbing blows or Mitchell's tip-tap jab.

The tenth began like the ninth, with me in the offensive and Mitchell on his bike. Now and then he would stop and hold on. I knew I needed to produce something jaw dropping – perhaps quite literally – and that I'd get no favours or largesse from the three American judges, much less the crowd.

The promoter of the show, Gary Shaw, also happened to be Mitchell's promoter and I knew he had some influence on the three apostles who would decide my fate. I'd resolved that even if they were going to take the fight from me, I needed to make sure those watching would have something to talk about for years to come. The odds were against me in a sport where allegiances can be swayed by cash and promises of favour and influence. Or all three.

I won the tenth and kept Mitchell on the backfoot in the penultimate round as his frustration mounted. My left hooks and straight rights were finding their mark, despite his holding tactics. He slipped and fell to the canvas as his mind whirred overtime in trying to find solutions to the puzzles I was posing. There was no count but he needed the time to catch his breath and process his thoughts, as he dilly-dallied in returning to his feet. The bell sounded and I felt I'd clearly won the round.

Going into the final round, I believed that should natural justice prevail I was already the new world champion. I deemed that Mitchell would need a knockout to win the fight. But I've never been knocked out in my career and the first time wasn't going to be here or now. I marauded forward in pursuit of what I saw as my destiny but the sweat-soaked sponsor's logo on the canvas made it as slippery as an ice rink and I had to watch my footing.

Mitchell, perhaps confident that only a knock down or knockout could stop him getting a hometown verdict, was content to keep running. He slipped again with no count while I fired off looping lefts and right hooks. Mitchell held on and seemed happy to let the clock tick.

When the final bell rang every fibre of my being said the fight was mine. But the big if was whether the judges saw it that way.

My misgivings were not misplaced as right before the ring announcer proclaimed the verdict I saw Gary Shaw whisper in Mitchell's ear, probably telling him that he'd got the decision. Seconds later my fears were confirmed. Mitchell had won with all three judges scoring it in his favour. The scorecard read like a travesty: Judge Debra Barnes, scoring it 118–110, Pierre Benoist 117–112 and John Stewart 115–113.

Disbelief was only eclipsed by anger as I processed the verdict. I could see looking at Mitchell's face, pockmarked with blood seeping from small wounds, that he was both relieved and surprised. Media, commentators, the crowd and millions who watched the fight on TV all shared my incredulity.

Years later, after I'd won the very same title and Gary Shaw was trying to lure me into his camp, he confirmed what I'd always known. 'You know, Lovemore if you'd been signed up with me at the time you would have won that fight. You would have walked away with the decision. No problem,' he matter-of-factly nodded.

As if I didn't know that, I thought, to myself. The decision didn't go my way but I won more fans than I lost and gained a measure of world recognition and respect. I also moved up the IBF rankings despite the loss. To me that spoke loudly what other people thought, and that I deserved to win that fight.

CHAPTER 26

THE 'KALINKA DANCE' THAT NEVER HAPPENED

'Our meeting never materialised but I feel we both did Australia proud as its adopted sons.'

With the controversial loss to Sharmba Mitchell my dream fight with Kostya Tszyu never materialised. In my view it would've been a showdown for the ages in the annals of Australian boxing. Tszyu was an extraordinary talent, a ferocious and powerful puncher whose demolition-style displays belied his diminutive stature. Strangely, during sparring I always felt in control of him thanks to the consistency of my jabs, but you can never judge a fighter based on a sparring session.

In May 1996 we journeyed together to Adelaide to promote his joust against American Corey Johnson. I was scheduled to fight Antonio Tunaco on the undercard. I'd only been in the Tszyu camp for a few weeks but we'd already covered plenty of mileage in the ring. I flew first class to the city of churches, along with Tszyu, Vlad Warton and Johnny Lewis. A ring was erected in a shopping centre for an impromptu sparring session between Kostya and me to generate some more interest in the fight.

My years of working with Philip Holiday and Brian Mitchell back in South Africa had taught me that you treat a public exhibition very much like you treat a fight. You never let your guard down, otherwise your sparring partner might just knock you out and embarrass you. In keeping with the maxim of being on guard and vigilant, I threw a jab into Tszyu's face, which opened up a small cut, more like a scratch. It was unintentional but I don't think Kostya interpreted it that way. Every time he sees blood in the ring he goes for the kill, as I'd seen countless times before in his fights. And this occasion was no different.

The mood in the ring took on a darker hue as Tszyu, peeved that a hired hand had the temerity to upstage him in front of an adoring audience, set about exacting some revenge. There was suddenly spite and intent in his punches but he was finding it hard to breech the defensive wall of my jabs, and I kept flicking blows back at him.

Sensing that things might be about to get out of control, Johnny cut the round short and curtailed the session. I knew things weren't quite right when Warton and Tszyu conferred afterwards, talking in their native Russian and firing accusing glances in my direction. The tension was palpable and I didn't have to be a genius to fathom that my name was being taken in vain. They didn't have to say anything directly to me, their body language said it all.

I wasn't going to apologise over inflicting a little nick on Tszyu's face. If he believed I had come to Adelaide to be a punching bag in front of a bunch of shoppers then he was wrong again. To hell with that, I thought to myself. Damn, I wasn't even getting paid for the session, so I didn't owe him anything. Least of all an apology.

Tszyu and Warton's displeasure was all too evident as they headed off without me to the hotel while I was left alone to grab a taxi.

The snub extended to the trip back to Sydney, where I was shifted to a separate flight and downgraded from first class to economy. This was the beginning of some serious antipathy between the pair of us and our sparring sessions were sombre and sometimes savage affairs from that day on.

I was retained though to help him prepare for his title defence against my compatriot Jan Bergman in Newcastle in September of 1996. In the final days of the build-up, when you're basically just ticking over and not looking to expend excess energy, Kostya decided to take a little slice of retribution after what he perceived as the indignity of Adelaide.

I was due to fight on the undercard of the same bill and we were cruising around the ring, throwing light punches when from nowhere

Tszyu decided to unleash a heavy blow to my ribs. The punch was delivered with malice, a forethought, and designed to inflict maximum damage. I winced and felt the beginnings of some bruising, with Tszyu quick to apologise. He explained later that for a split second he'd envisioned me as Jan Bergman and had let the blow go. I wasn't buying it and dismissed his explanation as a flimsy excuse for what resembled more a case of a payback.

I went into my fight with a sore rib but still managed a third round KO.

When I eventually moved up to super lightweight, where Tszyu was the reigning champion, I publicly called him out.

You must respect the guy and his achievements – in my view he's one of the greatest fighters who ever lived. But I also knew his lifestyle would eventually catch up with him. Tszyu used to balloon in weight between bouts, and in the great Aussie tradition – not to mention Russian – he loved his booze. That predilection even extended to times when he was in camp when he'd wash down his meal with a bottle of Corona. And I'm talking about only a week or two out from a scheduled fight.

We'd sometimes sit in the sauna after a sparring session and he'd use Corona to lubricate the sauna rocks instead of water to produce more steam. Incredulous, I'd ask him why and he'd reply in his Russian accent, 'It's simple Lovemore, I love the smell of beer!'

To me, as an abstainer, that was a sign of alcoholism. Perhaps I was wrong but that's how I saw it.

As a young fighter, dealing with weight fluctuations isn't a huge deal because, metabolically, you can easily take it off. But as the years encroach it becomes problematic and the yo-yoing can have a cumulative negative effect, including sapping your strength and durability.

This balloon-and-bust approach was Tszyu's undoing in his final fight against Ricky Hatton – a brawler who had his own battles with booze and drugs.

Hatton was tailor-made for Tszyu in terms of style but fought him at exactly the right time. At his best, Tszyu had the weapons and the delivery system to short circuit Hatton. But he came into their match-up with his batteries already running low and simply couldn't keep up with the Englishman's busy, come-forward style.

The first signs of erosion were there some two years earlier when Tszyu fought Jesse James Leija at the Telstra Super Dome in Melbourne. I was constantly calling him out in the media around that time because I sensed he was ready to be taken. It was a matter of who exploited those weaknesses, and I wanted it to be me. None of that should detract though from Tszyu's stature and standing when you gaze at boxing's pantheon of champions.

He's one of the best fighters of my, and probably any era, and was also a gentleman outside the ropes. Our meeting never materialised but I feel we both did Australia proud as its adopted sons.

CHAPTER 27

TRAINING WITH THE 'MONEY' MAN

'It's true what they say about money – it gives you power and will make grown-ass men act like puppets.'

There was scant opportunity for rumination or recrimination after being on the wrong end of a hometown decision against Sharmba Mitchell. Less than three months later I found myself back in the US, this time at Las Vegas's MGM Grand to take on the Puerto Rican power-puncher Miguel Cotto.

Cotto was a chip off the old block, in the enduring tradition of gladiators from the tiny US territory – wrecking machines like the great Felix Trinidad, Hector Camacho, Wilfredo Gomez and Edwin Rosario. He was on course to becoming a super champion, whose punches carried the sort of venom to which there is no known antidote. He also possessed a deftness and lightness in the ring which bordered on balletic, as he went on to win world titles in four weight classes. Along the way he out-pointed, out-manoeuvred and pulverised some of the world's best ring craftsmen.

My confrontation with Cotto came on the undercard of the Manny Pacquiao versus Juan Manuel Márquez world title bout, and it was another I took on short notice. A week to be exact.

Despite the minimal preparation time, I came within a whisker of victory, in an echo of the Sharmba Mitchell duel. Did I win or lose? It depends on who you ask. A lot of boxing sages thought I had edged it but the men with the scorecards begged to differ and gave Cotto a unanimous decision.

In an interview years later, after his retirement, Cotto wound back through the cogs of his career and described his meeting with me as his toughest ever twelve rounds in the ring. To hear his words brought a warm glow, especially when you consider that he fought the legendary Pacquiao and Floyd 'Money' Mayweather, in my view the most gifted pound for pound fighter of his generation.

In the later rounds I had him back-pedalling and reeling from a barrage of big right-hands. He wasn't exactly passive either, stinging me with some punishing body shots. He ultimately got the verdict but I've no doubt, had the fight taken place in Australia or South Africa, the judges would have seen it very differently.

On the morning after the fight, feeling clear headed if a little bruised and battered after the previous night's war, I bumped into the late Emanuel Steward, the doyen trainer, who drip-fed his genius to the likes of Thomas Hearns, Lennox Lewis and Vladimir Klitschko before his death in 2012 at the age of only sixty-eight. Steward was on HBO's expert panel analysing the fight. He spotted me sitting alone, sipping my hot chocolate, and wandered over. Before I'd spoken, he asked if he could join me for a moment. Smiling up at him, I pulled out a chair.

He got straight to the point, his hand touching me on the shoulder as he said, 'Great performance last night kid. Look, I see a lot of things in you I like. I think I can help you get even better. I'd like to work with you but you'll have to relocate to the States.'

I was stunned by these words from a man who was as big a celebrity as the fighters in his care. I could feel the avuncular warmth in his voice as he fixed me with an intense gaze.

'Look kid, you've got something, but the boxing market is in America. Here is where the money and the exposure is. You can make more money than you've ever dreamed of but you've got to get out of Australia. You need a top manager or promoter here, otherwise they'll just keep shipping you over at short notice and use you as a stepping stone to build up their own fighters. And forget about ever coming here and beating a marquee fighter on points. If you keep taking these type of fights from Australia you must know only a knockout is ever going to do it for you, right? I can make it happen for you here but you've got to take a leap of faith kid. Give it some thought.'

Everything he said made perfect sense and he was dead right. Non-American fighters with credible ambitions to become world figures needed to be part of the US landscape. Manny Pacquiao is a prime example, leaving his native Philippines and linking up with promoter Bob Arum and trainer Freddie Roach to make his dreams crystallise.

While the offer was tempting, the prospect of uprooting to America didn't sit well for a number of reasons. Firstly, I was settled and happy in my adopted homeland of Australia. And even more importantly, I was in the midst of a custody battle for my children and leaving the country would effectively mean me having to abandon them because Florence would have fought tooth and nail to prevent me taking them overseas. I would also have had to put my university studies on hold. The bottom line was it would have meant choosing boxing, wholly and solely, at the expense of everything else I held dear.

I politely declined the invitation and explained my rationale. He understood and wished me well. I sometimes wonder what twists and turns might have ensued had I taken his advice. But there are no regrets. I've got to spend priceless time with my kids and taken pleasure in watching them grow and blossom. Today, I'm a proud grandfather and there's nothing I enjoy more than hanging out with my granddaughters Aaliyah Whitney-Mabel Ndou and Jamilia Ndou. They say children are beautiful but grandkids are the best. I'm playing a leading role in raising them and it's giving me a new lease on life.

Losing to Cotto was no disgrace. His achievements are legion and Mayweather felt his full force in 2012 before holding on for a points decision that was met with derision from large sections of the audience at the MGM Grand that night.

I got up close and personal with Mayweather myself when I was invited into his inner sanctum by his business manager Al Haymon as a sparring partner after I'd won the IBF super lightweight title in 2007. I spent close to four months working out daily with Mayweather in his Las Vegas lair, helping him prepare for his upcoming showdown against Ricky Hatton. Hanging out with Mayweather and his entourage of yes-men, hangers-on, hired-hands and bloated bodyguards was as much vaudeville as it was boxing.

Trying to avoid being the butt of Floyd's non-stop jabs – many of which were of the verbal variety – was a daily battle. The fawning flock who swarmed into the gym to watch Mayweather train under the watchful gaze of his uncle Roger, a former world champion in his own right, laughed, clapped, chucked and guffawed on cue as Mayweather played ringmaster.

For the first week or so after my arrival at his training base, surprisingly located in a slightly shabby part of town, I just took it all in. I was recovering from jet lag and wanted to see how he conducted himself with his other training partners. Meanwhile, I worked a few sessions with Roger and Cornelius Boza Edwards, the Ugandan-born former WBC super featherweight champion who had spent most of his life in the UK before relocating to the States. He went on to work the corner at some of my future fights and until this day we remain in contact and closely aligned.

I couldn't help but notice that during Mayweather's sparring sessions he would belittle and berate the stooges on the end of his punches with a clockwork regularity. He spewed and spurted all sorts of profanity and obscenities amid a cacophony of chuckles and chirps from his ever-compliant audience of sycophants.

The sessions often descended into farce against a backing track of choreographed cackling as Mayweather inflicted almost as many verbal volleys on his unwitting ring partners as he did body shots, telling them they were bitches and not worthy of being in the same ring as him. I wondered whether the troupe of chumps were being paid to clap along with his antics, and maybe they were. Or maybe they were just trying to bask in reflected glory.

'I'm here to school you,' Mayweather bellowed in the ears of his dance partners, and the parrots on the other side of the ropes would repeat the same words in unison, much to their own amusement.

From the moment their cult leader emerged each day from a different fancy car his flock of sheep would follow just one or two steps behind, moving left moving right in step with the maestro, stroking his ego at every stride. It was the same after the end of each sparring session; they'd be following behind him, hollering hysterically to lame lines from Mayweather like 'I train 24/7'.

It's true what they say about money – it gives you power and will make grown-ass men act like puppets. Mayweather loves that stuff because he's all about being in control. I also suspect he suffers from ADHD because he couldn't sit still for more than an instant. He was like a hyperactive kid on a sugar high, infernally bragging about how much money he'd made that day, whether from placing bets on basketball or baseball or some mega property deal. I wondered whether it was all just bullshit and simply part of the carefully crafted persona. He loved to sit in an entertainment room adjoining the gym, in front of a giant plasma TV screen, flicking impatiently from one channel to another before jumping up to make a point about this or that, gesticulating excitedly to get his message across.

The supersized bodyguards were never more than a metre or two away but were packing so many pounds they shuffled with each step, as mobile as heavily laden oil tankers. They'd have been as much use as an igloo in the Sahara were Mayweather to face any sort of threatening incident. He'd probably have ended up protecting them.

Mayweather's antics weren't to my taste, and at times I was offended by some of his caustic comments, especially when there were women and children amongst the hordes packed into the gym. Call me a prude, but I thought as a world champion he needed to conduct himself with a bit more professionalism. But, hey this is boxing and Mayweather, with a family background more volatile than Vesuvius, was the embodiment of his dysfunctional past.

I watched him tear strips off his father Floyd Sr, the former featherweight champion and trainer, on live TV. Their tempestuous relationship goes way back and might have something to do with Floyd Sr using his son, then just two years old, as a human shield when he was staring down the barrel of a shotgun during a botched drug deal. To understand how toxic the family tree was, his assailant was none other than Tony 'Baboon' Sinclair, the brother of Floyd Sr's wife Deborah.

After my sneak previews into the mysterious ways of Mayweather and his charmless congregation I got on the blower to Al Haymon and informed him that while I was happy to work with his man I wasn't going to tolerate personal abuse and belittling behaviour. Haymon told me to chill out, insisting he'd take care of it. Despite Haymon's reassurances I knew I had to be ready for anything because Floyd wasn't used to taking counsel from anybody and wouldn't take kindly to being advised on matters of decorum by anybody, let alone an uppity sparring partner.

I suspected his mouth would be working overtime at some point. I'd always believed in reverse psychology and I knew I would need to use it to deal with him.

As our first session got under way, the gym, usually pumping along on the borderline of bedlam, was eerily quiet. I'm not sure whether Mayweather had told his minions to mind their manners while he was in the ring with me or whether Haymon had put them on notice, but the upshot was a strange serenity. Halfway through the session there was a loud comment emanating from the crowd, probably from a would-be wisecracker. I couldn't make out what he said and nobody repeated it. Mayweather turned his head and glared in the direction of the onlookers. All of a sudden the hangers on were collectively shaking their heads and telling the interloper to shut it.

You couldn't help but be impressed with Mayweather in the ring. He moved more smoothly than velvet and his hand-eye coordination and the speed with which he delivered his punches was blurring. He was harder to get to grips with than a vapour trail but I kept pressing him and made him work hard, which is what I had been paid to do.

Our second session followed the same script as the first and it was only during the third that Mayweather's mask slipped.

'Come on Jumanji, show me what you've got,' he goaded, referring to a mythical character from the jungle fantasia movie series.

Without hesitating, I responded, 'Jumanji isn't in Africa, try Shaka Zulu, fool.'

My reply set off titters of laughter in the crowd. Mayweather must have forgotten to tell them not to laugh at any one-liners from the hired help.

'You're still my little bitch,' he barked back.

'No, I'm the king of Africa and I feast on little girls like you,' I deadpanned.

Again, there was muffled mirth in the gym. I think it began to dawn on Mayweather that if he kept prodding, I would just keep delivering the comeback lines. And so he kept quiet and got back to business.

A few days later, he slid back into insult mode. But it rebounded on him on this occasion, but more through deeds than words. As he taunted me, I caught him with a sharp right-hand on his nose, which drew blood.

Grabbing the chance to talk crap right back at him, I teased, 'Any of you ladies got some spare tampons for this little girl? She's got her period.'

There was dead silence before an explosion of laughter erupted. Even Mayweather couldn't contain himself, convulsing into fits of giggles. The session came to a standstill for half a minute as we gathered our senses, Mayweather stomping around the ring and whooping in delight.

For all his bombast, showmanship, bragging and swagger there was a side to Floyd that was endearing. He'd often cruise around the city delivering food to the needy in acts of kindness which didn't fit with his image as boxing's bad boy.

I'd won his respect and that was the end of the shenanigans. From there on it was just hard work. He was capable of going nine straight minutes in a round at a frenetic pace. And then repeating it. Most of his sparring partners couldn't last the pace. That was another way I'd earned his respect because I had the endurance and fitness to keep pace with him. I didn't care if it was nine minutes or twelve minutes. Fitness has always been my forte and it didn't let me down.

His determination to keep going finally caught up with him after fifteen minutes of one particularly sapping round a few days later. Suddenly he held onto me very tightly, pushing me up against the ropes. He let go, retreated to his corner and started vomiting profusely into his corner bucket. He blamed it on something he'd eaten the night before but I think there was more to it than that.

I was well paid for my Mayweather gig but the truth was I'd have done it for nothing. It's not often you get to mix it with the best in the world and it was no surprise to me when he went on to stop Ricky Hatton in ten rounds.

I also saw that beneath the ostentation and the bluster there was a benevolent side to the self-styled bad boy. He won't thank me for highlighting his humanity. But what the hell.

CHAPTER 28

'A LUTA CONTINUA'

*'If you thwart someone from excelling because of their age,
gender, race or sexual preference then it's a form of apartheid.
It doesn't have to be written into legislation to exist.'*

When I swapped left hooks for law books I thought my days of fighting were over. I couldn't have been more wrong. I'm still slugging it out on a daily basis, the only difference being when I was in the ring I was fighting for a better future for myself and my children. Now I fight for justice. Where once you'd see bruises on my face after a fight, now it's the ego that's bruised after a bad day in court.

Just like boxing, the legal game has its share of charlatans and opportunists, some of whom will sell their souls for a pittance. They feed on material gain and power and cases of lawyers working hand in glove to aid and abet the dodgy deeds of corrupt clients are legion. Some are linked with supplying illicit drugs while others are caught as accessories after the fact to murder, tampering with evidence or falsifying documents. Sometimes it's a case of all of the above. That's not to say the rotten apples have poisoned the entire orchid. There are lawyers of honour and scruples out there and I like to think I'm one of them.

It's a profession where you are continually bombarded by other people's problems and if your mental health isn't robust the risk of falling into depression and darkness under the stress of it all is very real. One day you're a hero, the next a villain in the minds of your clients, some of whom expect you to deliver miracles, even in the face of overwhelming evidence against them. So long as they're paying you, they expect you to turn water into wine, no matter what the circumstances. Some expect you to toil 24/7 on their case for minimal recompense and will jump ship if another lawyer offers their services for a penny less.

The most challenging clients are those embroiled in family law litigation. A colleague summed it up succinctly, describing them as 'ferrets in a sack, who are either fucking or fighting'. I see the fighting part every day in court as estranged couples wage war over property and kids. The level of antipathy and antagonism can run so deep I sometimes wonder whether these people ever truly loved each other. Could they really have coexisted in harmony, slept next to each other, nurtured one another and produced children together? It beggars belief. Often the only emotion left between these former soulmates is unfettered hatred.

Rancour sometimes erupts too between the lawyers representing these fighting factions because we invariably come to believe in the merits of our arguments and can end up taking matters personally as we are sucked into the vortex. I've lost count of the number of times I've seen lawyers lash out at each other in undignified attacks that would make Rumpole of the Bailey wince.

And I'm not exempt, either. Subliminally we become personally involved. Representing an ex-boxer in a family law dispute I got into a heated argument with my opposing lawyer. Feelings ran so high it almost became physical. The hackles rose over who should supervise his time with his child after his ex-partner alleged he was using drugs and his parenting capabilities could not be trusted. I wasn't buying that. I knew the man, having trained with him in the past, and I'd concluded he led a clean, if not totally virtuous, life.

The judge had sent the parties outside the courtroom to try and reach an amicable agreement over a suitable supervisor. We offered up some of his family members but his ex knocked that idea back, claiming he had too much control over his family and they'd let him get away with anything. In return, she offered her family members instead. They too were rejected, my client saying they'd never got along with him and they might be looking to level vexatious allegations against him.

The impasse was deep and as the arguments went back and forth I could see my learned friend become increasingly frustrated. He wasn't alone. Eventually we offered up a woman who used to be a mutual friend of both parties. The wife's lawyer went away to get instructions and quickly returned, his face cherry red and his head shaking accusingly.

'You know that your client is fucking this woman you're suggesting and doing drugs with her, don't you?' he spluttered contemptuously. 'How dare he propose her to supervise anything, let alone something as serious as this. It's insulting.'

Unconvinced by this latest twist, I replied calmly, 'Well, I'm sure you know that's an unsubstantiated allegation. You know as much as I do. There's no shred of evidence to support what you say. As far as we know your client could also be using drugs. How would you know he's fucking this woman unless you've been a peeping Tom? Have you?'

My counterpunch didn't go down well, the cherry-red hue in his face changed to a deep purple and his eyes glared back at me as he barked, 'Don't you fucking dare talk to me like that.'

Keeping my cool, I replied icily, 'Or what? What are you going to do about it?'

It was the wrong answer. He fired back with a stream of invective, his voice quaking with rage as he told me that in all his years in law he'd never come across anybody as ignorant and arrogant as me.

I sat impassively, letting his words wash over me. Seconds later several security guards raced up to the floor in response to the commotion. Many of the guards around the court circuit are boxing fans and are well aware of my past life.

'What's wrong champ?' one of them asked. 'Is everything OK?'

I told them we'd had a disagreement which had got a little out of hand but that all was good. They were chuckling about it, and as they turned to go one queried, 'Who in hell would want to pick a fight with you? Hasn't he seen your fight record?'

About a week later I was back at the scene of the imbroglio and heard somebody calling my name. The voice sounded familiar and I turned around to be greeted by my learned friend again.

'Oh crap,' I thought to myself. 'What does he want now, another fight?'

This time though, he was smiling, reaching out to shake my hand and apologising over our last encounter. I reciprocated. We were both out of order and shouldn't have lost our cool. We'd become too involved in the drama of our jobs and it was a lesson to me to not let emotion cloud judgement.

Despite the inauspicious beginning, a friendship bloomed between us and we remain close, sharing stories about our clients each time we run into each other.

I enjoy helping to unravel seemingly intractable problems for people and while you have to make a living, I take on a number of pro bono cases each year, particularly for Indigenous people. The incarceration rate of Aboriginal people in Australia is disproportionate and there appear to be significant injustices visited upon them on a systematic basis. I have painful memories of my upbringing in South Africa where injustice was rife, and I am determined to do my bit to aid Australia's Indigenous folk in any way I can to make sure they are treated with respect and equanimity under the law.

The truth is I'd rather represent a grateful client who pays me with a box of chocolates than a filthy rich client with attitude who pays me hundreds of thousands of dollars. I value appreciation and respect more than money, especially in a profession where you are unintentionally always making enemies.

Every time you win an acquittal you become a fiend in the eyes of the victim and their family. There have been instances where I've run the gauntlet of verbal abuse from these aggrieved parties when leaving court. I politely tell them I'm just doing my job and that every suspect has a right to legal representation. Not that it ever cuts much ice.

My clients range from the privileged to the impoverished, and victims of domestic violence to people with mental health issues. I treat all with the same respect, no matter what their circumstances. I reflect on my own life, growing up in a corrugated-iron shack in Musina, then moving to Johannesburg and finally Australia. I'm mindful of the help I received on the journey and I use that kindness as a template for my life in the legal profession. Should, one day, I follow a political path back in my native country, those same principles will be my driving force.

I dream of playing some part in helping to rebuild South Africa as it is slowly descending into chaos and anarchy in the post-Mandela era. I want to help tackle the poverty which is the precursor to the crime that runs unchecked there, and still affects friends and family every day.

There have been times when I've pondered chucking in the law and doing what almost every ex-fighter does: train, manage or promote other fighters. I know I could excel in that sphere but, to me, there's no challenge in it. I like things that tickle my brain. For me, academia trumps fisticuffs.

I'm often asked what's been my biggest achievement: winning world titles or accumulating the university degrees that gave me a second career in the legal sphere. My response is unequivocally the latter.

Success in the ring gives you status, and theoretically a certain degree of wealth, but you're always going to be a former world champion one day, usurped by somebody younger and hungrier. Should you choose to ignore the corrosion of the clock, and linger like an unpleasant odour, you risk becoming a figure of ridicule, or even pity, as you lurch towards retirement.

Boxing might ultimately strip you of your dignity but education, on the other hand, can't be taken away from you. The degrees you work so hard for are yours in perpetuity.

People are often surprised that, in the midst of a fighting career which took me to all corners of the world, I was able to simultaneously pour through legal textbooks and single-handedly raise three young kids. Mischievously, I've been known to tell people I'm able to channel mysterious energies from my Venda spirit guides, but on the condition they are used solely for good.

Amidst much eyebrow raising, I quickly add that the more down-to-earth reason is simply hard graft, dedication, perseverance and too many sleepless nights.

The hardest part, for me, was setting up a strict timetable that I never deviated from, no matter how deeply exhaustion clawed at me.

On treks abroad to train and fight I'd take just a couple of changes of clothes and still have to shell out hundreds of dollars in excess baggage charges for the weighty textbooks I stacked in my suitcases. In between sessions, as my team would wind down with some sightseeing or congregate and chill in hotel lounges, I'd lock myself in my room, my head buried in assignments.

Other than to train, the only time I'd venture out would be to go to courthouses, no matter where I was in the world, to observe real life barristers, solicitors and judges or magistrates in their element. I was a willing sponge and would brazenly approach beaks and barristers in an attempt to pick their brains. Even in Mexico City, where my knowledge of Spanish was non-existent, I still sought out the nearest court, just to take in the atmospherics and theatrics.

Occasionally, enticing looking women with a predilection for boxers would position themselves strategically in hotel lobbies during camps in entertainment and gaming hubs like Atlantic City and Las Vegas, making it clear they wouldn't be averse to 'spending time' with me and my team. I can't vouch for the others, but amid the fluttering of eyelashes and come hither looks of the women in question, I'd smile benignly and march on up to my room, where reams of unread pages awaited me.

My routine, when at home in Sydney, was round-the-clock remorseless: I'd be up at 7 am on a typical morning, feed the kids breakfast and drop them off at school. I'd then be off to lectures at university. If there were no classes that day I'd head to my second home, the library. If there was a window of opportunity between studying I'd drop into the gym for an hour or so.

Sometimes the kids would go to after-school care, or they'd come to the gym with me for a second session late in the afternoon. Then it'd be home to prepare dinner for the kids, make sure they were bathed and had done their homework. When they were tucked up in bed I'd prepare their packed lunches for school and then retreat to my home office to immerse myself in legal precedent and the minutia of obscure sub-clauses in family and criminal matters. At midnight, with the streets deserted and dimly lit, I'd trudge out for sixty minutes of roadwork then head back to study some more, before sleep finally overtook me. It was then a matter of wake, rinse and repeat. I was sometimes so exhausted In class I'd sneak out to my car for a twenty-minute power nap.

As for weekends, there was no lounging around in coffee shops or trolling through shopping malls. I'd be in the library dissecting law books and to wind down I'd devour TV courtroom dramas like *Matlock*, *Boston Legal*, *LA Law*, *Perry Mason* and *Rumpole of the Bailey*.

———————

After my twenty-four years in Australia, I'm often asked whether or not I see it as a racist nation. That's not the way I'd put it but like every other country race does matter. As former US President Bill Clinton put it 'there's a little bit of apartheid in everybody's heart'.

He argued that in every situation in the world where people are prevented from realising their full potential there is an 'apartheid of the heart' at play. I agree. If you thwart someone from excelling because of their age, gender, race or sexual preference then it's a form of apartheid. It doesn't have to be written into legislation to exist.

While I maintain that Australia isn't a racist land by design, that doesn't mean I haven't encountered instances of what I call racial profiling. When I first became a lawyer, I'd enter the courtroom and go and sit by the bench, only for the court officer – usually a female – to approach me and say the area was reserved for lawyers only, and I should sit at the back. In other instances, I was asked pointedly, 'Are you a lawyer? These seats are reserved for lawyers only.' There's no doubt the officers made those comments based on my colour. I didn't see them ask any of the white lawyers whether they were sitting in their rightful place.

There's two ways to analyse it. The first is they quizzed me on the basis I stood out because lawyers in Australia are predominantly from an Anglo-Saxon background. That in itself raises an issue of apartheid in that only whites are expected to excel in that profession to the exclusion of those of colour. Secondly, it could be a case of those individual officers simply being racist. But that doesn't make the entire nation racist. Those three or four officers don't represent what is a multicultural country.

Initially, being singled out like this was a trigger for instant anger. 'Did you ask these other people if they're lawyers?' I'd complain. 'Are you targeting me because I'm black? So, a black man can't be a lawyer?'

-year-old Lovemore in February 1996 at Brendon Smith's gym in Charlton, Toowoomba posing for a photo the local newspaper.

Lovemore (left) after he knocked out Jerry Malinga in the fourth round at the Thirroul Rugby League Club on 21 August 1998.

Brendon Smith's gym in Charlton, Toowoomba, bruary 1996.

Lovemore's family at ringside during one of his bouts at the Gold Coast, Australia in 1999.
From left, daughters Maria and Maxine, and wife Florence. Sitting behind Maxine is Christine Coleman.

Lovemore's late sister, Patience Siphelile Ndou in Limpopo in 2001.

Left: Lovemore in his office assisting an Indigenous client on a pro bono basis.

Lovemore (left) and Floyd Mayweather Jr (right) sparring in Las Vegas in 2007.

Fenech training Lovemore for the Junior Witter fight in 2005 at the Marrickville Boxing Gym.

th Johnny Lewis (right) at Homebush, Sydney in
07 after winning the IBF world super lightweight
e.

With Kathy Duva, an American boxing promoter and
CEO of Main Events in 2007 in New York.

With boxing promoter Don King in Las Vegas in 2007.

Johnny Lewis presenting Lovemore with the IBF World Title belt in 2007 in Sydney.

ovemore and Florence in New York.

ovemore Jnr and his sister Marion posing in traditional ttire in South Africa in 2010.

Maxine dressed in the traditional attire of the vha-Venda people.

From left, Caroline Ndou (Lovemore's sister) and Lovemore's children Maxine, Marion and Lovemore Jnr in 2010 in South Africa dressed in traditional attire.

Lovemore and his children in 2010 at the Musina cemetery visiting his parents' graves.

vemore Jnr dressed as a Zulu warrior in 2010 in
uth Africa.

Lovemore in his final bout in 2012 before retiring and
becoming a lawyer.

Lovemore (right) in
his final bout in
2012 at the Gold
Coast against Gary
St Claire. Lovemore
won the WBF
welterweight World
Title.

Lovemore with his two granddaughters, Aaliyah Ndou (left) and Jamilia Ndou celebrating South African Heritage Day in Sydney, Australia and dressed in the vha-Venda traditional attire.

Lovemore posing with all his belts following his last bout in 2012 at the Gold Coast.

Lovemore holding his granddaughter Aaliyah and flanked by daughter Marion and son Lovemore Jr when he graduated with a Master of Human Rights Law and Policy in 2015 at the University of New South Wales.

These flare-ups cast a pall over the entire day and I'd ruminate about it for the rest of the week. I knew I needed to find a way to neutralise the issue, so I applied some psychology. I'd go back into a court, and whenever I was asked whether I was a lawyer I'd reply, 'Yes, and a damn good one – hot as fuck.'

They would laugh at my bluntness and leave me alone. On subsequent visits they'd smile at me, perhaps even share the story with female magistrates. There were times I'd enter the court to be greeted by a smiling magistrate who'd address me by name before I'd had the chance to say anything.

I shared my story with retired Supreme Court judge, Justice Terry Buddin, who was my lecturer when I completed my Master's for Criminal Prosecution.

He guffawed loudly before responding, 'But Lovemore, you can't really blame them. You show up in court dressed in fancy suits like those characters from the mafia movies. One could easily mistake you for a gangster!'

An even more blatant example of racial profiling reared its head during a period in my life when I dated sports star, swimsuit model and sometime boxer Lauryn Eagle. She was a celebrity in her own right and we'd hit it off after meeting at a boxing gym as I prepared for my world title defence in South Africa against the tall and talented South African Bongani Mwelase. He was eleven years my junior and a natural southpaw who carried malevolence in both hands. He'd only gone the distance twice in his career at that time and was a knockout specialist.

I needed a good southpaw to help me prepare and, as always, Johnny Lewis delivered with one of his up-and-coming fighters, King Davidson, who was perfect for the job.

It was on my first day sparring at Sydney University that Lauryn and I crossed paths, striking up a conversation for over an hour. She seemed in no hurry to leave and the longer we spoke the more I was struck by her movie star-like looks and infectious persona. She was a former water ski world champion who'd decided to dabble in boxing. It wasn't long before we became an item, and while I had reservations at her taking up boxing, I did what I could to support her.

Call me old fashioned, or a male chauvinist if you like, but I thought she was too beautiful to put herself at risk in such a brutal and violent sport. Only she knows why she ventured into the ring. Perhaps for the love of the sport, or maybe to deal with some inner demons. Boxing, it has to be said, can be therapeutic. I'm a prime example, taking it up as an angry teenager to channel out-of-control aggression. Boxing worked its magic on me, taming the desire to lash out indiscriminately and giving me discipline to quell my rage. I sometimes counsel troubled teenagers, using my own experience as an example of how the sport can transform people for the better. I tell them if it wasn't for boxing, I'd probably be buried beneath the dust in Musina alongside my parents, or locked up for life in a prison cell.

While I kept a lid on my misgivings about her career choice, I at least persuaded Lauryn to enrol in a journalism course at university. I don't know if she ever completed it but I knew with her charisma and charm she was blessed with the TV gene.

We were out together on an evening stroll near my home in Sydney's west one evening when the racial card came flying out of the pack at me. We were waiting for the traffic lights to change so we could cross the road, when a car pulled up. Its two Caucasian occupants turned to look at us and the window wound down on the passenger side.

'Hey Tupac,' a voice shouted out.

Lauryn and I exchanged glances and did our best to ignore them. But the guy in the passenger seat, black hair slicked back and a heavily tattooed and muscled arm hanging by the window, kept yelling 'Tupac' at us.

Then his buddy chimed in, upping the ante with, 'Hey Tupac's bitch … you like a big black cock?'

That's when my patience snapped. I can handle insults being directed at me, I'll let it slide. But if you're going to insult my girlfriend, my wife, my daughter, or my sister then you'll have something coming back your way. I told the meathead behind the wheel, 'So does your mother. Just ask her. She'll tell you.'

'What did you say nigger? You want to die?' he spat back.

The doors opened and both men stepped out, bristling with malice. I faced them off, replying, 'I'm not scared of you idiots. Come over here and I will show you what a real man does.'

Lauryn panicked and ran into a police station, situated obligingly less than 50 metres away back up the street, screaming, 'Please help, these two guys are attacking my boyfriend outside.'

The cerebrally challenged duo looked like body-builder wannabes, puffed up chests straining the seams of their T-shirts and tight jeans and trainers completing the picture. They fixed me with their most intimidating stares and waited for me to run. But when they realised I wasn't taking a step back, their body language changed and I saw doubt in their eyes.

I had my guard up and was ready to throw some hooks if necessary. I've never shied away from a street fight and wasn't going to start now. You could say I grew up street certified and became law qualified. That said, I wasn't going to throw the first punch and jeopardise my chances of pleading self-defence should charges ever be laid.

As we stood in the middle of the road shaping up to each other, a cascade of bodies charged out from the nearby police station with five or six officers shouting and screaming, 'Move back and get on the ground.'

But it wasn't the two knuckleheads that they grabbed ... it was me. They wrestled me to the ground as the two perpetrators stood there watching in disbelief.

It wasn't until Lauryn yelled, 'No you idiots, it was those two who were attacking my boyfriend. Get off him,' that they released their grip on me.

They belatedly grabbed the two guys instead. Up to this day I still don't understand how they mistook one black guy for two men attacking her boyfriend. Was it because they saw a black man and simply concluded he must be the aggressor? I judged that it was and I felt somehow diminished by an experience which invoked flashbacks of my childhood in Musina, where the law saw colour and little else.

The cops apologised and so did the two boneheads. The station sergeant, who knew who I was, also emerged and personally apologised on behalf of his officers. He told the two boneheads they'd been messing with the wrong man, unless, of course, they deliberately wanted to get knocked out. I was asked whether I wanted to press charges but was so upset about what had just transpired and just wanted to get the hell out of there.

Despite the incident I still consider Australia a great country to live in. Yes, it was a case of racial profiling but that incident doesn't define Australia as an entity. I'm grateful for the help the country has given me. It's a land of opportunity where if you work hard enough your rewards will come.

I'm less forgiving of Australians though when it comes to one thing: for changing my last name without consideration and non-consensually.

In the twenty-four years that I have lived in this country I'm yet to meet someone who can pronounce my last name, Ndou, properly despite the fact that it only consists of four letters. I have to admit though that my mother tongue, TshiVenda, is one of the most difficult languages to learn … even Africans from other tribes in South Africa find it hard to master. Someone once, jokingly, said to me the language is so unfathomable that Venda children don't start talking until the age of ten. I guess what makes the language difficult to master is the fact that its phrases are hard to spell, thereby making it phonetically impossible to pronounce them.

The word 'Ndou' is thus impossible to pronounce phonetically. No matter how many times I try to pronounce it I end up confusing Australians more. Almost everyone in this country calls me 'Nadoo'. Some even go as far as calling me 'Naidoo'. I am not sure when I became Indian, as Naidoo is a common Indian last name.

The problem all started with Fox Sports commentators. They would always introduce me as 'Nadoo' during commentary or interview and the nation followed suit. They even changed the way my name is spelt by adding an inverted comma between the first and second letters of my name, to spell it N'dou. It used to upset me so much in the beginning but after listening to this for more than twenty years I find I now sometimes refer to myself or introduce myself as 'Nadoo'.

My kids think their last name is 'Nadoo' and when I try to correct them, they tell me 'No, you are trying to change our last name.' Even court judges I come before cannot pronounce my name properly.

I have now made it a point that the next woman I marry will need to learn to pronounce my last name correctly first or there will be no wedding bells!

Despite the gravity of my job there's always a chink of light and laughter along the way. Like the two lesbians who retained me to prepare a parenting agreement for their chihuahua after they split up. Or the case of my dope-smoking surfer client who invariably turned up for court appearances as high as a kite, in shorts, a T-shirt and flip flops. I had to buy him a suit and pay for a haircut after he pissed off one magistrate too many over his attire. Or the serial robber who's failed in every heist he's attempted except for the one time when he successfully stole candy from a brothel.

I've also had moments of self-flagellation when I've successfully defended clients who in truth deserve to rot in jail for the crimes they've committed.

But there's also pride in helping somebody turn their life around. I've had plenty of those cases; some involving refugees from war-ravaged countries who ended up committing offences in Australia. Often the problem is they've post-traumatic stress disorders after suffering horror in their homelands and have never had an opportunity to address those issues. As a result, they've gone off the rails in their new country. Some have witnessed loved ones slaughtered and tortured and you can only imagine the mental scars that leaves. I'm more than a lawyer to these young people; perhaps something akin to a parental figure. I point them towards therapy and counselling and share my own story with them. Gratifyingly, many turn their lives around to become fully functioning, well-adjusted members of society. They might have been denied a proper start in life but it's never too late to pick up the pieces.

I try not to let work totally dilute the time available for my beloved family and I keep my personal life very private, particularly after the tempestuous way my relationship with Lauryn Eagle ended. We became the subjects of media scrutiny and there were rumours of a sex tape, which tickled the appetite of the tabloids. But what really upset me were suggestions our relationship ended because it was destructive, dysfunctional and volatile. The fact that Lauryn went along with the media pantomime to further her own profile irked me.

Ultimately though it all backfired on her because a few months after we went our separate ways she was arrested after an apprehended violence order was taken out on her by her own mother. It begs the question that if our relationship was purportedly so incendiary then who was lighting the matches.

There were further arrests for offences like driving under the influence of drugs and alcohol. I felt bad for her going through all that with a media pack on her back. It was hard to witness someone who I had loved and cared for go through that. Even after we separated, despite all the media innuendo and barefaced lies, we remained on good terms. What ultimately ruined our relationship wasn't self-destruction but more outside influence from some of her friends and family, who frankly thought I wasn't good enough for her. That's what really sowed the seeds of our demise.

Her mother and I never saw eye to eye and I know for a fact that much of the tittle-tattle peddled in the media didn't emanate from Lauryn, who I believe was pressured into making allegations about a supposed sex tape. I tried to take the high ground, refusing to be drawn into commenting publicly on my sex life. What we are referring to here is less than a minute of mobile phone footage which was subsequently deleted.

Even if we had made a sex tape it's a private matter that needed to remain that way. Even today people still ask me whether the tape exists and can they view it.

I guess this sums up why sex remains an issue of great importance in this world. No-one ever wants to see one of my boxing belts, or university degrees. It's always about the sex tape.

CHAPTER 29

BOOM-SHAKALAH

'My adopted home has given me so much to cherish but sometimes it's those childhood memories which reach the deepest recesses of your soul, and pull you back into their embrace, despite all the hardships and terrors of that time.'

There comes a time when you need the planets to align and, for me, that moment came when a certain Naoufel Ben Rabah came into my life in 2007. Just like me against Sharmba Mitchell, he'd tasted injustice at the hands of American judges in a doomed title shot against Juan Urango. And now we were scheduled to face off in a title match originally sanctioned as an eliminator with the winner to take on Englishman Ricky Hatton.

I was sceptical that would ever happen and sought assurances from the IBF, concerned that Hatton might choose to relinquish the crown rather than face me. The 'Hitman' knew I was a dangerous adversary and strategically not the sort of opponent he'd want to risk stepping into the ring with at this point in his career.

I wrote to then IBF president Marian Muhammad, asking for a guarantee that were Hatton to dodge me by vacating the title I'd be elevated to world champion status by prevailing against Ben Rabah.

As I suspected, Hatton was not forthcoming about honouring any commitments. Fortunately, the IBF decided to play hardball with him and proclaimed that should Hatton do an about-turn I'd be crowned champion by overcoming Ben Rabah.

Hatton had continually ignored my entreaties to test himself against me over the years and clearly wanted no piece of me. His father Ray, who later fell out badly with his son, once told me Ricky viewed me as a gamble not worth taking. He was too big a name to be jeopardising the cash train he was riding and was guaranteed future title fights with myriad sanctioning bodies were he to wave goodbye to the IBF.

I respected the IBF for standing firm, rather than putting self-interest first and letting themselves be manipulated by a marquee fighter with a massive audience. Sanctioning fees are the lifeblood of the IBF, WBC, WBA and the like and farcical duels like Floyd Mayweather's cash-cow clash with UFC demolition man Conor McGregor are the perfect case of an organisation blindly following the dollars. When the WBC jumped on board with their diamond-encrusted 'Money Belt' It was as tawdry as it was ludicrous. But when a fight is worth a billion dollars in revenue, principles are nowhere to be seen. Although Hatton was never in the Mayweather money league, he was still a magnetic figure for the various boxing bodies.

My collision with Ben Rabah was promoted by Billy Treacy, from the Grange Old School Boxing gym in Sydney. He was a shrewd man with boxing in his blood and I was grateful to him for putting the fight together because another title opportunity had been a long time in coming.

Going into the fight, my old adversary Jeff Fenech – the three-time world champion turned trainer – nominated Ben Rabah as the likely victor. He'd trained both of us in the past and in the papers and on TV he stated that Rabah, who at twenty-nine was six years my junior, had an edge on me. It wasn't just his youth, but his ability to slip and slither out of the danger zone that Fenech liked. And he wasn't the only one.

While I was edging closer to retirement, Ben Rabah was on the up. He didn't just have the years on his side, he was taller than me and had a longer reach, which he knew how to utilise.

About eight months before our scheduled meeting, I'd watched Ben Rabah's battle with Juan Urango at Florida's Seminole Hard Rock Hotel and Casino. I thought he'd done more than enough to win but boxing politics conspired against him as the judges rendered their hometown decision.

I was sitting ringside with the great Bernard Hopkins, who held multiple titles in two weight divisions during an enduring career. He was looking to lure the winner into a contest with his nephew Demetrius Hopkins. Shannon Briggs and hip-hop star Fat Joe were also there, and we all thought Ben Rabah had been robbed.

Prior to the Urango fight, I knew precious little about Ben Rabah, until receiving a call one morning from Harris Mores, a friend with an encyclopaedic knowledge of the sweet science. We'd first met in the 1990s when I first arrived in Australia and he was the go-to man if you needed fight tapes, footage, or inside knowledge on just about any fighter on the planet. If they'd laced on gloves this boxing librarian knew about it. He was an invaluable presence behind the scenes, helping me dive into the fine details of my opponents. Apart from the obvious like fitness, training and sparring it's essential to have footage of your foes so you can assess their strengths and fallibilities and strategise a game plan.

'Hey Lovemore, have you caught the fights on Fox Sports tonight?' he asked.

Before I could reply, he continued excitedly, 'Ben Rabah has just challenged you on live TV.'

'Who is Ben Rabah?' I answered. 'Is he Lebanese or something, the name sounds Arabic?'

'No mate, he's an African kid, originally from Tunisia. He's a very slick operator. He was part of that group of African fighters that claimed refugee status in Australia after the 2000 Olympics.'

In all honesty I'd barely heard of Tunisia, let alone its one-time inhabitant Ben Rabah. Africa is a vast expanse and many westerners assume that hailing from there imbues you with an intimate knowledge of all its fifty-four countries. Others assume we all speak the same lingo and share the same culture. I find it amusing running into westerners who regale me with a few words or a phrase they've picked up in Africa and expect me to understand. There was one instance of a recently returned tourist pulling me aside to say *'Hujambo'* after his trip to Kenya.

'Who jumped who?' I asked.

Mystified, he told me *hujambo* was hello in Swahili.

'How am I supposed to know, I'm from South Africa,' I explained to my not-so-learned friend. 'We have about eleven official languages and Swahili is not one of them.'

Another misconception is the matter of wives, and why I don't have a bevy of them awaiting me back in the old country. Truth is, not all Africans believe in polygamy and while my Venda tribe does, I don't. Hell, I don't even have one wife. It's a choice, just like it is with Muslims who can take up to four wives, though few do.

Sometimes, when asked, I'll play along, replying, 'Wives? I've six: three blondes and three brunettes.'

One inquisitor actually bought it, replying with a nod of the head. 'Oh yeah, of course, South Africa is now open to mixed relationships. Good on you Lovemore.'

After my conversation with Harris, I started paying closer attention to Ben Rabah, thanks to the footage he'd assembled for me. The more I saw the more I realised how adept he was at ghosting out of harm's way. But I also noted the calibre of opposition he'd faced was distinctly substandard. He'd also lost against Fred Kinuthia earlier in his career, a fighter I'd easily out-pointed.

He had improved since then, though, knocking out most of his opponents. I knew he could fight but I felt impervious to the threat he posed, assessing that against Urango he hadn't faced the same intense pressure I planned to unleash.

He also seemed lacking in the stamina stakes, taking deep intakes of breath after rattling off four or five punches from the footage I was privy to. It was as if he was gassed up, while I was always running on a full tank and felt I could hunt him down and ultimately knock him out.

That said, it was his second title shot after his loss to Urango, who had gone on to lose to Hatton. So, I expected him to be running as close to capacity as he could. Two years earlier, Hatton had ended Kostya Tszyu's incredible career with an eleventh-round stoppage in Manchester.

In addition to his other attributes, Ben Rabah was cocksure around the ring, a trait encouraged by his equally brash trainer, Perth-based

Craig Christian, a man with more ink than Tommy Lee and a sneering demeanour of 24/7 menace. Ben Rabah was also the chief sparring partner of probably Indonesia's best-ever fighter, Chris John. I knew I needed a fail-safe plan to leave all that cockiness in a crumpled heap on the canvas.

I remembered as a teenager watching a crocodile attack a buffalo in the shallows of the Limpopo River. It was in high summer and the temperature was soaring into the 40s. Parched and feeling the heat, the great beast stepped beyond the banks until the water lapped halfway up to its flanks. It was a fatal mistake. Suddenly, the croc's huge mouth emerged from the murky water and razor-wire teeth lacerated the buffalo's legs, gripping a limb and dragging it deeper.

The buffalo thrashed about, seeking to extricate itself from the jaws of impending doom but it was pulled further into the depths. On dry land the crocodile would have been sent packing but in its own domain the buffalo was helpless. The crocodile dined on rump steak that day and I knew I had to be the crocodile in this fight: taking Ben Rabah into deep water. In this case that meant the later rounds where I knew I had an advantage.

Ben Rabah danced and jigged his way into the ring at Homebush Bay State Sports Centre in Sydney's west on 4 February 2007, instilled with the belief that I was an obstacle of little relevance. It was as if the Fenech's praises had made him invincible. As always, Fenech's co-commentator that night, Mathew Brooks, provided a counterweight to his ravings, saying my passion and hunger should not be underestimated, despite my age.

It was my turn to be led into the ring by my trainer Graham Shaw, clad in red-and-white trunks and gown. I had 'Boom-Shakalah' inscribed in bold capital letters on my robe. And that's what I needed to do: slam dunk him onto the canvas and shut both him and his camp up for good.

The fight had been billed 'Bad Blood' and there had been plenty of it during the build-up. I'd declared my hatred for Ben Rabah in a lexicon of loathing which had peppered the preparations. Taking into account the usual hyperbole surrounding such occasions, the undercurrent of venom was undeniable.

Ben Rabah had disrespected me during the lead-up, brandishing a pink G-string in the ring after a previous victory, telling me I was a girl and should start wearing the said attire since I was running away from him. I didn't appreciate his antics. The reality was at that point fighting him was unviable. However, I told his camp when the money was right, I'd fight him. But that didn't stop him playing the lingerie card and I vowed to make him regret his little pranks.

It was time for bad blood to be spilled. Ben Rabah came in at 63 kilograms with a record of twenty-three wins from twenty-six fights, thirteen of which were by KO. He was smiling from ear to ear during the introductions, up on his heels, loose limbed and ready to paint his name up in lights.

I weighed 63 kilograms, with a record of fifty-three fights, forty-four wins, a draw and thirty-nine KOs. My kids and ex-wife were ringside and it was time to make them proud.

For all the ill feeling and angst between us, Florence and I were always able to agree on the importance of protecting our children from media and public intrusions. In public we acted as a functioning couple, and she'd be there at functions and fights offering her support. Coincidentally, Harold Volbrecht, the man who took me under his wing all those years ago in South Africa, was also there. He had three fighters on the undercard.

Referee Pete Podgorski called us to the centre of the ring. We touched gloves and as soon as the bell sounded I was on the attack, pounding the body and then, as Ben Rabah held on, inflicting blows to the back of his head. I was sending out an immediate message that this was going to get dirty and nasty. The referee stopped us and warned me about the hits to his head. I didn't care; I would've punched him on his heels if I could. The referee motioned for us to continue and I went back on the attack while Ben Rabah used his long reach to try and keep me at bay.

But I was always in his face, leading with short left hooks and right-hand combinations. I'd noticed during my homework that he had a tendency to leave himself open after a left jab or a right cross, with his hands down by his waist. He could normally get away with it because of his hand speed and fleetness of foot but I'd practised taking steps forward when he did that; invading his space and negating his long reach.

I kept throwing short jabs and body punches and whenever Rabah tried to wrestle I'd revert to punching the back of his head if the referee wasn't watching. It was a tactic to wind up Rabah and his corner. He was switching from orthodox to southpaw but it didn't faze me because that switch was also part of my armoury.

I was pleased with the way the fight was unfolding. He was dancing to my drum and I was already beginning to drag him into deeper waters like that crocodile in the Limpopo River.

I ratcheted up the pressure in the second round and already I could see him taking in huge gulps of breath. In the third I doubled and tripled up on my jabs, mixing it up with some right-hands while he countered with quick combinations. When we got up close, I was throwing punches to the sides of his head and I could see the frustration on his face as his ears got a clubbing. There was nothing illegal with those punches and I was going to keep unloading them unless the referee intervened.

Just before the bell at the end of the third, Rabah returned some of my medicine with a double punch, but I clearly won the round. Rabah's confidence was draining faster than beer kegs at Oktoberfest, and Fenech alluded to it in his TV commentary. His quick feet had slowed and his dancing skills were dimmed. The body shots were taking their toll. But he still caught me with a searing uppercut towards the end of the fourth.

I kept the jabs coming and a minute into the fifth I rattled him with a looping right-hand. He returned the favour with a ripping right uppercut and while I could see some of his punches coming some were landing because of his tremendous hand speed.

I kept pouring forward in the sixth, shaking Rabah with a powerful left hook thirty seconds into the round which brought the crowd to their feet. The volume of body punches and short hooks to the head were muddling his mind and eating away at his core. I had him where I wanted him … out in the deep waters.

Rabah was digging deep but I was digging deeper. As Fenech put it, 'Ndou would walk across water to get that title.' And he was right. I'd have marched through a field of fire for the crown and I wasn't going to disappoint my kids.

Rabah was taking too long to come up for the seventh, milking any moment of reprieve he could get while I was up on my feet, bouncing and ready to detonate more bombs in his direction.

Thirty seconds into the round Rabah threw a left hook which caught me on the back of the head as I simultaneously slipped on the sweat and water-slick sponsor's logo on the canvas and momentarily lost balance, making it appear I'd been badly hurt. Rabah certainly thought so and he went on the offensive, looking to capitalise, only to be hit by a left hook as he too slithered across the logo as he felt the full weight of my punch.

Rabah's mouth was gaping and gasping for air in the eighth, his juices beginning to run dry. I caught him with a short right-hand, which grazed him on the chin as he lost his footing and hit the canvas, the referee ruling it a slip. He was up and exchanging punches again, with Mat Brooks describing it as 'like a Rocky movie'.

I opened up a cut above his right eye and was enjoying what had turned into a war. This was my territory, on my terms, and I knew he could not last another five rounds at this pace. He was flat-footed and searching for answers.

With forty seconds left in the round I caught him with a flurry of left hooks to the head while he retaliated with haymakers that missed their mark. The crowd were getting their money's worth with Brooks labelling the round as one of the best he'd seen on Australian soil.

Rabah was moving in slow motion in the eighth, boxing off his back foot and trying to keep away from trouble. My plan never wavered and I knew I was wearing him down. I was warned for a body punch below the belt but wasn't bothered.

In the ninth, I felt as if I'd channelled Baby Jake Matlala – the tiny terminator from my homeland who won four world titles by never taking a backward step. At only 1.49 metres he was the shortest world champion ever, cutting down the big men like a little buzzsaw on steroids. I remained the aggressor, bullying Rabah around the ring while he held on out of sheer heart.

I knew he was ready to go and in the tenth, I was scoring freely. But he summoned something from somewhere to briefly pin me to the ropes deep into the round. It was his last hurrah, as I caught him with a huge left hook followed by two short right-hands which dropped him. The referee ruled it as another slip but I knew he was hurt. I just wanted him to get up so I could inflict more damage. He did and I unloaded with a cascade of punches. He tried to counter but I rocked him back with right-hands and left-hooks.

He survived the round but I told my corner I was going to take him out. The dream which had fermented back in the ramshackle gym at the copper mine in Musina was about to crystallise. It was time to deliver what I'd promised my mother and children and time to muzzle those who'd ever doubted me. Ben Rabah was still sitting on his stool trying to forestall the inevitable.

He finally rose to feet while I bobbed and bounced, the weight of Musina on my shoulders feeling feather light.

With twenty seconds left in the eleventh round, I unleashed a series of short hard blows, following up with the double punch. With ten seconds left, I could see the spirit drain from his face replaced by a sense of resignation. I caught him with a one-two combination to pin him to the ropes, and then a left hook to the head and another combination.

Rabah was out on his feet as the bell sounded and his trainer Craig Christian jumped into the ring to help him back to his corner, only for the referee to order him out. Rabah stumbled back to his corner and slumped on his stool, totally spent. It was over and I was a world champion.

The place was in pandemonium, one of my corner men hoisted me into the air and I was hugging my team. I saw my ex-wife and kids blowing kisses at me. Somebody handed me my son and I kissed him. Before long Marion was in the ring too, hugging me. When the ring announcer asked me what I thought I struggled to grasp my words as the emotions of the moment overwhelmed me. I thanked everybody and vowed to stop Ricky Hatton if he dared to take me on.

The fight never happened. I guess he wanted nothing to do with me after witnessing what happened to Rabah. He vacated his title and I was crowned IBF super lightweight champion. My fight with Rabah was voted the fight of the year in Australia.

Two years later I won the world IBO welterweight title and in my last fight I took out the WBF title at welterweight.

I dabbled with the dark arts of MMA after that, winning my one and only bout by a first-round submission and in 2019 I was inducted into the Australian Boxing Hall of Fame.

My adopted home has given me so much to cherish but sometimes it's those childhood memories which reach the deepest recesses of your soul, and pull you back into their embrace, despite all the hardships and terrors of that time.

The scents of the African savannah sometimes call me back: the sweetness of wild sage, the lily-like potato bush with its distinctive odour, the popcorn-like essence of leopard urine, the earthy aroma of elephant dung.

Perhaps one day we will be reunited.

ACKNOWLEDGEMENTS

There are many people who have touched and influenced my life on this great journey, and I'd like to dedicate this book to some of those most important to me.

Firstly, my childhood friend Phathu, who was cut down by a police bullet on the streets of my hometown Musina during an anti-apartheid demonstration aged just twelve. I share a similar sorrow for all the other South Africans who died in the struggle for freedom from oppression.

My mother Minah Emmah Ndou was the glue who kept me whole and inspired me to reach for impossible goals. Losing her at the age of just forty-one left a chasm in my life which can never be filled.

I also must thank my dear friend, sports journalist Dave Lewis, for helping me put my thoughts down on the page in a process which recaptured so many memories – good and bad. His exceptional writing and editing skills enabled this book to come to fruition.

My beloved brother Ruddock, who has been with me through the darkest of times and cajoled me into finishing what seemed like the impossible task of recounting a life visited so many times by turbulence.

My children Maria, Maxine, Marion and Lovemore Jr have given me more than I could ever ask for, and my beautiful granddaughters Aaliyah and Jamilia, who bring joy and laughter anew.

I must also acknowledge and give gratitude to my best friend Pete Moscardi, who helped me come to Australia. May his beautiful soul rest in peace.

Boxing encyclopaedias Bongani Magasela, of *The Sowetan* newspaper, and Australia's ring doyen and former IBF board member Ray Wheatley have both helped me immeasurably.

And it would be remiss to forget boxing-mad lawyer Adrian Joel who worked so hard to help me make Australia my permanent home. I would also like to thank Geoff Walkom from Walkom Lawyers who played a pivotal role in ensuring that I secured the custody of my children.

Kudos too to my agent Arthur Stanley, who foraged tirelessly to make sure my musings got published.

I must also thank and pay tribute to Chief Wilbert Mukandangalwo Madzivhandila, the Venda tribal elder who was and will always be a pivotal part of my life. The chief sadly passed away in October 2020 at the venerable age of ninety-two. Not only did he help me to work hard towards becoming a world champion boxer, but he was also a life mentor who instilled in me the importance of remembering and upholding my tribal and cultural heritage.

And to all the great fighters who died in the ring trying to provide a better life for their families, I salute you.

Last, but by no means least, a heartfelt thanks to my best friend Mirjana Adamsone, whose wisdom, love and support I would be lost without.